STRATEGIC COMMERCIAL MANAGEMENT

Commercial acumen is a critical skill that underpins the realisation of successful and high-value trading relationships.

This concise textbook provides knowledge of the principles of strategic commercial management together with a framework for critically understanding commercial practice within and between organisations. It also examines relevant commercial management best practice and aids the development of the intellectual skills to communicate the rationale behind the strategic commercial decisions made by organisations. Across each chapter, it presents practical and transferable skills for designing, negotiating, awarding and managing B2B transactions.

Strategic Commercial Management provides a practical and concise introduction for executive education students currently studying for MSc and MBA apprenticeship programmes, as well as supplementary reading for postgraduate students studying Strategic and Commercial Management.

David Lowe is Professor of Commercial Management, a joint appointment at the School of Energy Geoscience Infrastructure and Society and Edinburgh Business School, Heriot Watt University.

Management Practice Essentials

This series of Shortform and Supplementary textbooks has been developed to align with and support the Level 7 Senior Leader Master's Degree Apprenticeship (SLMDA). Each book concentrates on a key element of the SLMDA Standard and therefore covers a core essential of management practice. The series is centred around critical reflection on the underlying assumptions the individual leader or manager might make and their current practice, and collectively designed to enhance leadership knowledge, skills and behaviours. An ideal approach for any executive education course delivered through blended learning, and a useful alternative or supplement to traditional textbooks for a range of postgraduate Business & Management modules, the books:

- Combine theory and practice – providing students with knowledge and critical understanding of the theories, concepts and principles of leading organisations and focusing on the practical application and execution of these concepts;
- Are experience-led – providing students with the opportunity to develop their intellectual, practical and transferable skills and behaviours necessary to successfully analyse, develop and manage organisations.
- Include features to aid learning and understanding, such as chapter objectives, summaries, reflective questions and additional PowerPoint slides and cases available online.

Strategic Commercial Management
David Lowe

For more information about the series, please visit
www.routledge.com/Management-Practice-Essentials/book-series/MPE

STRATEGIC COMMERCIAL MANAGEMENT

David Lowe

Routledge
Taylor & Francis Group
LONDON AND NEW YORK

Designed cover image: Mak_Art/Getty Images

First published 2025
by Routledge
4 Park Square, Milton Park, Abingdon, Oxon OX14 4RN

and by Routledge
605 Third Avenue, New York, NY 10158

Routledge is an imprint of the Taylor & Francis Group, an informa business

British Library Cataloguing-in-Publication Data
A catalogue record for this book is available from the British Library

ISBN: 978-0-367-51029-9 (hbk)
ISBN: 978-0-367-51026-8 (pbk)
ISBN: 978-1-003-05215-9 (ebk)

DOI: 10.4324/9781003052159

Typeset in Optima
by KnowledgeWorks Global Ltd.

Access the Support Material: www.routledge.com/9780367510268

For Ruth

CONTENTS

FIGURES, TABLES AND BOXES

Figures

Tables

Boxes

ABOUT THE AUTHOR

David Lowe is Professor of Commercial Management, a joint appointment at the School of Energy Geoscience Infrastructure and Society and Edinburgh Business School, at Heriot Watt University. As Academic Lead for Executive and Professional Education, his remit is to develop executive education style programmes for senior leaders and professionals in sectors served by the schools.

Previously, David was Senior Lecturer (Associate Professor) in Commercial Management at the Alliance Manchester Business School, University of Manchester and the Academic Lead for Apprenticeship Programmes in Executive Education. Additionally, he was the Programme Director of the blended learning master's programmes in Management Practice, International Commercial and Contract Management, and Executive Management (Airport Operation & Services Delivery), plus several Executive Education programmes in commercial and contract management. Clients include Arriva, BAE Systems, BT, First Bus, Manchester Airport Group, Mitie, Northern Rail, Rolls Royce, Thales, the National Skills Academy Nuclear, and the Foundation Trust Network (NHS). His consultancy work includes benchmarking the engineering and project management provision of an international pharmaceutical company.

David's teaching interests include commercial management, commercial strategies and tactics, capture and contract management. Similarly, his research interests focus on commercial and contract management within the context of project-based industries, ranging from ICT/telecommunications to aerospace and defence.

David is the author of *Commercial Management: Theory and Practice* (Wiley-Blackwell, 2013) and the editor with Roine Leiringer of *Commercial Management of Projects: Defining the Discipline* (Blackwell Publishing, 2006). The latter is the first book to establish a theoretical framework for commercial management. Other book contributions include Transaction cost economics: governing the commercial interface, in the *Research Handbook on Complex Project Organizing* (Edward Elgar Publishing, 2023) and Contract Management, in *The Wiley Guide to Managing Projects* (Wiley, 2004). In addition, he has published over 100 academic papers and articles.

David is the Series Editor of *Management Practice Essentials* published by Routledge.

PREFACE

Intent

With the increased use of suppliers, third parties and partners to develop, manufacture and distribute products, as well as to deliver services and capabilities, leaders within organisations need to be aware of how the commercial transactions that underpin these relationships are formed, maintained and governed. Additionally, they require an understanding of how these external parties enable their organisation to meet its strategic objectives and how they personally contribute to these commercial exchanges.

This text is not intended to be an all-encompassing academic handbook, a fully fledged textbook or a management 'how-to' guide on commercial management. Falling somewhere between a textbook and a practitioner guide, the text seeks to combine theory and practice – providing readers with both knowledge and a critical understanding of the theories, concepts and principles of commercial practice, its strategic role in delivering the intent of an organisation and the practical application of these concepts by senior leaders to make informed, commercially driven decisions. The text is not aligned with a particular sector, and the material presented is generic and widely applicable.

Specifically, it aims to provide the essentials required by a leader to develop commercial awareness and to become commercially astute, presenting real-world frameworks, tools, techniques, processes and capabilities to support effective commercial practice. It enables leaders to comprehend and supervise the commercial practice of colleagues from the inception of an opportunity or proposal to its ultimate fulfilment.

Audience

The intended audience for the text is primarily senior and aspiring senior leaders and managers within private, public and third-sector organisations: adult post-experience practitioners who already have a wealth of knowledge and practice. While principally aimed at participants in the Level 7 Senior Leader Apprenticeship (SLA), the content is equally valuable for post-experience students undertaking an MBA or other postgraduate studies, as well as delegates on executive education leadership development courses.

Andragogical Approach

Given the demographic profile of the intended audience for the book – post-experience adults – the text adopts an andragogic perspective. For example, each chapter incorporates a series of reflexive activities and discussion questions intended to encourage the reader to critically reflect on their commercial awareness and practice, and on the commercially driven decisions a senior leader or manager might make. This is an ideal approach for any post-experience or executive education course delivered through blended learning.

ACKNOWLEDGEMENTS

Firstly, I would like to acknowledge the influence and support of my long-time partner in crime, Peter Fenn, Reader at the School of Mechanical, Aerospace, and Civil Engineering, The University of Manchester. Our endeavours to explore commercial management within a project environment have lasted more than three decades. Additionally, I would like to recognise the support of my former colleagues at Alliance Manchester Business School: Paul Evans, Carl Gavin, Mike Kennard, Eunice Maytorena-Sanchez, Irene Roele, Graham Winch, Mark Winter and last but most definitely not least, Janine May, Exec Ed manager extraordinaire! Plus, my current colleagues at Heriot-Watt University: Graeme Bowles, Neil Dunse, Bilge Erdogan, Fiona Grant, Ahmed Ibrahim and Craig Kennedy.

I also appreciate the constructive feedback received from the numerous students and delegates who have explored and applied the various concepts, tools and frameworks presented in the text, and from the executive education clients, especially BAE Systems, BT, BP, Manchester Airport Group, Mitie, Northern Rail, Rolls Royce, Thales and the Foundation Trust Network (NHS), that I have collaborated with.

Finally, I would like to thank Sophia Levine and colleagues at Routledge for their encouragement and patience over the extended period required to complete the manuscript.

1

MAKING COMMERCIAL MANAGEMENT STRATEGIC

Commercial acumen, commercial affinity and commercial management – How 'commercial' adds value to an organisation

Introduction

Commercial acumen is a critical skill that underpins the realisation of successful and high-value trading relationships. As the business world becomes progressively more complex, globalised and fragmented, individuals and organisations need to improve their planning, creation and management of complex inter-firm commercial relationships across their value network.[1]

During 2020–21, for example, the UK public sector spent £306bn (29% of its total spend) on external suppliers. In the private sector, BAE Systems spends £14bn approximately 61% of its revenue on procuring goods and services from 21,500 direct suppliers worldwide (2023), while the international infrastructure group Balfour Beatty expends two-thirds of its revenue on suppliers.

In this chapter, we will consider what the terms commercial acumen, commercial affinity and commercial management mean and how 'commercial' adds value to an organisation. The aim is to provide an overview of commercial management practice. This is predominantly within a business-to-business (b2b) context and from a projects and programmes' perspective. However, the concepts covered are equally applicable to major purchases and

DOI: 10.4324/9781003052159-1

outsourcing contracts. Essentially, we will examine the establishment and management of relationships between multi-parties – and in particular how organisations use third parties, suppliers and partners to deliver their commitments to customers.

Personal reflection

Before delving further into this chapter, spend a few moments considering what the term 'commercial' currently means to you and how it is interpreted and applied in your organisation or experience. To stimulate this reflection, generate a brief 'elevator pitch' definition of commercial management and statement of how the activity is applied in your organisation. If it helps, imagine that you have been asked to update your CEO or MD on the organisation's current commercial capability.

Commercial awareness (acumen)

The competency frameworks of many senior leaders include the requirement to be commercially astute or savvy. While the terms are frequently used, what does it mean to be 'commercial' or commercially aware?

It entails having a fundamental awareness of the economics of, and an interest in 'doing' business: the benefits and realities of an economic exchange for both the supplier and the buyer,[2] plus an appreciation of the context within which a transaction occurs and the impact the environment has on trading relationships.

It also involves having a broad understanding of an organisation's customers (clients) and suppliers. This requires senior leaders to:

- Know precisely who their customers and suppliers are, relate to them and help them fulfil their commercial objectives and achieve their strategic intent. This could be challenging, as organisations may adopt different positions in their supply network dependent on the specifics of a particular opportunity. For example, on one project, an organisation may be a prime – a Tier

1 supplier – dealing directly with the commissioner of a project (the customer/client). On another venture, it may be a subcontractor to a Tier 1 supplier – therefore, another supplier is their customer (in this instance, it could be a Tier 2 or Tier 3 supplier). Essentially, the organisation could be helping its competitors deliver their strategic intent. What does this mean for the organisation and do organisations fully understand this shifting nature of who their customer and suppliers are?
- Appreciate the culture or cultures involved in an economic exchange – not just relating to geographical location but also the values and norms within specific organisations. For example, some organisations are much easier to do business with than others – due to the organisation having a greater affinity with them in terms of management structures and the way they engage with their supply chain, etc.
- Be conscious of the language used when communicating with customers and suppliers. Organisations have a habit of developing their own jargon and acronyms – however, these may be unique to the organisation. When engaging with customers and suppliers, it is important, therefore, to use their language, as failing to do so might be interpreted as an inability to identify their precise needs and could undermine the ability to develop an appropriate relationship with the customer and frustrate the establishment of customer affinity.

In addition to understanding customers and suppliers, commercial awareness requires a clear appreciation of an organisation's competitors and the competitive landscape in which it trades. This involves monitoring, evaluating and understanding how one's competitors do business – an ongoing, evolving activity. To do this, an organisation needs to be able to establish the following:

- Who its competitors are, whether they are established, direct, indirect or disruptors.
- How they engage and position themselves in the market – their market share.
- Their corporate culture, plans and aspirations.

- Their revenue streams and profiles.
- Their weaknesses and strengths – their threat level or potential for collaboration, etc.
- How they respond when competing against it – their pricing policy or prices.
- How their brand compares to it – their reputation, brand, design values and media activity.
- Who their competitors' key customers are and importantly their level of intimacy with them – how does this compare with 'our' relationship with the customer? Are they a trusted advisor and able to influence the customer pre-award?

Certain individuals are considered to be more overtly commercially astute, minded or aware, etc., possessing an inherent commercial skill or aptitude; therefore, a personal dimension associated with the individual's mind-set, perspective, behaviour or predisposition. However, while some individuals might, at an intrinsic level, be 'mercantile', everyone can develop a degree of commercial awareness. Hopefully through this book, you will be able to refine and hone your commercial skills.

So how do you gain this competency?

Much is derived from experience – being engaged in building relationships – delivering projects and functioning at the commercial interface between organisations.

Context

This book is concerned with b2b relationships: the commercial activities and transactions (exchanges) related to the purchase and supply of products and services between businesses, and those associated with public sector organisations, business-to- government (b2g) contracts. In the former, the buyer in the relationship could be a manufacturer, service provider, consultancy, public sector or third sector organisation, etc.

The Commercial Exchange Model (Figure 1.1) illustrates the interconnectivity between the various parties to an economic exchange: the multiple interactions involved in delivering a solution, project or contract between a main/prime supplier, its customers,

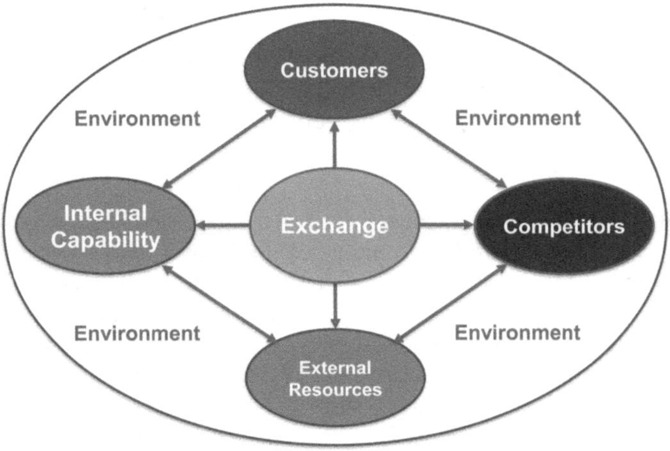

FIGURE 1.1 Commercial Exchange Model

external resources – third-party suppliers, subcontractors and partners and its competitors. All these interfaces need to be managed – the domain of commercial management.

Importantly, it also acknowledges the potential internal commercial transactions between the various business units of an organisation. Large organisations generally comprise multiple business units or trading entities. When these units collaborate to meet a customer's needs, internal trading agreements are required to configure and manage the commercial relationships between these discrete entities.

As discussed earlier, an organisation's role can vary from opportunity (project) to opportunity. For example, a competitor could be a supplier on one project, the customer on another or a partner in a joint venture. Alternatively, a supplier could also be a competitor on the same opportunity, dealing simultaneously with your competitors or working directly for your customer. The landscape is continually shifting depending on the configuration of a particular offering or solution – organisations need to have mechanisms in place to deal with this changing landscape and configure their trading relationships.

Environment

All exchange transactions take place within a context, its environment or 'atmosphere' in Transaction Cost Economics (TCE) and Essential Contract Theory terms, comprising both external and internal factors.

- **External factors**: include, for example, home and host government systems and intervention; cultural norms and values; legal systems and frameworks (civil codes and precedent-based models), procurement legislation and directives, competition or anti-trust laws, corporate governance legislation and regulatory obligations; organisation of labour; media attention; market structures and financial system imposed by funding bodies.

  The parties to an exchange require confidence in a judicial system's ability to enforce the terms of their contract(s). As a result, you may come across contracts in certain geographical locations where the contract is governed by English, Swiss or the law of a specific US state, etc., rather than the in-country's own legal system.
- **Internal factors:** include organisational and individual power and politics, the biases/predisposition of senior managers and inter-functional and business unit competition for key resources.

  For example, the decision to tender for a project may be determined by the biases of powerful leaders rather than objective criteria, while contracting strategies may be dictated by the historical practices of managers. Driven by familiarity, individuals generally favour the 'tried and tested' – 'what we've always used'. This can result in the adoption of suboptimal solutions that are not aligned with what is most appropriate for a particular opportunity.

  As most organisations have finite resources, frequently there is internal competition to assign the best staff to projects. Rather than allocate the most suitable candidate to a particular role, based on their abilities and the needs of a project, their appointment could be determined by the manager with the most influence/power.

Political	Economic	Social	Technological	Legal	Environmental	Regulatory

FIGURE 1.2 PESTLER analysis

There are various tools that can be used to collate information on the diverse environmental issues associated with an opportunity. For example, PEST (Political, Economic, Socio-cultural and Technological), PESTLE (which adds Legal and Environmental) and STEEPLE (which includes Ethical factors) analyses are frequently used.

Figure 1.2 presents a framework for a PESTLER analysis, which adds regulatory issues to the mix – as many organisations, such as energy, aerospace and defence organisations, rail franchisees and airport operators, etc., trade in highly regulated sectors.

If there is high public interest in a particular opportunity, media could also be introduced to the analysis – resulting in the acronym SMETLER. For example, in the construction sector, there is inevitably significant media interest in high-profile projects such as Wembley Stadium, Heathrow Terminal 5 (T5), Crossrail and HS2 – particularly, if they fall behind schedule or go over budget. In these circumstances, managing the various media channels and messaging is crucial.

Generally, these tools are used to scan the environment external to an organisation, but they can be used to examine the internal milieu of an organisation.

Customers (clients)

The first party we will consider is the customer (alternatively referred to as the purchaser or client), the originator and commissioner of an opportunity (potential project or contract). As stated earlier, for each new opportunity, we need to gain a clear understanding of our customer. Customer analysis involves addressing a series of questions. For example, who is the customer? Is the customer represented by an individual or group? What's their profile? What are their objectives – what are they seeking to achieve through this opportunity? How does it align with the customer's overall strategy? What are their current capabilities and assumptions? What's their capacity to collaborate and cocreate? What future opportunities do they offer – is there potential for further contracts? Who ultimately is the key decision maker? What are their drivers, their hot buttons, etc.? Answering these questions, however, may not always be straightforward, particularly where there are multiple demand-side stakeholders – as is common on major infrastructure projects.

Customer hot buttons

For a supplier, accurately identifying their customer's hot buttons is critical. Hot buttons are the comments, questions, symbols or images that instantly place an emotionally charged issue at the forefront of a prospective customer's mind: issues to be resolved or offloaded and desires to be sated that drive the buying decision. Hot buttons, therefore, are the lens through which suppliers scrutinise an opportunity or tender documents. They are subject to change and may vary from stakeholder to stakeholder; therefore, it is essential to determine those linked to the principal decision maker. Additionally, hot buttons inform the generation of win themes, which are utilised when developing propositions and bid proposals. When used effectively, win themes signal to the customer that the supplier fully appreciates their issues, challenges and desires.

How buyers see suppliers

Various models, such as Kraljic's (1983) 'Portfolio Matrix' and Piercy and Lane's (2009) 'How buyers see suppliers' model, can be used to establish the potential or likely trading relationship between customers (buyers) and suppliers (their upstream supply chain). Additionally, these models can be used by suppliers (contractors) to establish how they are possibly viewed by specific customers (downstream clients).

Having much in common, the Kraljic and Piercy and Lane models adopt a classic 2 × 2 grid (matrix) with dimensions comprising:

- 'Profit impact' (impact of supplier on cost structure and competitiveness) – this axis has been generally interpreted as including the importance and value of the purchase.
- 'Supply risk' (market risk/lack of choice) – similarly, this dimension is also deemed to include performance and complexity risk.

The four resulting quadrants are labelled:

- **Efficiency (noncritical)/recurring (low supply risk/low profit impact):** includes, for example, commodity suppliers, where there's generally no requirement to create a long-term relationship, as there are multiple suppliers in the market and purchases are often of low value.
- **Showstoppers (bottleneck)/continuity (high supply risk/low profit impact):** in this quadrant, while suppliers may not have a high impact on the firm's competitiveness/cost structure, they can delay production/delivery. In this instance, the customer is guided to implement just-in-time solutions or adopt alternative approaches that increase the potential pool of capable suppliers.
- **Leverage/best deal (low supply risk/high profit impact):** again, where there are multiple suppliers within a particular market but where these suppliers have the potential to have a significant impact on the customer's cost and/or competitiveness, the buyer should seek to leverage the best deal by managing any likely impact through price negotiation.
- **Strategic/cooperation (high supply risk/high profit impact):** where there's a lack of choice in the market and potentially a high impact on cost/competitiveness – particularly on complex projects or systems integration, it is recommended that customers should adopt a relational approach, creating strategic partnerships and alliances with key suppliers to create competitive advantage. Alternatively, they could encourage expansion of the supply base.

Similarly, an organisation can utilise these models to identify appropriate trading relationships with members of its upstream supply chain.

Competitors

In addition to scrutinising their customers, a supplier will also analyse their competitors. Again, competitor analysis involves addressing a series of questions. For example, who are our competitors? What are their profiles? What are their goals – what are they seeking to achieve? What are their current capabilities and assumptions? What's their capacity to collaborate and cocreate? What is their market strategy and how does it differ from ours? What are their weaknesses? What threats do they pose to our organisation? How do they react when competing against us? Do they have a more intimate relationship with the customer? Are they able to influence the customer's purchasing requirements or procurement approach? How can we compete against them? Answering these questions will enable an organisation to objectively assess its competitiveness within the market and evaluate potential outcomes if they were to competitively bid for a potential opportunity (project) or to develop a competing product or service (value proposition).

Internal capability (supplier)

For each new bidding opportunity or value proposition, a supply organisation needs to be aware of its internal capability to execute the opportunity or deliver the product/service line, establishing what aspects it will undertake internally 'make' and those it will look to third parties to perform – the 'buy' option. The classic 'make or buy' decision (we will cover this concept in Chapter 2).

Additionally, an organisation needs to consider its role and status within the wider supply constellation. Again, this analysis involves addressing a series of questions. For example, what is the perceived profile of the organisation? What are its goals? What are its strengths/weaknesses? What market strategy is it following? What is its current workload/order book and potential to undertake additional projects/opportunities? Once again, addressing these questions may not always be straightforward, particularly where the organisation is divided into autonomous business units and/or where there is internal competition for scarce resources.

Key partners/suppliers

Once a decision has been made over which aspects of an opportunity or value proposition will be executed internally and those that will be carried out by key partners and third parties, prospective suppliers need to be identified and selected. This requires an appreciation of the specific supply/value network, including, for example, knowledge of the structure and unique features of the market: is it competitive, with numerous potential suppliers, are there a limited number of suppliers or is there only a single monopolistic supplier? Is the market composed of local or global suppliers, or is there a combination? Does it contain long or short supply chains, or again is there a mix? Further issues to address concern the technological capability of strategic suppliers. For example, are there key aspects of the technology offered that need to be acknowledged; has the supplier the capability to work collaboratively or cocreate solutions? Also, what is the financial status of the supplier? We will address supplier selection criteria further in Chapter 8.

How buyers see suppliers

As mentioned earlier, suppliers can also utilise tools, such as Kraljic's (1983) 'Portfolio Matrix' and Piercy and Lane's (2009) 'How buyers see suppliers' model, to identify appropriate exchange relationships with members of both its upstream and downstream supply chains.

Strategic supply chain options

Similarly, a purchasing organisation needs to establish how it will engage with its supply chain. For example, will it focus only its direct contact with a selected number of Tier 1 suppliers, or will

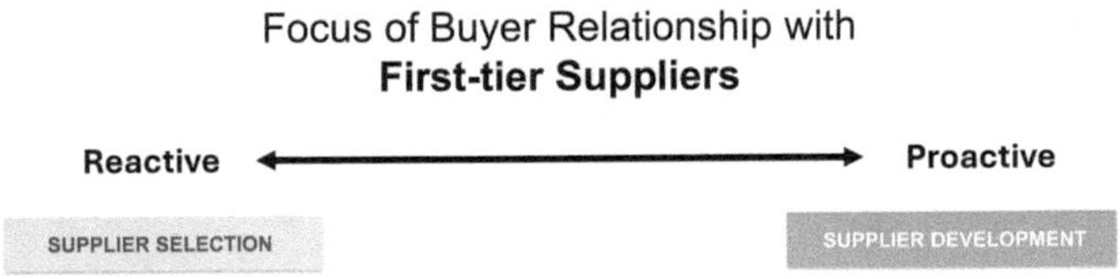

FIGURE 1.3 Strategic supply chain options (1)

it trade with the extended supply network? A subsequent decision involves determining whether this engagement will be on an ad hoc/reactive basis or take a more proactive and relational form. These decisions are illustrated by the following two continuums (see Figures 1.3 and 1.4), which are derived from the work of Cox and Ireland (2006).

The first continuum represents the case where the engagement is restricted to only Tier 1 suppliers. At one end of the spectrum, the interaction is reactive: the organisation appoints individual suppliers as and when their services are required from a pool of potential suppliers. Generally, there is neither a continuous relationship nor a requirement to develop a relational approach. Supplier selection and appointment, therefore, will typically be arms-length and transactional, while their management will potentially require limited oversight. At the proactive end of the spectrum, there will be a clear requirement for an ongoing relationship and for the adoption of a relational approach. In this case, the purchasing organisation may seek to develop these suppliers – for example, helping them to resolve production or delivery issues or improve their profitability to ensure investment and product/service development. This may involve embedding employees of

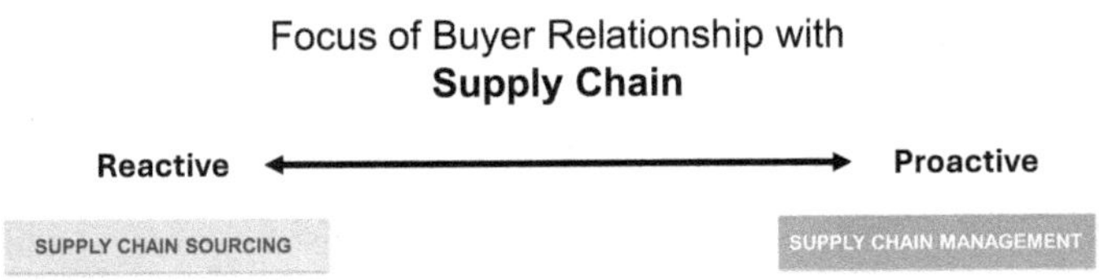

FIGURE 1.4 Strategic supply chain options (2)

the commissioning organisation in the supply company to help resolve these issues and improve performance, quality levels, etc. The logic being that improved supplier performance enables the purchaser to deliver on its value propositions and commitments more ably.

The second dimension incorporates the whole supply chain. Again, at a reactive level, the buying organisation will deal with specific Tier 1 suppliers, while considering its wider supply chain. At the other end of the spectrum, supply chain management entails the purchasing organisation building relationships across their entire supply network to develop and support its suppliers – thereby creating enhanced value propositions for the purchasing organisation and ultimately its customers.

How do we decide where to position an organisation's numerous suppliers and partners on these dimensions? For example, a few years ago, a UK utilities provider utilised 'overall spend with a supplier' as its primary criterion. Creating a scree plot based on overall spend, they identified the top 50 organisations with whom they would trade with on a relational basis. The remainder would be appointed using an ad hoc, transactional approach. However, on closer examination, there was no statistical difference in spending for numerous suppliers either side of the top 50 demarcation. In fact, there appeared to be only four suppliers that accounted for a significant proportion of their third-party expenditure. Imagine the impact such a move had on the organisation's supply base. While the organisation would see a reduction in their direct supplier management costs and potentially an improvement in the performance and quality of those organisations selected for supplier development, for those who were not, however, there undoubtedly would be a negative impact. These suppliers may well look for other customers who value their contribution or if they were to continue their engagement with the utility provider, they would potentially be more likely to behave opportunistically if presented with an occasion to do so. The message is to adopt a selection approach that is transparent, justifiable, consistent with the espoused values of the organisation and which does not alienate potential future suppliers.

Value transmission through an organisation (and its retention)

At its simplest, a distinct commercial organisation consists of a demand side (its supplier facing/buy side activities) and a supply side (its customer facing/sell side activities); it creates something, so has operations, and at its heart is its corporate core.

Organisational interfaces

In order to trade, sell its products and/or services, an organisation's customer facing function needs to define, create and deliver value for its customers. Simultaneously, its supplier facing activities must scan the wider supply chain and value network to identify potential value, acquire it and then exploit it. Thereby establishing throughput of value from its supply chain to the purchaser of the organisation's product and/or services.

However, from a commercial perspective, we are also interested in the value an organisation retains from the exchange. For example, achieving higher margins, enhancing its brand, generating market growth or delivering organisational regeneration/avoiding wane depression. For an organisation to survive and prosper, it needs to retain a proportion of this value. The proportion will vary from sector to sector and from organisation to organisation depending on the type of enterprise, the complexity of its products or services, its efficiency or the degree of competition and uncertainty in its market.

Governing the commercial exchange

Value is transmitted at the point of exchange between organisations and is distributed throughout the supply/value network. How organisations choose to govern these commercial/economic exchanges (interfaces) can be place on a continuum that spans from arms lengths contracting, where there is little or no integration between the demand side and its supply chain, to a more relational and integrated approach to its engagement with customers and supply network alike.

A market-based, transactional, 'arms-length' contracting approach, where an external supplier is selected via competition and the exchange relationship is governed via contracts, standards and rules, is appropriate where there is certainty in the process and product, for example, when buying or selling commodities. In these circumstances, contracts can be relatively simple and performance/contract execution easily determined. If the product/service is delivered on time, to the required standard or specification and in the right quantities, then the agreed payment can be made.

However, at the other end of the spectrum where the supply of products and services is both complex and uncertain, a traditional arms-length contract might not be the most appropriate way of structuring the relationship or governance framework to support a successful outcome. In these situations, a collaborative approach, a third way between market and hierarchy (a 'make'/in-house solution), may well be preferable. Utilising, for example, an integrated, relational contracting approach based on trust, such as partnering or alliancing, where the purchaser's demand-side activities are co-located with those of the principal Tier 1 suppliers' (supply-side) delivery activities.

An example is the alliance formed to construct the Queen Elizabeth-class Aircraft Carriers, which comprised BAE Systems, Thales, Babcock and the Ministry of Defence (MOD) at Tier 1 – plus Rolls Royce, Wärtsilä, Corus Group and numerous other suppliers at Tier 2. However, even with only four participating Tier 1 organisations, the approach results in a complex set of interrelationships that need to be judiciously managed.

If we compare this example with the Heathrow Terminal 5 project (T5), on which there were between 60 and 80 Tier 1 suppliers appointed using the innovative T5 agreement plus a further 120 Tier 1 suppliers appointed via a derivative of the NEC form of contract. In total, approximately 200 Tier 1 suppliers collaborated on T5 through an integrated demand/supply team to deliver a programme of 157 projects. All these interfaces had to be managed; consider the consequences of managing these relationships within a relational environment – it is complex, costly and requires a high degree of customer engagement. With this form of procurement, the customer would be unwise to fully abdicate their responsibilities to third-party consultants.

Therefore, as an organisation moves away from an arms-length, non-integrated approach to one where it actively engages with and integrates with its supply chain, processes and frameworks become more complicated, time-consuming and costly to establish and maintain.

Moreover, when the wider supply-chain network is included, the number of organisational interfaces significantly increases. For example, if we consider T5 again, there were in the region 2,000-plus Tier 2 suppliers engaged on the endeavour, requiring a significant number of interorganisational interfaces to be governed – and adding a further level of complexity to an already complex venture.

In subsequent chapters, we will explore relevant theory, principles and concepts, plus tools and techniques that will enable us to place a particular exchange on this contracting continuum.

Personal reflection

Before we move on to discuss commercial affinity, consider the following questions in the context of the organisation you work for (or one that you have previously worked for):

- How does your organisation position itself in its supply/value network? Illustrate the position of the organisation in its supply/value network and show how it configures its relationships and interacts to achieve its stated aims, etc.
- What proportion of the organisation's activities are carried out by third parties/partners, etc.?
- How are these trading arrangements established and governed?
- Who is responsible for determining strategy and for negotiating and managing these relationships?

The purpose of this exercise is to tease out where you perceive your organisation to be placed in its network. You can then consider the multiple relationships and interactions that are required with the resulting supply network: partners, suppliers, customers and competitors – and how they are best configured.

Later in the book, we will consider how to determine the most appropriate frameworks/agreements to govern these relationships between the multiple parties involved in delivering/executing successful contracts (products, services or projects).

Commercial affinity

According to Weatherly (2005), 'Commercial Affinity' is an *'intangible yet powerful force'* present in successful, enduring business relationships. Resulting from mutually advantageous commercial relationships, it is the attractive magnetism that binds the parties together derived from a need to continue doing business with each other when it makes economic sense for both parties to do so. Stated another way, it is the glue that unites the parties, underpinned by an appreciation of mutual value in the exchange and requiring an ongoing relationship.

For example, to Weatherly, "... a customer will have commercial affinity with a supplier who constantly strives to meet its needs and who demonstrates that it is the best supplier in the market". While irrespective of any contractual obligation, a supplier will be highly motivated to continue doing business that generates further profit. If either the customer or supplier becomes dissatisfied, for any reason, it simply informs the other party, who will seek to find a solution. If they are unable to do so, the parties simply "... walk away from the relationship".

Based on the concept of mutually assured destruction (MAD), Weatherly suggests that the principle applies equally to commercial relationships: as neither party is likely to be *'trigger happy'*, as walking away is likely to significantly disrupt both businesses. Generally, the principle that either party could potentially exit (terminate) the relationship is sufficient to encourage the other party to behave fairly and preserve the relationship. According to Weatherly, this is a further example of commercial affinity.

It is the antithesis of where one party to an exchange resorts to the contract provisions, for example, through third-party involvement (dispute resolution boards, arbitration or litigation) to enforce commitments (contractual obligations) once their fulfilment becomes no longer economically viable or problematic.

Customer attractiveness

Commercial affinity is closely aligned to customer attractiveness – at the heart of both is the acknowledgement of reciprocal value. Generally, if both parties perceive value in a relationship, then it will continue and be fruitful. When this is no longer the case or is absent from the beginning, it can create an environment where conflict and adversarial behaviours may arise. Successful contracts and relationships are, therefore, ongoing and based on mutual value.

However, not all customers are equally attractive. So, what makes a customer attractive? The following features have been identified (see Figure 1.5). Attractive customers are those that provide a route to market – opening markets, enable a supplier to enhance their brand or act as an advocate for the supplier. They allow their suppliers and partners to make reasonable or enhanced profits. For example, if a customer is continually seeking to drive down a supplier's prices – what does that say about their

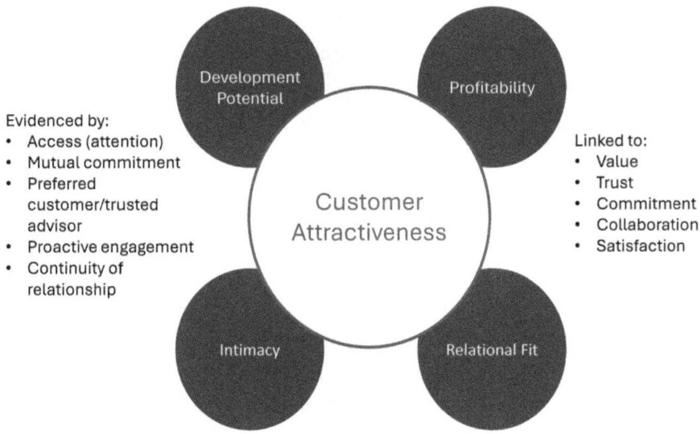

FIGURE 1.5 Customer attractiveness (Developed/derived from La Rocca et al. 2012)

perception of value (mutuality of value) in the supplier's product or services? In terms of relational fit, some customers are easier to work with than others; for example, where there's a closer relational fit, organisations do not need to engage as intensely in relationship/contract management. Ultimately, over time, this creates customer intimacy.

In addition to mutual value, customer attractiveness is also linked to trust, commitment, collaboration and satisfaction – recurring concepts and themes throughout this book.

Customer intimacy

Commercial affinity and attractiveness are closely related to 'customer intimacy', which Brock and Zhou (2012) define as "... a customer's perception of having a very close and valuable relationship with a supplier, characterized by high levels of mutual understanding".

So, what denotes customer intimacy?

Where customer intimacy exists, customers are available when suppliers need to contact them – their calls are answered rather than being blocked by gatekeepers; there is a mutual commitment to resolve issues and support projects; a preferred customer/trusted advisor relationship is evident; relationships become more proactive as opposed to reactive. Crucially, there's an ongoing relationship – opportunities for repeat business. Customer intimacy, relationships and appropriate behaviour on projects and contracts are contingent on the continuity of the relationship. If the engagement is a one-off or a commodity purchase, then perhaps the following principles are not as relevant when compared to a complex, ongoing project that offers the potential for follow-on work or commissions.

Consider the case of a one-off/sporadic customer of a particular market – illustrated, for example, by a Premier League football club seeking to construct a new stadium. As the club does not procure a new stadium very often (say once every 90 years), there is limited potential for an ongoing relationship to be formed with the stadium construction supply chain. As a result, there's an increased likelihood that the parties may behave opportunistically.

Customer intimacy and mutually beneficial relationships are not developed instantaneously. For example, before introducing the innovative T5 agreement on Heathrow Terminal 5 (T5) – the client, British Airports Authority (BAA), already had well-established business relationships with their supply chain. Generally, there tends to be a transition: the parties may start off in a transactional relationship but over time this association can develop, becoming more relational (intimacy is linked to ongoing relationships).

Crucially, as customer intimacy is based on the customer's perspective of the relationship, suppliers need to be able to objectively assess the quality of their relationship and the degree of intimacy with key customers. However, customer relationship management (CRM) activities in themselves do not necessarily generate intimacy.

Creating strong customer relationships

According to Allen et al. (2005), strong customer relationships are created by achieving the following:

- Designing the right propositions for the right customers; to achieve this, suppliers need to understand what the customer actually wants.
- Delivering the commitments made – projects and contracts involve making promises – therefore, to create intimacy, organisations need to establish a track record of delivering on their promises.
- Finally, developing capabilities – as customer requirements change and evolve, suppliers need to be open to and respond flexibly to potential new opportunities with customers. Identifying customer needs as they arise and offering pertinent solutions help develop 'trusted advisor' status and can lead to follow-on business from existing projects and contracts. It involves cultivating the capabilities to repeatedly deliver consistent products and services. Again, this requires and is founded on ongoing trading relationships.

Commercial affinity also entails customers appreciating and creating strong trading relationships with their supplier chain.

Commercial management

This section explores the nature of commercial practice at the buyer–seller interface and introduces a commercial management framework.

In many organisations, 'Commercial' exists as a distinct function, reporting to a group or business unit level commercial director. Instead, it may report to a Finance Director or General Counsel, while in other organisations, the activity may fall under marketing and sales, business development, finance, legal and corporate affairs, procurement/purchasing, supply chain or project/programme management. Commercial is particularly viewed as a dynamic capability within project-oriented organisations.

The effect of globalisation, servitisation and collaboration on b2b exchanges (economic transactions) has been the formulation and management of complex inter-firm contracts, agreements and relationships across the resultant value networks/constellations. Predominantly, the commercial function is responsible for the design, negotiation, award and management of these b2b transactions.

While traditionally 'commercial' might have its roots in Anglo-Saxon organisations, increasingly the competency is gaining more acceptance globally as a valuable business activity.

Definitions

The following definitions of commercial management have been proposed:

> The management of contractual and commercial issues relating to projects, from project inception to completion.
>
> *(Lowe and Leiringer, 2005, 2006)*

> Commercial and contract management refers to the wider process of managing a contract across a project's lifecycle.
>
> *(National Audit Office (NAO), 2016)*

> Commercial management is the activity which defines the overarching policies and practices that provide a framework for trading relationships.
>
> *(Cummins, 2024)*

The term commercial manager has been defined as follows:

> ... a person controlling or administering the financial transactions of an organisation with the primary aim of generating a profit.
>
> *(Lowe et al. 1997)*

> The role of the professional commercial manager is to provide the stewardship at the heart of the investment, and ultimately the benefit realisation processes.
>
> *(RICS, 2016)*

Alternatively, as contracts place obligations on the parties, IACCM[3] proposed the term Commitment Management:

> ... a method through which an organisation applies quality principles to business terms, policies, practices and processes to drive improvement in negotiation, contract performance and governance standards. It is a systematic way of ensuring that business requirements and capabilities are aligned to formal commitments, to ensure that opportunity selection is optimized and business relationships are fulfilled as agreed.
>
> *(IACCM, ND)*

However, this term has not been widely adopted in practice.

Commercial management framework

Lowe (2013) provides a commercial management framework (see Figure 1.6), which exemplifies the multiple interactions and connections between the purchaser's procurement cycle and a supplier's bidding and implementation cycles: from the inception of an opportunity or the realisation that an organisation has a

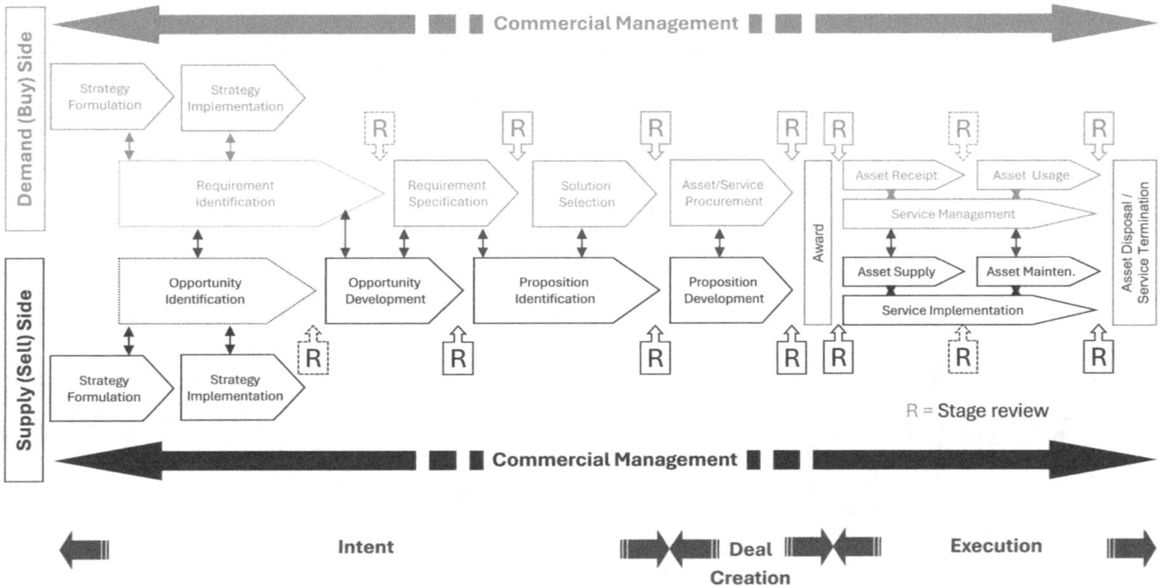

FIGURE 1.6 Commercial management framework (Lowe, 2013)

requirement that needs satisfying through to the end of life of that asset or termination of a service. In some respects, the framework may be aspirational or an ideal, as in many organisations the commercial function may become engaged in the process at a later stage, for example, after the identification phase. Alternatively, it may be subdivided into two separate functions linked to pre- and post-contract award activities.

While the commercial management framework appears to be a linear process, in practice, it is more iterative – 'looping' through some phases several times, while progressing through a project's/contract's commercial lifecycle.

The framework contains three discrete stages:

1 **Intent**: includes the front-end activities that link the opportunity or requirement (acquisition) to the strategic intent of the organisation. For example, why would an organisation invest in an asset or service if it did not align with their strategy or help them to deliver on their strategic intent? Similarly, from the supply side – why would an organisation pursue an opportunity that was not aligned with or supported its strategy?

Once the customer has established a requirement it needs to be specified, alternative solutions for delivering the requirement considered and a preferred solution selected. Similarly, during this stage, as mentioned above, the business winning team within supply organisations seek to identify potential opportunities, engage with and influence buyers, develop opportunities and identify viable propositions.

At this stage of the model, supply-side activities are positioned slightly ahead of those linked to the demand side. While an exchange is predominantly driven by the demand side, during this initial phase, the supply side attempts to influence demand-side decision-making. For example, by persuading the customer to appoint them as a single-source supplier or, failing that, if the opportunity goes out to tender, to be invited to tender and potentially to gain an advantage by embedding elements of their products or services that are exclusive to their organisation (a unique selling proposition/point (USP)) in the customer's solution. Thereby placing the supplier in a much stronger position compared with their competitors.

2 **Deal creation**: involves the customer instigating a procurement process, in response to which the prospective supplier (bidder) would develop and submit a proposition (bid). Submitted supplier proposals are evaluated, a preferred bidder selected and a deal negotiated, culminating in the award of a contract. We will explore elements of procurement best practice, how suppliers respond to opportunities and the negotiation stage in later chapters.
3 **Execution** (implementation stage): the framework differentiates between the supply of an asset and a service. For an asset, the stage includes asset delivery and receipt, following which the resource will be used and maintained. Ultimately, at the end of the products usefulness, a decision must be made either to sell, dispose of or to demolish the asset. For a service, there's an implementation and management phase. Similarly, at the end of the service or outsourcing contract, a decision must be made either to continue with the existing supplier, retender the work or to bring the activity in-house (insourcing). The impact of these decisions should be considered during the earlier stages of the commercial framework and accounted for in the contracts entered into by the parties.

Personal reflection

Before discussing the actions and components that constitute commercial management, consider your current participation across the commercial management framework – from inception through to completion. For example, when do you personally become involved; what's your sphere of influence and how do you engage in or support commercial activities?

Commercial management practice

Activities undertaken by commercial practitioners include contract management (contract strategy/selection, negotiation, formulation and administration), risk management, dispute resolution and bidding. Plus development appraisal, estimating, price formulation, cost management, payments, cost–value reconciliation, cash flow management, value management, the creation of outline proposals, acquiring approvals and permits, determining procurement strategy, supplier evaluation, supply chain management, subcontracting administration, performance measurement, quality assessment and claim formulation. They may also provide support to business development, marketing and sales, image/reputation management and innovation management. As a result, commercial practice is underpinned by an eclectic mix of academic disciplines and principles.

Lowe (2013) collates these disparate tasks in the following model (Figure 1.7), which focusses on the processes, activities, knowledge and capabilities that support commercial interfaces and highlights the multiple interconnected disciplines involved.

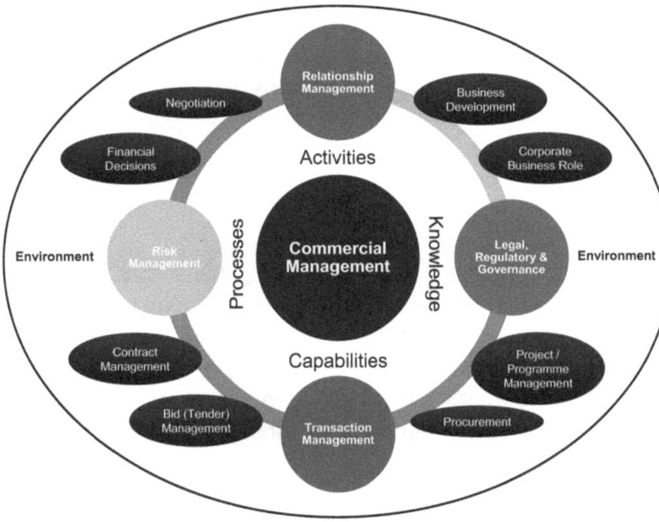

FIGURE 1.7 Model of the activities, processes, capabilities and knowledge that underpin commercial practice (Lowe, 2013)

The four main components of commercial management are risk, relationship and transaction management plus legal, regulatory and governance. It also encompasses contract and bid management; procurement and project management; financial decisions and negotiation plus support for business development and the organisation's corporate activity.

Commercial practitioners, therefore, undertake and contribute to several business processes – in management, operational and supporting roles – each involving a range of interrelated structured tasks and activities. Figure 1.6, presented earlier, identifies multiple gateway (decision) points required throughout a contract's/project's lifecycle. In the following chapters, we will explore how to combine and apply the concepts, frameworks and techniques from the relationship, transaction and risk management – plus legal, regulatory and governance fields to make informed 'commercial' decisions from the perspective of both the customer and the supply chain.

Commercial roles across various industry sectors and even within organisations can comprise different combinations of these components. Different prominence may be given to aspects of the role due to the dominance of other functions within the business, for example, marketing and sales, finance and accounting, legal, procurement/supply chain management and project management. It may also be influenced by the different 'histories' (backgrounds) of individual commercial practitioners. Similarly, where commercial 'sits' within an organisation can also influence its role and impact. For example, if the commercial activity reports to 'finance', there is a potential for it to focus on cost benefits or the bottom line of a potential opportunity rather than alternative sources of value in the prospect, while those that report to 'legal' may become risk averse.

Further, not all organisations will have a discrete function called commercial. However, the organisations, particularly those in the infrastructure, construction, aerospace and defence space that structure their delivery systems around projects, programmes and portfolios, tend to have a separate commercial function.

If an organisation chooses not to have a distinct commercial discipline, then these activities will need to be undertaken by other functions within the organisation. A potential disadvantage of distributing these activities across several business functions is that the organisation loses its high-level overview of the entire commercial landscape. Plus, it creates the problem as to how it collates these activities to offer a 'joined up' commercial response.

Commercial management capabilities and competencies

According to Lowe (2013), effective commercial management practice is underpinned by a combination of capabilities and competencies (see Table 1.1).

TABLE 1.1 Top 20 'Commercial' capabilities and competencies

1	Communication and presentation skills	11	Contract Management skills
2=	Commercial acumen/ awareness	12=	Decision-making skills
	Relationship/people management skills		Staff development skills
4=	Leadership skills	14=	Creative/innovative thinking
	Negotiating skills		IT/IS skills
6	Team/collaborative working skills	16	Strategic thinking
7	Influencing skills	17=	Problem-solving skills
8=	Analytical skills		Time Management skills
	Project Management skills	19=	Change Management skills
10	Financial acumen/ awareness		Cost Management skills

Source: Analysis of 90 commercial functional frameworks/job specifications (Lowe, 2013).

Personal reflection

At this point, spend some time considering the following questions:

- How does your organisation currently coordinate its commercial activities? What's its logic for adopting this structure?
- How is the commercial/commercial management competency currently perceived? Is it viewed as a dynamic/distinctive capability?
- How might that change in the short/medium term? Why do you believe this?

How does 'commercial' add value?

As highlighted, the commercial function undertakes and/or supports a combination of activities that underpin and deliver an organisation's, business unit's or project's strategic aims and objectives, and particularly their commercial intent.

The value of the role is its ability to develop and deliver innovative commercial solutions derived from a diverse mix of activities and its integrating features that focus on value creation, maximising (generating or optimising) profit margins and/or return on investment, driving growth (improving market penetration/increasing market share and/or revenue), acquiring and delivering competitive advantage[4] and protecting and enhancing an organisation's commercial and reputational interests (via contracts and relationships). For example, ensuring that the contracts and relationships entered into with customers and the wider supply chain are constructed to support the organisation's strategic intent or programme/project deliverables, protect its interests, for instance, in respect of its exposure to risk, generate value for both the organisation and its customer and provide an opportunity to create additional competitive advantage.

The benefits of a discrete commercial function are focussed on its ability to encompass an eclectic mix of activities, possess a wide vocabulary derived from all these disparate disciplines, provide a 'helicopter' view of all the commercial elements of exchange relationships and constitute an integrating capability. Further, a commercial function provides the cohesion (glue) that holds the commercial elements of an organisation together – particularly in terms of focussing on value creation and protecting an organisation's position via contractual and relational mechanisms – to foster more informed commercially driven decision-making.

Definitions of terms

Profit (or margin) is the money (income/revenue) retained by an entity from a commercial exchange, its investments or business interests once all the costs and taxes of producing its goods and/or services, etc., have been accounted for.

Profit margin is generally taken to be the net income (profit generated by an entity) expressed as a percentage of the total revenue generated before deductions are made.

Value, according to Porter (2008),

> ... is measured in terms of total revenue (an expression of the price a product and or service realizes) and the units it can sell. Profitability is achieved when the value an organisation achieves exceeds the costs incurred in creating the product or providing the service offered. Porter believes that the aim of any generic strategy is to create value for buyers, which exceeds the total cost of manufacture and supply.
>
> *(Porter, 2008, p. 38)*

Value for money

> ... is the optimal use of resources to achieve the intended outcomes. 'Optimal' means 'the most desirable possible given expressed or implied restrictions or constraints'. Value for money is not about achieving the lowest initial price.
>
> *(NAO, 2004)*

It is obtained via *'the effective, efficient and economic'* utilisation of resources.

Value management has been defined as follows:

> A structured approach to defining what value means to the organisation and the project. It is a framework that allows needs, problems or opportunities to be defined and then enables review of whether the initial project objectives can be improved to determine the optimal approach and solution.
>
> *(APM, 2006)*

Commercial management maturity

Commercial management maturity is

> ... an indication of an organisation's present 'commercial management' sophistication and capability, for example, its managers know which technique to apply, appropriate to an exchange's needs.
>
> *(Adapted from Ibbs et al. 2004)*

To improve their commercial and contract management capabilities, organisations need to objectively assess their current performance against perceived best practice within the discipline. To facilitate this, a few commercial management maturity models have been developed. These include the following:

The World Commerce and Contracting's Capability Maturity Analysis enables organisations to obtain objective insights into their current commercial and contract management performance and business impact for both its buy-side and sell-side. Additionally, its reporting mechanism provides benchmarking comparisons to equivalent organisations and recommendations for improvement. It comprises the following sections, which measure the 'extent' of an organisation's:

1 **Leadership:** executive level leadership and accountability for commercial and contract management performance.
2 **Customer vendor experience:** the 'ease of doing business'.
3 **Execution and delivery:** the range and effectiveness of current performance metrics.

4 **Solution requirements management:** integration of commercial and contracting practices with product and service development/supply.
5 **Financial:** integration of commercial/contracting and financial indicators and performance.
6 **Information systems and knowledge management:** relating to contract and relationship performance.
7 **Risk management:** effectiveness in identifying, mitigating, managing and eliminating commercial risk.
8 **Strategy:** how the organisations commercial/contracting process impacts and underpins its strategic intent.
9 **People development:** the capability to effectively develop the skill base of its commercial/contracting practitioners.[5]

Alternatively, the National Audit Office (NAO, 2016) published their Commercial Audit Framework based on insights and emerging best practice derived from their audits of UK government contracts. The framework consists of a series of questions that allow organisations to evaluate their commercial capability under the following themes: commercial strategy, commercial capability, market management and sourcing (procurement), contract approach, contract management, contract lifecycle and termination and transition.

We will examine the Commercial Audit Framework in more detail in Chapter 7.

Conclusion

Many organisations operate (trade) using commercial approaches (contracts and practices) based on what they are familiar with, rather than utilising solutions designed to address the specific conditions and context of the exchange. A key feature of this book is to look beyond established practices – the tried and tested. It will provide objective mechanisms to inform commercially driven decision-making, for example, that will support the identification of frameworks and contracts that have the best likelihood of delivering successful commercial outcomes.

Notes

1 Interconnected entities that exchange value in order to create and deliver superior value through products and services.
2 The terms buyer, purchaser, client and customer are used interchangeably, as are the terms supplier, contractor, subcontractor, third party and partner.
3 International Association for Contract & Commercial Management (IACCM) – now known as World Commerce & Contracting.
4 Factors that place an organisation's product and/or services above those of its competitors, enabling it to generate value and higher profits. Generally, such features cannot be easily duplicated.
5 For more information, see https://www.worldcc.com/Research/Capability-Maturity-Analysis-Benchmark

Further reading/resources

For additional information on the role of Commercial Management and Commercial Awareness, see

Cummins T (2024) *The Difference between Commercial Management and Contract Management*. World Commerce & Contracting. https://news.worldcc.com/news-from-worldcc/the-difference-between-commercial-management-and-contract-management (Accessed 9 July 2024).

Greasley A (2020) Chapter 15: Supply chain management. In *Absolute Essentials of Operations Management*. Routledge, Abingdon, Oxon. pp. 84–92.

Lowe D J (2013) *Commercial Management: Theory and Practice*. Wiley-Blackwell Publishing Ltd, Oxford.

Lowe D J, with Leiringer R (2006) *Commercial Management of Projects: Defining the Discipline*. Blackwell Publishing Ltd, Oxford.

Stoakes C (2011) *All You Need to Know about Commercial Awareness 2011/2012: What It Is and Why You Need It to Become a Successful Professional*. Longtail Publishing Limited, London.

Witcher B J (2020) Chapter 3: The external environment. In *Absolute Essentials of Strategic Management*. Routledge, Abingdon, Oxon. pp. 16–28.

World Commerce and Contracting (Formerly, IACCM). https://www.worldcc.com

Commitment Matters: Managing Trading Relationships in the Global Networked Economy – a blog run by Tim Cummins President and Head of Research and Learning at World Commerce and Contracting. See, for example: What does a commercial manager do?

References

Allen J, Reichheld F F, and Hamilton B (2005) The three "Ds" of customer experience. *Harvard Management Update*, 10(10), 1–4.

APM (2006) *APM Body of Knowledge: Definitions*. APM, High Wycombe.

Brock J K-U and Zhou J Y (2012) Customer intimacy. *Journal of Business and Industrial Marketing*, 27, 370–383.

Cox A and Ireland P (2006) Strategic purchasing and supply chain management in the project environment – theory and practice. In: D J Lowe (ed.) with R Leiringer, *Commercial Management of Projects: Defining the Discipline*. Blackwell Publishing, Oxford, pp. 390–416.

Cummins T (2024) *The Difference between Commercial Management and Contract Management*. World Commerce & Contracting. https://news.worldcc.com/news-from-worldcc/the-difference-between-commercial-management-and-contract-management (Accessed 9 July 2024).

IACCM (ND) *What Is the Definition of Commercial Management?* IACCM, Ridgefield, USA. http://www.iaccm.com/about/faq/?questionid=15 (Accessed 22 August 2012).

Ibbs C W, Reginato J M and Kwak Y H (2004) Developing project management capability: benchmarking, maturity, modeling, gap analysis, and ROI STUDIES. In: P W G Morris and J K Pinto (eds.) *The Wiley Guide to Managing Projects*. John Wiley & Sons, Hoboken, NJ, pp. 1214–1233.

Kraljic P (1983) Purchasing must become supply management. *Harvard Business Review*, 61, 109–117.

La Rocca A, Caruana A and Snehota I (2012) Measuring customer attractiveness. *Industrial Marketing Management*, 41, 1241–1248.

Lowe D J (2013) *Commercial Management: Theory and Practice*. Wiley-Blackwell Publishing Ltd, Oxford.

Lowe D J, Fenn P and Roberts S (1997) Commercial management: an investigation into the role of the commercial manager within the UK construction industry. *CIOB Construction Papers*, 81, 1–8.

Lowe D J and Leiringer R (2005) Commercial management in project-based organisations. *Journal of Financial Management of Property and Construction*, 10, 3–18.

Lowe D J and Leiringer R (2006) Commercial management — defining a discipline? In *Commercial Management of Projects: Defining the Discipline*. Blackwell Publishing Ltd, Oxford, pp. 1–17.

National Audit Office (NAO) (2004) *Getting Value for Money from Construction Projects through Design*. The Stationery Office, London.

National Audit Office (NAO) (2016) *Commercial and Contract Management: Insights and Emerging Best Practice*. NAO External Relations, London.

Piercy N F and Lane N (2009) *Strategic Customer Management: Strategizing the Sales Organization*. OUP, Oxford.

Porter M E (2008) *Competitive Strategy: Techniques for Analysing Industries and Competitors*. Free Press, New York.

RICS (2016) *Commercial Management of Construction*, RICS guidance note, UK, 1st Edition. Royal Institution of Chartered Surveyors (RICS), London. https://www.rics.org/profession-standards/rics-standards-and-guidance/sector-standards/construction-standards/black-book/commercial-management-of-construction (Accessed 10 July 2024).

Weatherley S (2005) Pathclearer: a more commercial approach to drafting commercial contracts. PLC*Law Department Quarterly*, October-December, 39–46. https://uk.practicallaw.thomsonreuters.com/3-201-3377?contextData=%28sc.Default%29&transitionType=Default (Accessed 9 July 2024).

2

FOUNDATIONS OF COMMERCIAL RELATIONSHIPS

Transaction cost economics, relational contracting, power and trust

Introduction

As we discovered in the last chapter – commercial (the commercial activity/function) is an amalgam of disciplines and concepts appropriated from economics, finance, organisational behaviour, strategy, marketing, legal and project management to name a few. This chapter provides an overview of key theories and concepts that underpin commercial practice.

According to Lumineau (2017), inter-organisational relationships are predominantly regulated concurrently by two key governance mechanisms: one utilising formal contracts to safeguard against opportunism and conflict (Transaction Cost Economics [TCE]), the other harnessing relational governance, and especially trust (Relational Contract Theory [RCT]).

The following sections cover TCE, relational contracting/RCT, power and trust and present key frameworks and models to aid commercially focused decision-making. In subsequent chapters, we will explore how these concepts can be combined and applied to enable us to make informed commercial decisions.

The foundations of commercial relationships

Throughout this book, you will encounter several recurring concepts and themes – for example, trust, relationships, collaboration, opportunism, commitment, uncertainty, value, conflict, power,

DOI: 10.4324/9781003052159-2

FIGURE 2.1 Theories and concepts underpinning the commercial function

etc. – as we consider various commercial frameworks, best practices and models. Figure 2.1 illustrates several of these principles and concepts.

Transaction Cost Economics (TCE)

TCE is an interdisciplinary concept that integrates aspects of economics, contract law and organisation theory and can be used to determine both 'Economic Governance' – the boundaries of the firm and 'Governance Structure' – the framework within which economic exchanges (transactions) are conducted. Moreover, I consider TCE to encapsulate commercial – both the commercial function and the management of the commercial interface between organisations through its specific combination of disciplines. Additionally, it provides both a theoretical framework and common vocabulary for us to explore and explain commercial practice.

Utilising the lens of contract, TCE employs the cost of the transaction as its unit of analysis and governance as the mechanism through which order is introduced to the exchange, thereby assuaging conflict and delivering reciprocal benefit. Williamson (1981) states that a transaction cost is incurred, whenever a product or service is '... transferred across a technologically separable interface', demanding investment in new skills and abilities, resources and the processes through which the product is manufactured, or service delivered. It comprises the costs incurred in scanning the market, determining who to trade with (for example, execute a project), drawing up the contract, negotiating with them, striking the deal, recording commitments made and then managing the relationship and commercial interface post-award, that is, providing oversight to ensure that the supplier delivers on the commitments they've made or applying sanctions when they do not. It is, therefore, the cost of procuring a product or service via the market rather than producing or supplying them from within the firm: the costs incurred in an exchange.

Mostly, TCE texts assume a demand-side perspective; however, transaction costs are incurred by both the purchaser and supplier. While the purchaser (demand side) incurs the direct transaction costs associated with the activities outlined above, they will, probably, also pay the costs incurred by suppliers in complying with and responding to these activities. These indirect costs are frequently recouped by suppliers as an overhead, which is only recovered on executed contracts.

Economic governance

When considering the boundaries of the firm, the classic 'make or buy' decision, there are essentially two options:

1 **Markets:** where products and services are procured external to the organisation, and
2 **Hierarchies:** where a product or service is manufactured/supplied from within the organisation.

In certain circumstances, an alternative hybrid approach, which seeks to combine the advantages of markets and hierarchies, is appropriate.

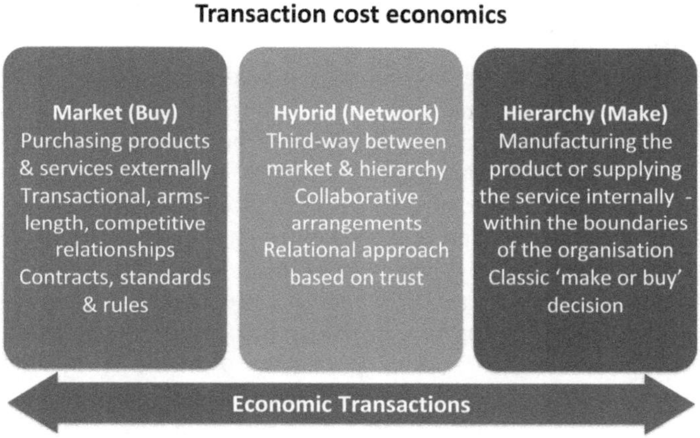

FIGURE 2.2 Economic transactions

TCE theorises that when the cost of purchasing the product, service or capability becomes prohibitive (i.e., complicated, time-consuming or costly), the purchaser would bring that activity into the organisation, i.e., make (hierarchy) rather than buy (market).

If we select the buy option, purchasing options can be placed on a continuum that has a pure market-based approach at one end of the spectrum and a hybrid approach at the other (see Figure 2.2).

At the market end of the spectrum, the approach is transactional, incorporating arm's length, competitive relationships and the use of contracts, standards and rules to enforce compliance. At the opposite end of the spectrum is a hybrid approach; a third way, founded on collaboration and trust-based relationships, which incorporates partnering and alliancing principles, is applied. The latter approach seeks to attain the benefits of 'making' but without the associated costs of ownership.

We can prudently use a market-based approach for simple, discrete purchases where we can precisely specify our requirements in terms of quality, cost and time pre-award, for example, when purchasing commodities such as basic materials and common components. In such instances, we can draw up contracts and select appropriate terms and conditions to adequately protect the interests of the parties.

However, in respect of complex projects and systems integration where the purchase and supply process can become more convoluted and potentially entail bespoke procurement and contracting solutions, a hybrid approach is more appropriate. One that incorporates elements of collaboration, relationships and trust. In these circumstances, the resulting contracts can become more challenging to formulate and take longer for the parties to come to an agreement. Consequently, the process can become very costly with the parties incurring significant transaction costs. For example, UK PFI projects have, in some instances, taken up to five years to negotiate, requiring significant legal involvement and incurring transaction costs of several million pounds. As mentioned earlier, if this becomes too prohibitive, it may be in the purchaser's interest to bring the activity in-house.

I would like to dispel the notion that relational approaches are inevitably less expensive than traditional procurement/contracting methods. There are specific costs related to collaborative working and in maintaining associated inter-organisational relationships. Frequently, suppliers initially undervalued the cost of relational contracting and the amount of unpaid work they feel obliged to undertake.

Governance structure

You may have come across TCE before – in relation to the 'make or buy' decision. Additionally, the concept can be utilised to evaluate alternative governance frameworks and contracting approaches in respect of specific opportunities and projects.

How does TCE influence contracting strategy?

Predominantly, in business, contracts (governance structures) are used to safeguard exchange transactions, incorporating complex terms and conditions to deal with aspects of change management, the valuation of additional work and determining issues between the parties. For example, through the inclusion of third-party dispute resolution techniques. Clauses, post-award (ex post) control mechanisms, are constructed to prevent or moderate opportunistic behaviour – defined by Williamson (1985, p. 47) as *'self-interest seeking with guile'*. Essentially, opportunism involves cheating, stealing and lying to fraudulently gain a partisan advantage – primarily, a financial one, thereby using stealth to get more from a contract than the party is contractually entitled to. Other examples could include overpricing variations post-award or where an organisation utilises their position or power to extract more value out of a project or opportunity than is warranted.

TCE, therefore, focuses on post-award (ex post) governance, especially the inclusion of control mechanisms to restrain or moderate opportunistic behaviour by an exchange partner. However, opportunism can occur both pre-award (ex ante) and post-award (ex post) and frequently involves subtle, active and passive forms of deceit. While many trading partners will not behave opportunistically, it is difficult to predict pre-award those that will. However, it is assumed that most partners will *'have their price'*, the point at which the incentives for acting opportunistically are too high for them to ignore.

A key aspect of governance structures is their inability to provide suitable or effective adjustment (maladaptation) post-award, i.e., during the contract execution phase. Except for simple commodity or spot purchases, change is inevitable in most projects due to unforeseen circumstances and technical advancement. For example, where a purchaser is unable to completely specify their requirements pre-award or where they wish to avoid committing themselves to potentially obsolete solutions/technology on lengthy projects or where technology is rapidly advancing. The objective during the pre-award phase, therefore, is to endeavour to foresee probable contractual hazards, identify appropriate control mechanisms and incorporate these into the proposed governance structure (contractual arrangement).

In the context of western exchange transactions, legally binding contracts are primarily used to protect the interests of the parties and mitigate the potential impact of opportunistic behaviour.

Moreover, the standing orders of organisations generally preclude its representatives from committing the business to an exchange relationship without a contract. Although, there are many instances of smaller entities trading for many years without a formal written contract.

Legal agreements and contracts lie on a continuum ranging from simple discrete to complex bespoke contracts – the costs of drafting, negotiating and agreeing these contracts increase significantly as one progresses from simple to complex. As mentioned earlier, ultimately, it may become more cost-effective to vertically integrate the activity (product or service).

Drivers of transaction governance

How does TCE aid the selection of an appropriate governance framework?

TCE utilises three attributes, with associated behavioural characteristics, to describe exchange transactions:

1 **Asset specificity**: is associated with the degree to which trading parties can reallocate specialised assets purchased to manufacture a product or deliver a service, and the importance of these resources to the commercial relationship. The following specific assets have been identified: physical, human, site, dedicated, brand name and temporal. Where a party is unable to reutilise these resources or recover their investment in them elsewhere a bilateral dependency is created. As a result, it is assumed that this increases the potential for opportunistic behaviour.

The behavioural characteristics linked to asset specificity, therefore, is opportunism. As discussed above, this is exhibited when a party goes beyond the pursuit of self-interest to engage in dishonesty, double-dealing, deception and falsifying information to deliver financial gains.

For example, if one party expends more resources than the other when entering into an agreement the dependency or imbalance of power created can drive opportunistic behaviour by the party that has invested the least in the transaction. For example, when the customer (buyer) has invested more time and effort in the procurement process than the supplier. In these circumstances, there is a potential for the supplier to behave opportunistically up to the cost of switching. Switching costs are the costs incurred when changing suppliers mid-contract, terminating a contract and appointing an alternative supplier, which can be significant. As a result, a customer may pragmatically tolerate a certain degree of opportunistic behaviour. Likewise, where a supplier has higher investment costs in the exchange than the buyer, for example, where they are required to purchase specialised equipment, plant or software in order to execute a contract, undertake extensive project specific personnel induction activities or co-location as part of an integrated project team, and they are only able to obtain a return on their investment through this particular contract or customer, again this creates a dependency. If the other party is aware of this disproportionate investment, potentially they may seek to manipulate this power for their own advantage, that is, behave opportunistically.

Disappointingly, there have been instances where parties have opportunistically exploited aspects of partnering – for example, with suppliers being asked/required to undertake additional work at their own expense – as it was perceived to be building the relationship and supporting the partnering approach. This is despite the supplier potentially having a contractual right to an additional payment.

High asset specificity, therefore, creates dependency (an imbalance in the distribution of power between the parties) that can lead the independent/more powerful entity to behave opportunistically.

Asset specificity and opportunism are key features of TCE. Theory asserts that transaction costs will increase as the exchange parties (transactors) invest more in specialised assets, driven by the need to safeguard themselves against the potential opportunistic behaviour of the other party. Further, according to Williamson (1991), 'asset specificity increases the transaction costs of all forms of governance'.

2 **Uncertainty**: as indicated above, bespoke, long-term contracts (projects) are particularly subject to change and variations due to unforeseen circumstances. If we consider a major project, there is generally a high degree of uncertainty; its complexity leads to a lack of awareness and understanding, and clients may not want to commit themselves to solutions at an early stage particularly if there is a long gestation period. Flexibility, therefore, creates further uncertainty. To accommodate this need for adaptability, contracts generally incorporate mechanisms to facilitate and value these adaptations. Uncertainty can produce ex ante environmental and ex post behavioural costs.

The behavioural characteristic associated with uncertainty is bounded rationality. There are limits to a decision-maker's mental faculty and knowledge, particularly during the early stages of a project's (contract's) development: the parties do not have perfect information or all the answers or solutions, and face time constraints in which to reach a decision. Additionally, some projects will be inherently more uncertain than others, for example, when innovative solutions/components are utilised. Further, one party to the exchange may be privy to certain knowledge that the other party might not be aware of leading to issues of asymmetry of information (an imbalance of power). Moreover, the party in possession of key information may seek to benefit from this and use the power gained to extract additional value from a contract. It is theorised that, when complex and uncertain environments are encountered, bounded rationality will result in hierarchy.

3 **Frequency**: regular, recurring transactions support the establishment and continuation of relationships due to the potential value to be gained from future exchanges. The experience gained from regular exchanges, therefore, engender self-interest trust, foster intimacy (as mentioned in Chapter 1) and incentivise the parties to invest in specialised governance structures. As a result, it is in a party's interest to behave appropriately because if they do so then they (the supplier) are likely to get obtain future/follow-on work from the customer.

Supplementing formal contracts, the relationship/intimacy gained from frequent engagements can moderate the potential for opportunistic behaviour.

In addition to trust, Winch (2006) has proposed a further behavioural characteristic linked to frequency: learning. The more often and longer two parties contract with each other, the more they discover about the other's requirements, aims, processes, etc., and their stimulus to transact. Experience gained from the frequency of engagement, therefore, drives learning and trust.

Ideally, this knowledge, linked with the principles of creating strong customer relationships: customer intimacy, places the supplier in a preferential position in relation to their competition. However, this knowledge can be a disadvantage, particularly in a highly competitive environment where new entrants, unaware of a customer's standards and expectations, may undervalue the work involved and underbid established suppliers.

To misquote Milton Friedman: *One man's opportunism is another man's* gamesmanship. The point here is that, for some, opportunistic behaviour is part and parcel of doing business. For example, in the case of the hypothetical football stadia project mentioned earlier, it could be argued that, as there will be no ongoing relationship, no frequency of engagement: why wouldn't the parties behave opportunistically? Conceivably, such opportunistic behaviour would result in the organisation gaining a poor reputation in the market and act as a deterrent, but experience doesn't always seem to substantiate this.

The main governance structures (frameworks) derived from TCE are Market Governance (otherwise referred to as Classical Contracting), where market forces prevail; Trilateral Governance (Neo-classical Contracting), where issues can be referred to third parties to mediate or pronounce on an issue, for example, by a Dispute Adjudication Board; and Transaction-specific Governance or Relational Contracting and Bilateral Governance also known as Obligational Contracting. Finally, there is vertical integration (Hierarchy) where a supply chain activity is brought within the boundaries of the firm.

Personal reflection

Before we move on to the next section, in the context of the organisation you work for/previously worked for or a project/contract that you are familiar with, consider the following questions:

- How does TCE explain the behaviours of the organisation or those of its trading partners?
- What 'insights' does TCE provide on the relative position of the main parties involved?

Relational contracting

Shortcomings in classic contracting as a governance structure of transactions led critics to consider alternative approaches and fields of research that exploited informal mechanisms within an exchange. Ian Macneil, for example, a key proponent of relational contracting, rather than choosing to label exchanges based on their governance structure, described the behaviours within an exchange. Initially adopting the term 'relational contract theory' (RCT), he subsequently labelled the approach 'essential contract theory' (Macneil, 2000), although RCT is more commonly used in the literature. Further, he determined that economic transactions should be placed on a continuum: discrete to relational exchanges, contingent on the intensity of the relationship between the parties (Macneil, 1983).

Contract behavioural patterns and norms

Macneil (2000) identified ten common contract behavioural patterns and norms, evident in all contracts, that underpin and drive relational behaviour (see Figure 2.3). However, he considered the power norm to have the most influence on exchange relationships.

Relational contracting, based on relational norms and behavioural patterns, is regarded by some authorities as an alternative

Role integrity Reciprocity Implementation of planning Effectuation of consent Flexibility Contractual solidarity Restitution, reliance, and expectation interests Creation and restraint of power Propriety of means Harmonization with the social matrix

FIGURE 2.3 Essential Contract Theory (developed/derived from Macneil, 2000)

to explicit, complex contracts and vertical integration. Further, relational contracts – 'informal agreements sustained by the value of future relationships' – are widely used in ongoing, collaborative b2b exchanges (Baker et al., 2002).

Figure 2.4 identifies the key features that underpin relational contracting – these include the appropriate allocation of risk, joint working, problem solving and mechanisms to jointly share any potential savings or additional costs incurred on the project. At its core is good communication between the parties. For example, an underlying factor in the difficulties experienced on both the Wembley stadium and the Olkiluoto 3 nuclear reactor projects was the breakdown of communication between the principal parties.

RISK ALLOCATION
JOINT WORKING
NO-BLAME CULTURE
PROBLEM SOLVING
MUTUAL OBJECTIVES
GAIN & PAIN SHARING
CONTINUOUS IMPROVEMENT
PERFORMANCE MEASUREMENT
A
T
I
O
N

FIGURE 2.4 Components of relational contracting (developed/derived from Frydlinger et al., 2016)

Incorporating collaborative working, relational contracting utilises partnering and alliance contracts (see Chapter 4). Specifically, Galvin et al. (2021) have established that:

- alliance contracts are underpinned by relational norms
- to foster collaboration, exchange parties should integrate governance, trust and culture, as the potential for opportunistic behaviour persists
- for collaboration to be established, significant investment is required
- to establish and sustain collaboration between members of an alliance, a holistic and integrated approach is necessary, requiring continual effort throughout a project's lifecycle.

However, there are critics of relational contracting and collaborative working. For example, Cox et al. (2000) challenge procurement and supply management perceived best practice (received wisdom), which advocates long-term collaborative approaches upheld by trust. Further, Cox (2001) maintains that '... the best defence of the buyer's position, and the one that ensures that suppliers innovate and pass value to buyers, is the maintenance of perfectly competitive (or highly contested) supply markets, with low barriers to entry, low switching costs and limited information asymmetries'.

While not fully embracing Cox's position, particularly in respect of complex, bespoke projects with potential for follow-on business/opportunities, there are, however, circumstances where the development of a relationship is potentially not necessary or advisable, for example, in respect of a commodity-related purchase or 'one-off' spot transaction. The parties, therefore, should objectively consider the circumstances surrounding the exchange and address the question: is it in the party's interest to build a relationship? Again, if the exchange is merely a one-off engagement, then it is probably not appropriate to spend the time, effort and money in building a long-term relationship.

To illustrate this point, on the Emirates stadium project, Arsenal FC elected to adopt a collaborative approach with their main contractor Sir Robert McAlpine. However, instead of restricting their engagement to a single project: the new stadium, Arsenal FC was shrewd and created the potential of a follow-on project: the remodelling of the existing Highbury Stadium. Thereby establishing an ongoing relationship with Sir Robert McAlpine, which supported certain beneficial behaviours.

Personal reflection

Before we move on to the next section, in the context of the organisation you work for/previously worked for or a project/contract that you are familiar with, consider the following questions:

- How does relational contracting explain the behaviours of the organisation or those of its trading partners?
- What further 'insights' does relational contracting provide?

Two recurring concepts in the first part of this chapter are power and trust. The following sections explore these issues further.

Power dynamic

As previously mentioned, unequal investments during the formation or execution of a contract (asset specificity) can create a dependency where the investment made by the dependent party can only be recouped via the specific exchange. This dependency produces a power imbalanced, which can then be leveraged or exploited by the independent party (the party with less invested in the exchange). Therefore, we need to be aware of the relative power (dominance) between the buyer and the supplier (a feature of both TCE and RCT/Essential Contract Theory), as this will inform both the type of contracting solution we adopt and our strategy when negotiating both the initial contract and post-award changes. Further, as the distribution of power can change over the lifecycle of a contract/project (a dynamic situation), both the buyer and the supplier need to be able to identify, in advance, potential pivot points. Similarly, the power dynamic can be influence by market conditions, for example, during 'boom' periods the power pre-award is generally held by the supplier due to over demand of supply capability, and during periods of 'bust' the power position is reversed with the purchaser in the dominant position, as they hold the potential of income where there is under demand of supply capability. Where these two situations occur, the parties can adopt appropriate strategies; however, issues arise where the exchange occurs during a period of instability between these extremes. The parties, therefore, need to be aware of dynamic changes/inflection of power in the market.

The power perspective: buyer power/supplier power

The following questions, therefore, need to be addressed. Who is dominant? Is it the buyer or the supplier? Is this likely to change between the pre-award and post-award stages of a project? Can we identify potential turning points during the contract/project lifecycle or in the market?

Generally, in stable markets, the buyer is dominant during the pre-award phase, as they're the ones initiating the contract/project. However, once a contract has been awarded (referred to as the 'Fundamental Transformation' in TCE), then power generally transfers to the supplier, due to the switching costs incurred by the purchaser if they decide to change supplier. As mentioned earlier, a supplier can potentially 'hold things up' and behave opportunistically due to the customer's higher asset specificity (dependency) resulting from their investment in the procurement process. However, as discussed, this norm can vary in times of recession and boom or where a particular sector is dominated by a monopolistic supplier or customer.

Conflict in buyer-supplier relationships

Additionally, conflict is inherent within buyer-supplier relationships, as each party is driven by their own unique and often conflicting commercial intent. Simplistically put, while buyers seek to maximise value, suppliers are motivated by combinations of profit maximisation, market share/penetration, brand enhancement and return on investment from an exchange. (For more detail, see Cox and Ireland, 2006). We will consider aspects of conflict management in Chapter 4.

The power matrix

As both commercial and operational outcomes in an exchange transaction are influenced by the relative power between the purchaser and the supplier (Cox and Ireland, 2006), it is essential that both parties determine which of them is dominant at each stage of a contract's/project's lifecycle. One model at our disposal to establish this is Cox and Ireland's (2006) Power Matrix. The Power Matrix (Figure 2.5) is underpinned by the notion "... that all buyer and supplier relationships are predicated on the relative utility and the relative scarcity of the resources that are exchanged between the two parties" (Cox et al., 2002). The model can be used to place the parties to the exchange in one of four quadrants: Buyer Dominance, Supplier Dominance,

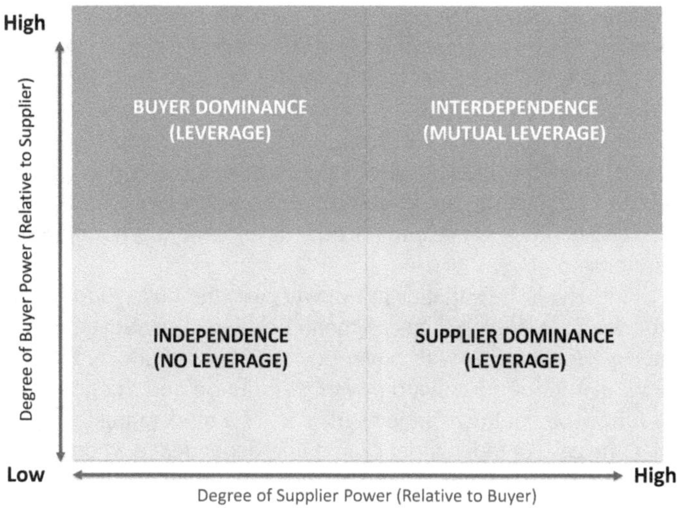

FIGURE 2.5 The Power Matrix (adapted from Cox and Ireland, 2006)

Independence and Interdependence. Initially, this would be based on the issues influencing the pre-award stage, then on those affecting the deal creation stage (for example, if a single preferred bidder is selected), then on the factors prevailing during the execution stage of the contract/project and finally on experienced at the contract resolution/final account stage. Thereby plotting the transition of power between the parties across the contract/project lifecycle.

Application of the power matrix/perspective

For example, if at the pre-award stage the power lies with the buyer, they're able to exert their power over supplier(s) potentially forcing them to only achieve minimal profits in the exchange, resulting in lower tenders or at worse the submission of 'suicidal' (at or below cost) tenders. However, the buyer should ask themselves if it is in their best interest to exert all their potential power. If they do, the danger is that by forcing a supplier into accepting very low or zero margins, this may well drive negative and adversarial behaviours post-contract award in order for the supplier to recoup their costs or generate a profit. This would increase the buyer's enforcing/oversight (contract management) costs due to the need to closely monitor the supplier. Moreover, if the exchange is a 'one-off' contract, without the potential for future exchanges, or if the power transfers to the supplier post-award, then the likelihood of opportunism on the part of the supplier significantly increases. Also, the behaviour undermines trust and could negatively impact the development of a long-term relationship.

Similarly, if the supplier has power over the buyer during the pre-award stage, then they can theoretically realise above normal returns. However, as with buyer power discussed above, the dynamic nature of post-award power distribution and the potential for follow-on contracts/projects may act as a moderating factor.

In the case of independence and interdependence where there is no imbalance of power, market prices and quality will prevail.

We can also utilise this approach to consider where the power lies between a main/prime contractor and its supply chain. For example, if a main contractor was dealing with a monopolistic supplier, then the power is with sub-contractor; the main contractor is obliged to engage with them. Again, this will drive certain behaviours and different approaches in terms of negotiating and contracting strategy.

Personal reflection

In relation to the power perspective, consider the following questions:

- Have you experienced the case where an organisation has extracted the maximum amount of value it could from a relationship at contract formation? If so, what were the consequences over the course of the engagement?
- Have you experience of where an organisation has forgone exercising its full power when negotiating a contract? Again, if so, what was the outcome?

Trust

'Trust' and 'self-enforcing' agreements have been recognised as an alternative mechanism to contracts. Trust, according to Rousseau et al. (1998), is:

> ... a psychological state comprising the intention to accept vulnerability based upon positive expectations of the intentions or behaviour of another.

The principle is based on reciprocity: a relationship based on mutual and cooperative behaviours and actions.

Several categories of trust involved in transactions and associated with the development of long-term relationships have been identified. These include contractual, competence, goodwill (altruistic), socially orientated and self-interest trust (Sako, 1992; Lyons, 1995). However, I consider that the principal form of trust in business-to-business relationships is self-interest trust. As noted in the last chapter, customer intimacy is fostered where both parties perceived value in a relationship – a key feature being self-interest trust.

While some authors suggest that formal contracts undermine trust and, as a result, promote opportunistic behaviour, others, such as Poppo and Zenger (2002) believe that formal contracts, relational norms and trust act as complementary mechanisms. Moreover, Blomqvist et al. (2005) suggest that contracts and trust are critical success factors for unequal relationships and that collaboration demands trust. In most exchange agreements, there is a relational dimension. Further, if the intention of the parties is to interact relationally, then this can compensate for the formal contract adopted. Therefore, suitably selected and applied contracts, aligned where applicable with relational approaches, provide highly appropriate governance structures (frameworks).

Trust (from either the buyer or supplier perspective), however, can easily be undermined. Ekici (2013) has collated, from both perspectives, the activities that undermine trust. He has also identified under what circumstances the parties may continue their relationship despite a deterioration in trust.

Trust – buyer perspective

For example, a buyer's trust in a particular supplier can be undermined by the opportunistic actions of the supplier or because of disappointment, arising from having unrealistic expectations of the product/service provided or being undervalued, exploited or expected to go the 'extra mile'.

To illustrate this, if a supplier's sales team oversells a solution (exaggerates its capabilities), or if they fail to correct erroneous misconceptions/assumption made by a customer during the pre-tender stage, the customer may develop unrealistic/incorrect expectations of what they are to receive through the exchange/contract. Ultimately, the buyer's trust in the supplier will be eroded when the supplier does not deliver on their promises/commitments or meet the client's expectations. (As noted in Chapter 1, delivering contractual commitments and promises is a key aspect in developing customer intimacy).

As a result, low levels of trust between the parties may drive further adversarial behaviours and could ultimately lead to the termination of the contract. However, Ekici (2013) suggests that there are certain factors that could prompt the parties to continue with a trading relationship despite the existence of low levels of trust. These include conformity with company policy or agreements, the size and reputation of the supplier, the lack of viable substitutes, particularly if the supplier has a monopolistic position in the market, or where substitution would negatively impact a project's goals, and prohibitively high switching costs. As a result, a customer may have to continue with a contract even though the parties have a low-trust relationship and would ideally prefer to terminate the relationship.

Trust – supplier perspective

Similarly, from a supplier's perspective, trust can be undermined by duplicity (for example, where the customer is found to be mendacious), the unreasonable behaviour of a customer, or where a customer engages in freeloading or generally exploits the relationship.

The following is an example of the latter. A supplier was engaged to construct a new wing at an existing school. As they were on site, the site team were frequently asked to carry out remedial work on the existing building, such as replacing/repairing a broken toilet. This work was not covered by their contract. Initially, the supplier absorbed the cost of such work in the belief that it would build trust and develop their relationship with the client. However, as they received further requests to undertake non-contractual activities, they felt exploited but were reluctant to pursue legitimate claims for additional payment for fear of negatively impacting their relationship with the client. Moreover, this position could be cynically exploited.

Again, these behaviours erode trust. However, as with the case of the buyer, a supplier may still be motivated to continue with an agreement. For example, the organisation may operate in a highly competitive market and consider this behaviour to be a function of their specific environment. Likewise, due to the size of the account or their reliance on the client, they may not be able to say no to the customer. For example, where they have invested a disproportionate amount of money in tendering for and mobilising the resources to undertake a project, or where terminating the contract would precluded them from obtaining future work from the customer or via their consultants. On a positive note, it could be that where a contract is highly profitable, despite the negative behaviours of the customer, they may be prepared to tolerate lower levels of trust. Alternatively, there could be relatively low levels of risk in the work being undertaken.

Personal reflection

In relation to trust, consider the following questions:

- Is trust established at the individual or organisational level? Why do you think this?
- When individuals leave an organisation, can you still assume the same level of trust and relationship between the organisations? Why do you think this?
- How might your actions undermine the trustworthiness of your organisation and its trading relationships?
- While it takes a long time to establish trust, it can be lost very quickly. Plus, once things start to go wrong, participants can very quickly revert to a more adversarial stance. What steps can you take to prevent these instances from occurring or mitigate their effects?

Application

Risk allocation via contracts

As described earlier in the chapter, contracts can be placed on a continuum based on the amount of risk the parties seek to transfer or are prepared to accept. Considering that contracts are generally instigated or determined by the purchaser pre-award – they are the party driving the engagement – it is essentially how much risk they wish to retain or pass on to their supplier.

At one end of this continuum, there is a market-based approach where fixed price/lump sum contracts are used. As mentioned earlier, these forms of contract are appropriate when the purchaser can precisely define their requirements/needs (for example, regarding time, cost and quality) but to be effective, there needs to be certainty both of process and of product. At the other end of the spectrum, for example, where there is uncertainty in terms of product and process or where the purchaser wants to retain a high degree of flexibility, there are relational and collaborative approaches. For example, on Heathrow Terminal 5 (T5), the client, BAA, didn't want to fix their solution at the outset – preferring to preserve the flexibility to amend their designs, enabling them to incorporate the latest technology and products. To facilitate this, cost reimbursable/fee-based approaches can be adopted.

In the middle, there are incentivised contracts – including guaranteed maximum price contracts which cap the purchaser's liability and guaranteed maximum liability contracts, which limit the liability of the supplier.

However, while there is a wide range of contracting approaches at our disposal – contracting solutions are often chosen based on the decision-maker's familiarity with the various options or preference for a particular contract rather than as a result of an objective evaluation of the contract's appropriateness to the given circumstances. My position is that, rather than using a standardised/dogmatic approach, contracts (governance frameworks) should be selected according to whether they are most likely to best serve our purposes and support the successful delivery of a particular project.

Contractual governance matrix

The final model presented in this chapter is adapted from the 'Suppliers strategic relationship positioning matrix', which is based on the principles of TCE (Cousins et al., 2008). Cousins et al.'s model utilises 'level of uncertainty' as its X axis and 'level of dependency' (asset specificity) as its Y axis indicate the potential for opportunistic behaviour by the parties and suggest an appropriate purchasing approach.

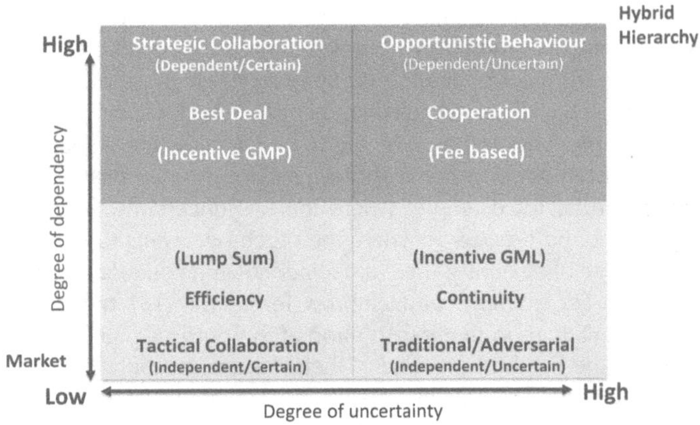

FIGURE 2.6 Contractual Governance Matrix (developed/adapted from Cousins et al., 2008 and Kraljic, 1983)

The Contractual Governance Matrix (see Figure 2.6) has flipped the polarity of the X dimensions of Cousins' model and added the contracting strategy continuum to the diagonal of the model, ranging from a market approach (where there are low levels of dependency and low levels of uncertainty) to a hybrid approach (where there are high levels of dependency and high levels of uncertainty). In the latter case where these levels go beyond those acceptable to the commissioning organisation, the activity can be brought in house (Hierarchy). Based on this contracting strategy, continuum contracting solutions are allocated to each quadrant enabling an organisation to identify and allocate appropriate contracting strategies.

Additionally, as there is a high degree of commonality between the axes of Kraljic's (1983) Product and Service Positioning Matrix and the Contractual Governance Matrix. Kraljic's relational descriptors have been added to each quadrant to enable the contracting solution to be cross-referenced to an appropriate relational approach.

For example, at the market end of the contracting strategy continuum, where the exchange comprises low levels of uncertainty (i.e., greater certainty of product and process) and low levels of dependency (i.e., independence and low asset specificity), a market-based, arm's length approach is preferable, consistent with 'tactical collaboration' and the features of 'efficiency' (where substitute products are readily available and a competitive supply market exists), for example, and associated with the purchase of commodities or a fully designed solution. In this quadrant, lump sum forms of contract are appropriate, as the customer can specify in advance their precise requirements, changes to the brief are unlikely and there are numerous potential and capable suppliers.

At the other end of the contracting strategy continuum, where the exchange involves high levels of uncertainty and high levels of dependency, there is a greater potential for opportunistic behaviours to be exhibited; a third way or hybrid approach is recommended. This is consistent with both Cousins' and Kraljic's matrices, which recommend the development of cooperation, particularly when a custom design or unique specification is required, the purchaser is unable or unwilling to commit to a specific solution at the outset of the contract, supplier technology is critical, and substitution is too difficult or costly. In this quadrant, the recommendation would be to utilise a relational form of contract that incorporates a fee-based approach. Again, if this approach becomes too expensive or time-consuming to utilise, the purchaser could consider bringing the activity into the organisation (Hierarchy).

Example: This approach was adopted on Heathrow Terminal 5 (T5). The project had an 18-year gestation period, due to the lengthy public inquiry process it went through. The client rightly did not want to commit themselves to a specific solution, thereby restricting themselves to old technologies. Further, they created uncertainty by embracing the need for design evolution post-contract award and incorporating a high degree of flexibility. Add to this the size and complexity of the project, and the need to construct the terminal next to a fully operational airport and runway, a fee-based approach was deemed to be the most appropriate contracting methodology. Although, they adopted mechanisms to maintain commercial affinity between the parties.

Where there are low levels of uncertainty and high levels of dependency, the optimal relationship would be strategic collaboration (Cousins, 2002) with the objective of seeking the best deal (Kraljic, 1983). In this instance, substitution is possible as a competitive supply market exists with several capable suppliers. The recommended contracting solution entails incentivising the parties but capping the liability of the customer by incorporating a guaranteed maximum price in the contract.

Finally, where there are low levels of dependency and high levels of uncertainty, the relationships encountered are potentially traditional and adversarial (Cousins, 2002). The objective here is to establish continuity, as the specification tends to be unique, supplier technology is critical, production-based scarcity exists due to low demand and/or few sources of supply and demand is unpredictable (Kraljic, 1983). Again, the recommended contracting solution involves incentivising the parties but, in this case, capping the liability of the supplier by incorporating guaranteed maximum liability clauses in the contract.

Customers can utilise the model to identify appropriate contracting strategies for their Tier 1 suppliers aligned to the prevailing circumstance and that are most likely to support project success. Similarly, Tier 1 suppliers can allocate their Tier 2 suppliers to these quadrants to identify appropriate contracting strategies. The process then flows up the supply chain. Alternatively, suppliers can utilise the model to establish the optimal contracting strategy between themselves and their customer to support their contract negotiations. Particularly, when the customer is seeking to impose a suboptimal approach, for example, by using a lump sum contract to pass on unmanageable risk to their supply chain or where there are high levels of uncertainty and dependency.

Summary

In this chapter, the key features of TCE, relational contracting, power and trust have been presented, together with Cox and Ireland's Power Matrix and the Contractual Governance Matrix. These concepts and models will be applied in later chapters to inform commercially driven decision-making.

Personal reflection

Finally, attempt the following reflexive questions:

- How are/how may the concepts and models introduced in this chapter be applied in your business or on specific projects/ programmes you are involved in?
- How may they explain the behaviours adopted by your organisation and its trading partners?
- What personal 'take-aways/insights' have you gained from engaging with this material?
- How does the material covered aid your understanding of your organisation's strategy and commercial practices?

Further reading

For additional information on the concepts covered in this chapter, see

Transaction cost economics and project governance

Lowe D (2023) Transaction cost economics: governing the commercial interface. In: G M Winch, M Brunet and D Cao (eds.) *Research Handbook on Complex Project Organizing*. Edward Elgar Publishing, Cheltenham, pp. 78–88.

Müller R (2011) Project governance. In: P W G Morris, J K Pinto and J Söderlund (eds.) *The Oxford Handbook of Project Management*. Oxford University Press, Oxford, pp. 297–320.

Winch G (2006) The governance of project coalitions – towards a research agenda. In: D J Lowe (ed.) with R Leiringer, *Commercial Management of Projects: Defining the Discipline*. Blackwell Publishing, Oxford, pp. 324–355.

Relational Contracting/Trust

Gil N, Pinto J and Smyth H (2011) Trust in relational contracting and as a critical organizational attribute. In: P W G Morris, J K Pinto and J Söderlund (eds.) *The Oxford Handbook of Project Management*. Oxford University Press, Oxford, pp. 438–460.

Swan W, McDermott P and Khalfan M (2006) Trust and commercial managers: influences and impacts. In: D J Lowe (ed.) with R Leiringer, *Commercial Management of Projects: Defining the Discipline*. Blackwell Publishing, Oxford, pp. 172–191.

Power perspective

Cox A and Ireland P (2006) Strategic purchasing and supply chain management in the project environment – theory and practice. In: D J Lowe (ed.) with R Leiringer, *Commercial Management of Projects: Defining the Discipline*. Blackwell Publishing, Oxford, pp. 390–416.

References

Baker G, Gibbons R and Murphy K J (2002) Relational contracts and the theory of the firm. *The Quarterly Journal of Economics*, 117, 39–84.

Blomqvist K, Hurmelinna P and Seppänen R (2005) Playing the collaboration game right - balancing trust and contracting. *Technovation*, 25, 497–504.

Cousins P D (2002) A conceptual model for managing long-term interorganisational relationships. *European Journal of Purchasing and Supply Management*, 8(2), 71–82.

Cousins P D, Lamming R C, Lawson B and Squire B (2008) *Strategic Supply Management: Principles, Theories and Practice*. Pearson Education, London.

Cox A (2001) The power perspective in procurement and supply management. *Journal of Supply Chain Management*, 37, 4–7.

Cox A and Ireland P (2006) Strategic purchasing and supply chain management in the project environment – theory and practice. In: D J Lowe (ed.) with R Leiringer, *Commercial Management of Projects: Defining the Discipline*. Blackwell Publishing, Oxford, pp. 390–416.

Cox A, Ireland P, Lonsdale C, Sanderson J and Watson G (2002) *Supply Chains, Markets and Power: Mapping Buyer and Supplier Power Regimes*. Routledge, London.

Cox A, Sanderson J and Watson G (2000) *Power Regimes: Mapping the DNA of Business and Supply Chain Relationships*. Earlsgate Press, Boston, UK.

Ekici A (2013) Temporal dynamics of trust in ongoing inter-organizational relationships. *Industrial Marketing Management*, 42 (2013), 932–949.

Frydlinger D, Cummins T, Vitasek K, and Bergman J (2016) *Unpacking Relational Contracts: The Practitioner's Go-To Guide for Understanding Relational Contracts*. Thaslam College of Business, The University of

Tennessee, Knoxville, IACCM and CIRIO. https://www.vestedway.com/wp-content/uploads/2022/03/Unpacking-Relational-Contracting_Jan-31-2019.pdf (Accessed 10 July 2024).

Galvin P, Tywoniak S and Sutherland J (2021) Collaboration and opportunism in megaproject alliance contracts: The interplay between governance, trust and culture. *International Journal of Project Management*, 39(4), 394–405.

Kraljic P (1983) Purchasing must become supply management. *Harvard Business Review*, 61, 109–117.

Lumineau F (2017) How contracts influence trust and distrust. *Journal of Management*, 43(5), 1553–1577.

Lyons B R (1995) Specific investment, economies of scale, and the make-or-buy decision: a test of transaction cost theory. *Journal of Economic Behavior and Organization*, 26, 431–443.

Macneil I R (1983) Values in contract: internal and external. *Northwestern University Law Review*, 78, 340–418.

Macneil I R (2000) Contracting worlds and essential contract theory. *Social and Legal Studies*, 9, 431–438.

Poppo L and Zenger T (2002) Do formal contracts and relational governance function as substitutes or compliments? *Strategic Management Journal*, 23, 707–725.

Rousseau D M, Sitkin S B, Burt R S and Camerer C (1998) Not so different after all: A cross-discipline view of trust. *Academy of Management Review*, 23, 393–404.

Sako M (1992) *Prices, Quality and Trust: Inter-firm Relations in Britain and Japan*. Cambridge University Press, Cambridge.

Williamson O (1981) The economics of organization: the transaction cost approach. *American Journal of Sociology*, 87, 548–557.

Williamson O (1991) Comparative economic organization: the analysis of discrete structural alternatives. *Administrative Science Quarterly*, 36, 269–296.

Williamson O E (1985) *The Economic Institutions of Capitalism*. Free Press, New York.

Winch G (2006) The governance of project coalitions – towards a research agenda. In: D J Lowe (ed.) with R Leiringer, *Commercial Management of Projects: Defining the Discipline*. Blackwell Publishing, Oxford, pp. 344–355.

3

IDENTIFYING, ALLOCATING AND MANAGING RISK AND VALUE

Risk and value management methodologies and techniques to inform commercially focused decision-making

Introduction

As identified in Chapter 1, risk and value management are key components of commercial practice and business decision-making and are fundamental business leadership capabilities.

Risk management is the process by which risk, both opportunities (positive, upside events or circumstances) and threats/hazards (negative, downside events or circumstances), is proactively managed when determining whether to invest in a new asset, product or service (buy-side decisions) or to tender (bid)/supply specific assets, products or services (supply-side decisions). In some project-oriented organisations, risk management is a discrete business function, either in its own right or in association with legal, regulatory or governance – applied by risk practitioners. However, senior leaders within organisations need to be aware of the inherent risks underlying their potential choices and of the means and probable effectiveness of alternative approaches to managing them.

Value management is a solutions-generating methodology focused on defining and enhancing value and prompting innovation. It is applicable at the organisational, portfolio, programme,

DOI: 10.4324/9781003052159-3

project, product, process or service level to define and add tangible benefit (value).

Generally, risk management and value management are considered systematic, iterative processes or group of management policies, processes or procedures that are associated with an organisation's internal control, governance, strategic management and decision-making. They also incorporate coordinated sets of activities, approaches, practices, principles and structures that are applied to risk and value (benefit analysis) at the corporate, business and project levels and underpin many if not all management activity. Therefore, a key aspect of organisational management/leadership. At the project level, risk and value management are applied throughout the project/contract lifecycle.

The aim of this chapter is to provide an overview of risk management and value management. It introduces the concepts of risk and value, including definitions of terms and an overview of risk management and value management processes, and commonly used tools and techniques.

Risk management

Increasingly, organisations operate within VUCA conditions:

- **Volatility:** unstable, unpredictable, hazardous and/or changeable environments.
- **Uncertainty:** indecision and ignorance (lack of knowledge) of conditions, events, issues and/or solutions.
- **Complexity:** multifaceted, intricate, complicated relationships, solutions and/or environments.
- **Ambiguity:** vague, unclear and/or indefinable causes of events, or confounding alternatives (options).

These conditions result in an increased risk (threats and opportunities) when trading: engaging in economic exchanges. Senior leaders, therefore, need to be aware of potential risks within their sector and how they may be managed.

Definitions

There are numerous definitions of risk and risk management. Over the years, our perception of risk has changed from one focused on threats and hazards to one that encapsulates both negative/downside and positive/upside events and outcomes. For example:

> ISO 31000:2018 states that risks "... can include anything that generates uncertainty related to an organization's objectives or creates a deviation from the expected. This involves not only threats to the strength or viability of the organization, but also opportunities to be gained. Reputation, political changes and climate change impacts are examples of what needs to be considered when managing risk effectively".
>
> *(ISO, 2021)*

Similarly, the Association for Project Management (APM, 2024) define risk as "The potential of a situation or event to impact on the achievement of specific objectives ..." while the Project Management Institute (PMI, 2021) describe it as "An uncertain event or condition that, if it occurs, has a positive or negative effect on one or more project objectives".

Additionally, APM (2024) define project risk as "The exposure of stakeholders to the consequences of variation in outcome". Whereas the APM Body of Knowledge 7th edition defines risk management as:

> ... a process that allows individual risk events and overall risk to be understood and managed proactively, optimising success by minimising threats and maximising opportunities and outcomes.
>
> *(APM, 2019)*

Typically, definitions of risk include five key aspects: source, context, consequence, probability and timeframe. Risk, therefore, is clearly associated with an event (an action, decision, function or process) or series of events, the atmosphere (circumstances or environment) in which it occurs and is time framed. Further, events have a potential consequence, either a positive opportunity or a negative impact, for which a probability or likelihood of occurrence can be determined together with an estimation of the magnitude of its likely impact. In the context of business exchanges, this impact is ordinarily expressed as the sum of money the organisation may directly lose/gain, or the adverse/beneficial influence its occurrence may have both monetarily and reputationally on the concern.

Further, a distinction is often drawn between risk and uncertainty:

- **Risk:** where the probability of an event occurring can be determined in advance and its consequences forecast from existing data
- **Uncertainty:** where there is a lack of understanding/data regarding the probability of occurrence (opportunity or threat)

However, while more recent definitions of risk contain both positive (opportunity) and negative (threat) dimensions, in practice, the term is still predominantly viewed as having negative connotations. Something to be mitigated, reduced and avoided. Likewise, many definitions of risk management still focus on the potential hazards faced by an organisation. For example, the Chartered Management Institute (CMI) define risk management as:

> … the range of activities undertaken by an organisation to control and minimise threats to the continuing efficiency, profitability, and success of its operations.
>
> *(CMI, 2024)*

This book assumes the term risk captures both opportunities (positive, upside events or circumstances) and threats/hazards (negative, downside events or circumstances), while risk management is the process by which these threats and opportunities are proactively managed.

Risk, therefore, is a key component of business decision-making, be that determining whether to invest in a new asset, product or service (buy-side decisions) or to tender (bid)/supply specific assets, products or services (supply-side decisions). Senior leaders within organisations consequently need to be aware of the inherent risks (threats or opportunities) underlying their potential choices and of the means and probable effectiveness of alternative approaches to manage them.

Perspectives of risk

According to Maytorena (2013), the importance of risk and its management has been established through studies in several disciplines, for example, behavioural and cognitive psychology, decision theory, economics and business/management domains. She identifies four principal perspectives:

- **Rationalist:** This perspective has underpinned the development of probability, mathematical and economic theory, all highly influential in our understanding of decision-making. Leading to the conceptualisation of expected utility, expected value, modern utility theory, subjective probability and subjective expected utility theory.
- **Behavioural:** This perspective considers the behaviour of individuals when making decisions. Key concepts include 'bounded rationality', where an individual's judgements are constrained by their information processing capacity. It further considers the impact of an individual's beliefs and values when deciding on a course of action.
- **Cognitive:** This perspective utilises managerial and organisational cognition (individual and social processes) to develop our comprehension of organisational decision-making. Studies in this area have sought to provide insight into how decision-makers (senior leaders/managers) comprehend and model the environment within which they operate, how they process information and how this impacts their behaviour.
- **Cultural:** This perspective focuses on the social and cultural aspects of decision-making, particularly those factors that influence an individual's responses to risk (acceptance and aversion). For example, the impact of power, social status and political views on risk perception at the individual, team or organisational level.

For those interested in delving further into these various perceptions of risk, see Maytorena (2013).

Risk management standards and guidance

Numerous good practice guides and risk management standards have been produced by various professional organisations, international institutes and government bodies. These include:

- **ISO 31000 Risk Management Standards and its related documents:** published by ISO® (International Organization for Standardization, 2021).
- **BS 31100:2021 Risk management – code of practice and guidance for the implementation of BS ISO 31000:2018:** published by BSI (British Standards Organisation, 2021).
- **Management of risk in government:** published by the Cabinet Office (Cabinet Office, 2017).
- **Orange Book: Management of risk – principles and concepts:** published by HM Treasury (Government Finance Function and HM Treasury, 2023).
- **The Risk Management Standard:** published by the Institute of Risk Management (IRM), The Association of Insurance and Risk Managers (AIRMIC) and ALARM (The National Forum for Risk Management in the Public Sector) and adopted by the European Federation of Risk Management Associations (FERMA) (IRM, 2002).
- **Enterprise Risk Management – Integrating with Strategy and Performance:** published by COSO (Committee of Sponsoring Organizations, 2017).
- **Management of risk – RICS guidance note:** published by the Royal Institution of Chartered Surveyors (RICS, 2015).
- **M_o_R® (Management of Risk: Creating and Protecting Value):** published by AXELOS (AXELOS, 2022a).

These standards provide advice on risk management practices, principles, tools, techniques and templates, including exemplar risk management models and frameworks, establishing a common vocabulary for risk management, and maintaining effective risk management processes and procedures. While some are aimed at risk practitioners, senior leaders in government and programme and project Senior Responsible Officers (SROs), others are aimed at business managers (see also Chapter 7: Applying rigorous and consistent commercial processes and procedures).

Benefits of effective risk management

Effective risk management is considered to deliver the following benefits:

- Enhanced future-oriented thinking
- Enhanced/informed decision-making
- Improved planning
- Improved productivity
- Safer working environments
- Improved communication
- Improved resource allocation
- Continuous improvement
- Enhanced reputation/prevention of reputational damage
- Enhanced competitive advantage

As a result, risk management is a critical business activity, as inadequate management of risk can result in significant financial and reputational losses.

Projects and risk

More and more, projects are used to realise and deliver organisational strategic intent. While risk has always been a feature of economic exchanges and projects specifically, the ever-changing environment in which they are now undertaken, leading to increased complexity and uncertainty, significantly impacts the approach by which an engagement or project is established, and its inherent risks are addressed. For example, the emergence of new/disruptive technologies, increased regulation, the globalisation of supply chains, the impact of the UK's withdrawal from the EU and other changes to international trade, issues around cyber security and evolving business practices have given rise to risk and uncertainty.

Risk management/project risk management process

There are many risk management and project risk management protocols; however, these generally adopt a similar structure: that is, a systematic approach to identifying, analysing, responding to, monitoring and controlling risk/project risk. Additionally, it is an iterative process or group of management policies, processes or procedures – a defining feature of the culture of the organisation, which is linked to its internal control, governance, strategic management and decision-making. The aim is to encourage robust risk management processes, ensure appropriate oversight of the investments and exchanges/projects undertaken by the entity and enhance contract/project execution.

These standards and best practice guidance documents divide the risk management process into several iterative stages, requiring stakeholder collaboration and the consideration of the context (internal and external) in which the endeavour (investment/opportunity) will take place. ISO 31000:2018, for example, utilises the following steps:

Step 1: Communication and consultation

Undertaken throughout the process to enable stakeholders and the wider project team to comprehend the risks inherent in the endeavour, communication and learning are key elements of successful risk management. Examples include engaging with both internal and external stakeholders to surface information that is clear, accurate, apt and well-timed to support informed commercially driven decision-making and promoting risk awareness across those involved.

Step 2: Establish context

A clear appreciation of the circumstance under which the endeavour will occur, the internal and external environments in which the organisation operates need to be determined as part of the risk management process. Tools frequently used at this stage are SWOT and PEST analyses. A SWOT analysis or matrix is a decision-support tool that facilitates a situational assessment of the internal and external factors (strengths, weaknesses, opportunities and threats) related to a business investment or opportunity. Alternative, dimensions include SOAR (strengths, opportunities, aspirations, and results) and SVOR (strengths, vulnerabilities, opportunities, and risks). Likewise, a PEST analysis involves the consideration of the macro-environmental (political, economic, social and technological) factors surrounding the endeavour. Generally taken to encompass a business' external environment: its inter-organisational relationships and affairs. The approach can also be used to capture its internal environment, internal or inter-business unit power and politics, resource constraints and technological capacity. Particularly, in respect of large global corporations comprising multiple business units. Derivatives include PESTLE, which further incorporates legal and environmental factors, PESTLER, which adds regulation, and STEEPLE, which contains ethics. The decision-support tool 'the Business Case Framework' introduced in Chapter 5 incorporates both SWOT and PESTLER analyses.

Risk assessment

A systematic, cooperative, iterative and research underpinned process of identifying, analysing and evaluating risk. Risk assessment is subdivided into the following three steps: identification, analysis and evaluation.

Step 3: Risk identification

The process of identifying, distinguishing and labelling potential risks that may prevent an endeavour from attaining its objectives or support it in achieving its anticipated benefits. Box 3.1 collates potential risk under the following headings: 'Overview and context of the opportunity', PESTLE+R analysis and the components of the 'Total Solution' introduced in Chapter 5.

BOX 3.1 POTENTIAL SOURCES OF RISK

Overview and context of the opportunity

- *Opportunity*: rationally, the client (buyer or asset owner) should retain a substantial proportion of the inherent risk in an investment/opportunity. They identify and define the business need/opportunity, develop and evaluate its business case (determining the feasibility of the investment/opportunity), allocate or raise the necessary finance required, determine the development or procurement approach and oversee the manufacture/delivery of product, asset or service, etc. Issues often arise when clients attempt to transfer inappropriate levels of risk to third parties, that is, those risks that will always revert to the client on the default of others. Further issues may occur when clients fail to provide sufficient funds or complete a viable business case.
- *Stimulus*: business risks will also arise where an investment/opportunity fails to address a clear business need or is incompatible with or duplicates an existing business system or process, is vague, incomplete or not fit for purpose.
- *Strategic fit*: further business risks occur when client requirements (buy-side perspective) and opportunity selection (sell-side perspective) are inconsistent with an organisation's intent/strategy, parties rely on or fail to revise an erroneous strategy, or have incompatible organisational cultures.

PESTLE+R (SMETLER) analysis

Risks associated with the context, environment or 'atmosphere' in which business (exchange transactions) occurs:

- *Political risks*: include those arising from shifts in the political climate within a home nation (e.g. the UK) and globally. These could include, for example, uncertainty resulting from general labour disputes, civil disturbance, terrorism and conflicts, or a change in government, trading agreements and alliances (such as the withdrawal of the UK from the EU), and the impact of political decisions associated with global pandemics. Additionally, risk can ensue from internal politics, those within an organisation. For example, risks associated with competition for internal resources, powerful/influential business functions and inter-functional rivalry.

- *Economic risks*: include those stemming from market volatility (general and specific), loss of market share/competitive advantage, instability in exchange rates, disruption of supply chains, or changing customer behaviour, which lead to uncertainty of costs and the viability of any price predictions that may impact the utility of the underlying business case of an investment/opportunity.
- *Social risks*: include those resulting from public disturbances, vandalism or damage, public inquiries (objections) or referrals to an ombudsman, changes in public attitudes, tastes or standards (for example, purchasing behaviour, working patterns – remote/in person, ethical practice (Corporate Social Responsibility (CSR)/Environmental, Social, and Governance (ESG)) – including an organisation's record on human rights, protection of the environment, treatment of animals and the behaviour of its trading partners.
- *Technological risks*: include those associated with technology change. For example, long project gestation periods generally require post-award design changes to avoid consigning a project/solution to utilising obsolete technology. Moreover, variation clauses in contracts are linked to cost and time risks, while lack of data concerning the lifespan or operation of innovative solutions creates uncertainty. Additionally, IT-based technologies may introduce data/information security issues or generate recruitment/training requirements.
- *Legal risks*: include those ensuing from changes in or the enforcement of legislation and regulations: for example: tax changes, bribery and corruption (in the UK, the Bribery Act 2010 is the principal instrument for prosecuting corruption offences by both individuals or companies from both the private and public sectors), modern slavery (the Modern Slavery

Act 2015 provides guidance on compliance with modern slavery legislation), competition and anti-trust (Competition Act 1998), and equality, diversity and inclusion (Equalities Act 2010).

- *Environmental risks*: include hazards resulting from inclement weather (floods, snow/ice, storms, tornadoes, etc.), earthquakes, pollution (air, noise and water), deforestation and soil erosion. Plus, sustainability risks, for example, excessive or noxious waste produced in the manufacture of a product/execution of a project/delivery of a service.
- *Regulatory risks*: include those stemming from changes in or the enforcement of rules and regulations instituted by central government or local authorities, which companies need to observe. For example, those associated with the Health and Safety Executive (HSE), Data Governance and Cybersecurity (GDPR) or international trading practices. Additionally, there are sectoral regulations, for example those regulating aerospace and defence (The Defence and Security Public Contracts Regulations), nuclear (Office of Nuclear Regulations), pharmaceutical (Medical and Healthcare products Regulatory Agency), etc.
- *Media risks*: high-profile projects, such as HS2 (High Speed 2) attract significant media interest particularly concerning budget and time over runs, plus breaches of health and safety regulations. The resulting negative publicity can lead to reputational damage.

The total solution

- *People risks*: include those linked to the following:
    - *Leadership*: as executive support is a key driver of project success; risks arise from executives failing to support or disassociating themselves from the endeavour or undermining it due to inter-managerial discord or senior level churn.
    - *Stakeholders*: similarly, these include risks resulting from stakeholders failing to support or distancing themselves

from the endeavour or undermining it due to inter-stakeholder discord or stakeholder turnover, for example, the emergence of new stakeholders with additional, conflicting or inferior requirements. Additionally, stakeholders may hold erroneous expectations of the investment/opportunity.

- *Resources and teams*: include those risks associated with skill shortages and staff turnover (the attraction and retention of appropriately qualified/experienced personnel), poor performance linked to incompetent and/or inexperienced staff, and the inability to provide adequate training. Additional team risks occur when members are required to work under unacceptable pressure, inter and intra team conflict arises, low staff motivation is present, poor oversight is prevalent and where there is a lack trust.

- *Project management risks*: include those due to the failure to comply with contractual obligations or apply project management processes/methodology, including errors in these processes/methodologies resulting in delays and scheduling errors, or an absence of project management/control. Additional project management risks are associated with ill-defined or poorly understood project schedules, the need to include unplanned work/additional requirements, and changes that impact the viability of the project's business case. Plus, where project managers lack the authority or where it's unclear who has the authority to make timely decisions, when customers exceed approval deadlines or there are delays in releasing finances or in procuring goods and services, or delays generally in making decisions or resolving issues, or where these decisions are inadequate, incomplete or vague. Finally, this category includes risks associated with ineffective and ill-timed communication, leading to ill-informed stakeholders, misunderstanding and inappropriate expectations, and poor information management.
- *Solution or service risks*: include those arising from ill-defined, incomplete or errors in scope definition, and scope creep, for example, due to poor change management. Similarly, where

the resulting solution (design/engineering/architecture) is not fit for purpose, inflexible, includes errors and/or omissions, fails to obtain sign off or is delivered later than anticipated. Further, technical components/systems integration are of poor quality, not fit for purpose, noncompliant, volatile, outdated/unsupported or fail to integrate with existing systems/processes, etc. Plus, uncertainty resulting from the need to incorporate technological innovations.

- *Supply chain risk*: the execution of a project/investment/opportunity or delivery of an asset, product or service invariable necessitates the involvement of third parties (suppliers) resulting risks include: no or poor-quality responses to invitations to tender, leading to the engagement of unsuitable suppliers, delayed start dates, failure to meet obligations (poor-quality work, components or service), conflict with and between suppliers, and theft of raw materials, equipment and potentially intellectual property.
- *Implementation risks*: encompass those risks associated with execution, performance and quality. For example, accidents and unforeseen events that delay or terminate the project, an endeavour fails to achieve/deliver its intended benefits/results, meet its quality standards or doesn't interface with existing systems and protocols, leading to reduced productivity, cultural misalignment, missed deadlines, rejection of the asset, product or service, reputational damage and financial loss (from negative impact on organisational performance or the levying of non-performance penalties: liquidated and ascertained damages) and future investment/collaboration opportunities.
- *In-service support/operational risks*: in-service support risks include those stemming from the obsolescence/unavailability of components, computer software and systems, etc., the insolvency of suppliers, manufacturers and service suppliers, failure to honour warranties and guarantees, the inability to undertake repairs due to access issues, skill shortages, etc., and the termination of licensing agreements. Likewise, operational risks include accidents and unforeseen events that delay or terminate business operations.

- *Commercial risks*: in addition to the commercial impact of the political, economic, social, technological, legal, environmental, regulatory/compliance, security, media risks identified above, these include risks intrinsic to a specific project/contract, or the market in which the participating organisations are active. For example:

  - *Business conduct*: include risks arising from the duplicitous behaviour of individuals and third parties (fraud, theft and embezzlement), noncompliance with contractual terms and trading conditions, leading to litigation, prosecution, reputational damage and loss of intellectual property.
  - *Commercial viability*: include risks associated with the endeavour ceasing to make its anticipated return on investment, a new value proposition (product/service) doesn't perform or sell as projected or is defective, operating costs of an asset exceed predictions, leading to cashflow problems, negative media attention and reputational damage.
  - *Procurement risks*: include risks related to specific procurement and tendering approaches, leading, for example, to an organisation being unable to effectively negotiate or forced to accept unreasonable contract terms and conditions. Other risks arise where inexperienced or arrogant clients ignore the advice of their consultants, or suppliers take on work outside their core expertise.
  - *Cost/financial management*: risks occurring from inaccurate cost estimates, budgets and forecasts, inadequate cost control, mishandling project finances, failure to maintain adequate cashflow (liquidity risk), the inability to procure material and/or components within agreed targets, failure to raise necessary funding, unanticipated or unaccounted for inflationary price rises, late payment from or payment default by client/customer, customer/supplier default on credit obligations (credit risk), insolvency of client/suppliers.
  - *Contract management*: risks associated with inadequate or non-existent change control/management procedures, increased complexity arising from excessive, ambiguous or late

variation orders/change requests, stakeholder disagreement over requested revisions to scope, etc., prioritising trivial changes, inadequate or non-existent dispute resolution/conflict management procedures, delayed escalation of issues that may lead to conflict/disputes, delays resulting from litigation/arbitration, etc., the impact of acts of nature, for example, extreme weather events (Force Majeure), inadequate or inability to obtain appropriate level of insurance cover.

The above risks have been presented as hazards: threats to be avoided, reduced or offloaded. However, many of these risks may be viewed as prospective upside opportunities, enabling organisations to potentially generate additional rewards/benefits if retained/accepted and appropriately managed.

Risk classification/categorisation

According to Kim (2012), risks are usually classified based on the level of knowledge about a risk's occurrence (known or unknown) and the quality of acquired knowledge on its impact (again, known or unknown), resulting in four potential categories:

- **Known–knowns (knowledge):** Risk
- **Unknown–knowns (impact is unknown, but existence is known, i.e. undetermined knowledge)**: Impacted information
- **Known–unknowns:** Identified uncertainties
- **Unknown–unknowns (unk-unks):** Unidentified uncertainties/ unfathomable uncertainty) (Cleden, 2009)

Numerous tools and techniques are available to assist individuals and teams at the risk identification stage. Maytorena (2013) has categorised these as follows:

- **Lists:** checklists, risk registers (see Figure 3.1), risk breakdown structures and risk taxonomies generated using group brainstorming sessions or via interview

ID Number	Risk Category	Risk Description			Probability	Impact	Confidence		Risk Score	Response		Target Date	Risk owner	Status of response
Identification number	Commercial, Political, Environmental, Supply chain, People, Solution (Technical), Implementation, etc.	Outline the risk and its likely effect on the endeavour/project mission			Probability of risk occurring	Potential impact of the risk	Level of confidence in ratings (90% CL)		Probability x impact	Proactive	Reactive	Completion date for each mitigation action	Identity of the individual responsible for managing the risk	**Red** - unlikely to be met **Amber** - may not be achieved **Green** – going according to plan
		Risk Source	Risk Event	Risk Effect			P	I						
1														
2														
3														

FIGURE 3.1 Risk register

- **Soft techniques:** cognitive and causal mapping, soft systems methodology (SSM), etc.
- **Strategic techniques:** future and horizon scanning, scenario planning/analysis, etc.
- **Technical/engineered system techniques:** failure mode effects analysis (FMEA), hazard and operability (HAZOP) studies, utilising structured brainstorming sessions.

Cognitive mapping

Cognitive mapping is an approach, comprising a set of sense-making techniques, that can be utilised in complex situations. Employing text and connecting lines/arrows, it enables a 'visualisation' of reasoning to be generated. By 'mapping' concepts and their interrelationship, it captures the ideas, views, thinking and experience of the various parties involved in the exercise (generally, stakeholders). A proactive approach, it is particularly helpful when generating strategies.

Proposed benefits of cognitive mapping:

- It enables the visualisation of the inherent risk and uncertainty associated with an endeavour (project, opportunity, etc.).
- It generates a shared understanding of the situation/ circumstances.
- It engenders a questioning attitude.
- Especially, it discourages the implementation of a mechanical/ token approach to risk identification.

However, the following limitations have been levelled at the approach:

- Despite being a comparatively uncomplicated and easily learnt approach, it can be a length, convoluted process to undertake
- Its effectiveness is determined by the motivation of individuals (stakeholders) to fully participate in the process.
- Ultimately, the map is an incomplete model of the situation.

For an example of a risk map (applying cognitive mapping) using Decision Explorer® Banxia Software, see Williams (2017) and for cognitive mapping generally, see Ackermann et al. (1992).

Step 4: Analysis

This stage of the process involves a thorough analysis of all the classified risks, taking into account their source, cause, likely occurrence, potential impact and management (including the effectiveness of potential means of control). Risk exposure and risk appetite are major aspects, that is, the likelihood and impact of the identified risk and the willingness of the parties to accept/retain risk.

Again, underpinned by research, this step utilises both quantitative and qualitative analysis methods. Including, for example:

- **Probability/impact matrixes:** where risk = probability × impact. A prediction of the likely loss/gain associated with the risk (see Figure 3.2).
- **Quantitative analysis:** involves the application of statistical and mathematical techniques to analyse potential risks.
- **Deterministic approaches:** such as sensitivity and uncertainty analyses, where mathematical models re-compute outcomes linked with alternative assumptions surrounding a risk.
- **Probabilistic approaches:** for example, Monte Carlo analysis.

It must be remembered that risks are not generally independent variables, having many sources and potential effects, which can impact multiple objectives or benefits of an endeavour.

FIGURE 3.2 Probability/impact/manageability matric (Maytorena, 2013)

Step 5: Evaluation

Used to support business investment or opportunity selection decision-making, this stage of the process involves evaluating the results of the risk analysis for each identified risk criteria with the aim of determining if further action is required. The outcome of this stage is a decision to either accept/retain, avoid, mitigate, transfer or reject a potential risk.

Step 6: Risk treatment

During this stage of the process, a series of managerial actions are generated, selected and employed, which seek to lower the probability of an identified and analysed event occurring or moderate its impact if it does (for example, see Box 3.2). Similarly, these actions will include measures aimed at maximising the benefit derived from an opportunity. Maytorena (2013) identifies two categories of response: proactive, such as building in resilience or eliminating risk exposure by redesigning solutions or reactive, for example, the inclusion of contingency sums to cover any potential liability if a risk effect materialises. Senior leaders and commercial actors play a significant role during this phase.

BOX 3.2 PROJECT RISK MITIGATION/ MANAGEMENT APPROACHES

Key functions of a business leader include having an awareness of the potential risks inherent in an endeavour and knowing how to mitigate/manage them. In the context of a project, this may involve:

- *Knowledge*: obtaining, analysing, updating and applying appropriate information/data, including lessons learnt from previous projects; market and supply chain analysis, exchange rates, internal and external factors that could impede the design, execution and use/sale of an endeavour: to effectively analyse customer/project needs and requirements, complete a business case, design and select an optimum solution; identify and appoint suitable suppliers, track and monitor progress and address sources of delay.

- *Communication*: ensuring and facilitating communication: for example, establishing and applying a communication plan (utilising appropriate communication channels), conducting workshops with team members and/or stakeholders, conducting regular meetings of all team members and project-related personnel and encouraging participation.
- *Personnel and resources*: appointing subject matter experts to address deficiencies in expertise/capability, motivating staff to perform, monitoring staff performance – rewarding good work and instigating remedial action where necessary, analysing, assembling/obtaining and ensuring access to all necessary resources before undertaking the endeavour/project and then utilising them efficiently, plus employing additional staff where required/possible to avoid work overload.
- *Project/contract management*: utilising appropriate contracts and agreements, incorporating contingencies, ensuring work schedules allow sufficient time and resources to complete the task, surfacing and resolving potential sources of conflict and dispute, instigating and ensuring the application of quality management principles, providing health and safety facilities, instigating and ensuring safe working practices.

The principal risk in any investment/opportunity is the attainment of its primary objectives. Ultimately, this risk is always borne by the purchaser (the project instigator). Additionally, the purchaser will carry the strategic risks of any project, for example, those associated with deciding to initiate a project/investment/opportunity, defining the project's scope and specification, determining a contract strategy, and identifying and selecting a supplier(s). Other risks, such as those concerning the design, implementation and execution of a project, are generally allocated to the parties via contracts. However, irrespective of any contract entered into both parties may be at risk, for example, when forces outside their control frustrate the work.

Ideally, the allocation of risk between exchange parties should be based upon the following principles:

- **Managerial**: in preference to demanding guarantees and relying on contract terms that impose rights to damages for default (liquidated and ascertained damages), successful project completion is more probable if effective planning, management and supervision is undertaken.
- **Commercial**: based on the premise that risk should be borne by the party best able to control, manage or insure against the risk and its effects.
- **Legal**: the avoidance of penalties. Ultimately, unfair contract terms, for example, terms designed to punish rather than compensate a party will commonly be unenforceable.

Overlaid on the risk classification matrix (Figure 3.3) are four potential responses to these classifications of risk/uncertainty by suppliers when responding to a bid opportunity:

- **Technical contingency:** a contingency based on measurement included within a tender by a supplier to cover any complicated (known/knowns) contractual elements (responsibilities).
- **Management contingency:** a contingency based on judgement to address complexity (known/unknowns), hidden (unknown/knowns) and elements of chaos (unknown/unknowns) – depending on the proposed contractual terms.
- **Business risk:** a supplier may accept a degree of vulnerability in order to 'win' work (Risk to win). This may include further elements of complexity (known/unknowns), hidden (unknown/knowns) and chaos (unknown/unknowns).
- **Retained client risk:** those elements of complexity (known/unknowns), hidden (unknown/knowns) and chaos (unknown/unknowns) not transferred to a third party/supplier.

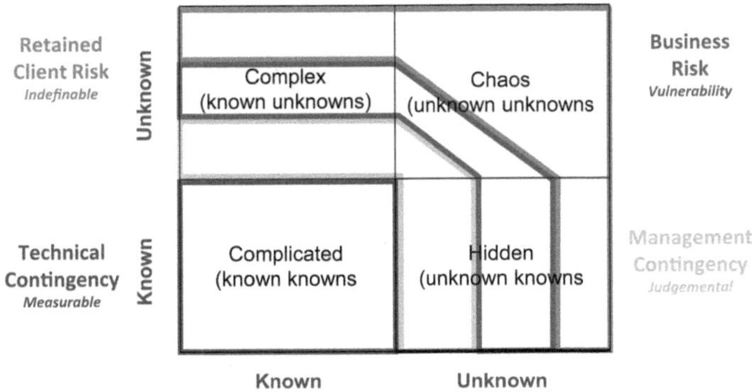

FIGURE 3.3 Risk classification matrix (developed by Maytorena and Lowe 2016-24)

However, generally it is not in a purchaser's ultimate business interest to require a supplier or their supply chain to absorb all risks and particularly uncertainty (chaos) associated with an exchange contract/project. For example, if a supplier were to become bankrupt as a result of accepting risks/uncertainty outside their control generally the responsibility of delivering the project, product or service would revert to the customer. This is particularly the case where government clients are involved.[1]

A purchaser's interests are probably better served through the utilisation of contractual terms that motivate their supplier(s) to complete on time, within budget and to the required standard, etc. Plus, ensuring that no risks are transferred that would negatively impact the stability of either party in the short or long term. This principle was appreciated by BAA when formulating their contracting approach for the Heathrow Terminal 5 (T5) project.[2] After significant research into other airport and major infrastructure projects, they concluded that they were unable to effectively transfer the inherent risks of the project to their supply network. As a result, they elected to retain and manage the risk themselves.

For each risk identified, an appropriate risk owner should be identified and to whom accountability for the risk allocated.

Step 7: Monitor and review

A further iterative activity, again undertaken throughout the process, that establishes a control and assurance process to monitor and review the effectiveness of the adopted risk responses and the risk management process as a whole. Monitoring involves an ongoing appraisal of the identified risks, the adopted risk treatments and their current status; whereas controlling determines and ensures that any residual levels of risk are acceptable and that any remedial actions are instigated. The activity is a key component of the implementation/execution phase of contract management.

Personal reflection

Before we consider the next topic, value management, in the context of the organisation you work for/previously worked for or a project/contract that you are familiar with, consider the following questions:

- What were the key risks identified on the project?
- How were they identified and evaluated?
- On what basis were they allocated to the parties or otherwise managed?
- Were they successfully managed over the project/contract lifecycle? What contributed to this?

Value management

Risk management and value management are complementary processes. The latter seeks to create/maximise value and optimise the cost and delivery time of a benefit, while simultaneously reducing any associated risks (threats). Utilised appropriately, it is not merely a cost-cutting exercise. Value management is applicable to organisations/businesses across the entire supply constellation.

Definitions

Often applied in conjunction with risk management, value management – based on the notion of value and the principles of function-informed thinking – has been defined as follows:

> A structured approach to defining what value means to the organisation. It is a framework that allows needs, problems or opportunities to be defined and then enables review of whether these can be improved to determine the optimal approach and solution.
>
> *(APM, 2024)*

> ... an underlining concept applied within existing management systems and approaches based on value and function-orientated thinking, behaviours and methods, particularly dedicated to motivating people, developing skills, promoting synergies and innovation, with the aim of maximising the overall performance of an organisation.
>
> *(BS EN12973:2020)*

While the Institute of Value Management (IVM, 2024) consider value management to be "... all about: Organisational Improvement, setting clear goals, improving productivity, creativity and return on investment".

Its aim, therefore, being is to create and maximise value and strike the optimum sustainable balance between the desires and requirements of all the stakeholders involved in the endeavour and the necessary resources to satisfy them. In this context, value has been defined as:

> A standard, principle or quality considered worthwhile or desirable. In value management terms, value is defined as the ratio of 'satisfaction of requirements' over 'use of resources'.
>
> *(APM, 2024)*

$$\text{Value} = \frac{\text{Satisfaction of needs}}{\text{Consumption of resources}}$$

Therefore, "Value is based on the relationship between satisfying needs and objectives and the resources required to achieve them" (BS EN12973:2020). While in accounting terms, value is:

> ... the monetary worth of an asset, business entity, goods sold, services rendered, or liability or obligation acquired. In economic terms, value is the sum of all the benefits and rights arising from ownership.
>
> *(Corporate Finance Institute (CFI), 2024)*

Perceptions of value are idiosyncratic and value judgements are unique to each stakeholder.

Value management, therefore, is a solutions-generating methodology based on defining and enhancing value and prompting innovation. It can be applied at the organisational, portfolio, programme, project, product, process or service level to define and add tangible benefit (value).

Value management standards and guidance

Several good practice guides and value management standards have been produced by various professional organisations, international institutes and government bodies. These include:

- **BS EN 12973:2020 Value management:** published by BSI (British Standards Organisation, 2020).
- **Value management and value engineering – RICS guidance note:** published by the Royal Institution of Chartered Surveyors (RICS, 2017).
- **MoV® (Management of Value):** published by AXELOS (AXELOS, 2022b).

Again, these standards provide advice on value management practices, principles, tools, techniques and templates, include exemplar value management models and frameworks, establishing a common vocabulary for value management, and maintaining effective value management processes and procedures.

(See also Chapter 7: Applying rigorous and consistent commercial processes and procedures.)

Benefits of effective value management

Effective value management is considered to deliver the following benefits:

- A clearer grasp and ordering of the stakeholders' requirements and of the potential means of satisfying them.
- Improved stakeholder alignment with project/endeavour values, goals/objectives, and critical success factors.
- Enhanced/informed business/investment decision-making.
- More effective use of finances, time and resources to delivering the required outcomes/objectives.
- Enhanced competitive advantage driven by innovation, increased productivity and resource efficiency.
- Superior value (potentially delivering 10–25% savings).
- Enhanced communication, learning and collaboration.

Note the similarities between the benefits of value management and risk management identified earlier in this chapter.

Value management process

There are several value management protocols that promote systematic and iterative approaches to identifying, analysing, acquiring, implementing, maximising and monitoring value. Plus, outline principles, drivers, methods and techniques to support these actions.

Grounded on value and function-orientated thinking, BS EN 12973:2020 Value management identifies four 'essential' guiding principles:

1 **Strengthen value orientation:** by aligning an organisation's value culture to its strategic intent and creating an awareness of the concept of value across all its stakeholders, together with an understanding of how it acquires, implements and monitors value.

2 **Apply function thinking:** by utilising tools and techniques that enable the function or purpose of a project, process, product, service or component of them to be identified. Permitting the generation of innovative and creative solutions that reduce the allocation of resources, while simultaneously delivering superior value and benefits without negatively impacting its performance or quality.
3 **Apply a structured, holistic approach:** by integrating value management into an organisations management and governance systems, adopting integrated cross-functions teams and considering the views of all stakeholders.
4 **Manage complexity, risk and uncertainty:** by taking into account the impact of these stimuli on cost, resource utilisation, performance and quality to ensure the attainment and maximisation of value (the intended/anticipated benefit) (BSI, 2020).

The above principles are further underpinning by the following four features (referred to as drivers or levers):

1 **A collaborative style of managing fundamentals:** requiring and facilitating collaborative teamworking and encouraging free thinking and expression.
2 **Allowing for a positive human experience:** recognising and respecting diversity and different perspective and empowering participants.
3 **Considering both the internal and external environments:** specifically, their influence and the ability to modify these circumstances.
4 **Applying proven methods and tools:** requiring an understanding of the various value management techniques and approaches and when they may be effectively utilised (BSI, 2020).

Similarly, Management of Value (MoV®) is based on the following seven principles:

1 **Align with organisational objectives:** each initiative should support the delivery of an organisation's strategic intent.

2 **Focus on functions and required outcomes:** concentrating on those functions that will deliver the required benefit(s), the aim is to enable informed decision-making resulting in increased stakeholder value.
3 **Balance the variables to maximise value:** identifying key stakeholders, reconciling their diverse aspirations and requirements, understanding how these needs can best be delivered and balancing any financial, quality, time and resource constraints.
4 **Apply throughout the investment decision:** applying value management across the whole project/contract lifecycle.
5 **Tailor to suit the subject:** adapting the value management approach to meet organisational needs and to account for issues, such as the size of the endeavour/project and its complexity, environment, culture and inherent risk.
6 **Learn from experience and improve performance:** using lessons learnt to inform future proposals.
7 **Assign clear roles and responsibilities and build a supportive culture:** to support value-creating activities (AXELOS, 2022b).

Implementation of Management of Value (MoV®) is via the following seven processes:

1 **Frame the programme or project:** applying value management techniques to discern the purpose and strategic intent of the proposed endeavour/project.
2 **Gather information:** collating relevant information on the endeavour/project, establishing expectations, identifying stakeholders and categorising their specific requirements and identifying potential team members.
3 **Analyse information:** scrutinising this information and developing alternative means to deliver the intended benefits.
4 **Process information:** utilising the data to create value-adding propositions.
5 **Evaluate and select:** balancing stakeholder requirements and desires, available resources, inherent risk, and time, quality and funding constraints and potential benefits, then selecting an appropriate solution that is both practical to execute and will provide the maximum benefit.

6 **Develop value improving proposals:** generating alternative fully developed proposals and presenting them to the decision-makers.
7 **Implement and share outputs:** using previous lessons learnt to generate an execution plan for the accepted proposal, monitor its realisation and initiate continuous improvement (AXELOS, 2022b).

Likewise, BS EN 12973:2020 includes five core value management methods, which are to be selected as dictated by the prevailing circumstance. These comprise:

1 **Value analysis/value engineering:** applying, in combination, various methodologies, such as brainstorming, creative thinking, function analysis and function cost analysis to identify, evaluate and prioritise stakeholder (customer and end user) requirements (to resolve issues and satisfy desires) to surface and promote innovation, superior design, organisational change or project, product, service or system improvement. APM (2024) define value engineering as being:

   ... concerned with optimising the conceptual, technical and operational aspects of deliverables.

2 **Function analysis/function analysis system technique (FAST Diagram):** identifying, describing, classifying and validating functions to derive a mutual appreciation between stakeholders of the purpose/aims of the project/endeavour through effective communication.
3 **Function cost:** a significant feature of value management, this method allocates a value (cost) to each necessary function, connecting individual endeavour/project requirements expressed in terms of their functionality and associated cost.
4 **Functional performance specification (FPS):** in which the stakeholder requirements are presented in terms of 'user-related functions' (URFs) without, however, identifying potential practical solutions. On completion, the FPS is disseminated to the relevant designers, engineers and suppliers enabling them to propose potential solutions to address the URFs.

5 **Design to cost (DtC) and Design to objectives (DtO):** grounded on value analysis, value engineering and functional analysis, DtC develops into DtO when alternative non-cost criteria are accounted for. For example, balancing factors, such as time, quality, performance (efficiency and durability) and environmental impact, in addition to merely cost (BSI, 2020).

Additional tools and techniques include brainstorming (mind showering), benefits management, cost–benefit analysis, cost modelling, criteria weighting technique, excursion/metaphors, 5 Ws and H, Ishikawa technique (fishbone analysis), issue generation and analysis, Kaizen, lean management, lessons learned value management technique, lifecycle costing, objective hierarchy, pair wise comparison, Pareto analysis, process mapping, risk management, scamper, stakeholder analysis, SWOT analysis and TRIZ (Theory of Inventive Problem Solving).

Value management stage reviews

BS EN12973:2020 Value management includes the following key decision points:

- Value management 0 (VM0): *Defining the business need*
- Value management 1 (VM1): *Understanding, challenging and validating the business need*
- Value management 2 (VM2): *Deciding on the best business solution*
- Value management 3 (VM3): *Re-validating the project objectives and design development*
- Value management 4 (VM4): *Signing off the design*
- Value management 5 (VM5): *Keeping the project on track*
- Post-occupancy evaluation (POE1): *Learning lessons*
- Post-occupancy evaluation (POE2): *Learning lessons and validating outcomes meet the business need* (BSI, 2020).

Personal reflection

For a project/contract that you are familiar with, consider how value was management at each of the above value management decision points (VM0-VM5) and evaluated post-occupancy (PEO1 and PEO2):

- What tools and techniques were used?
- How effective were they in ensuring/delivering the anticipated benefit?

Application

Risk and responsibilities

As contracts apportion risk between the contracting parties, effective project/contract management necessities a common awareness of how these risks are distributed. Moreover, studies have identified significant differences in the perception of risk allocation across supply chains, especially by upstream suppliers. To address this, decision-makers are encouraged to involve, consult and communicate broadly with stakeholders. The use of contracts in economic exchanges is explored in more detail in Chapter 4.

Application of risk and value management

In Chapter 8, we will examine the application of commercial practice (including risk and value management) throughout the project lifecycle from both the supply and demand perspectives. In respect of risk and value management, this includes:

- **Intent stage:** a critical aspect of the business justification gate review for both demand-side and supply-side participants is the evaluation of the inherent risk and potential value (benefits) associated with or derived from a purchase/sales opportunity (asset, product or service) or organisational change, arising from a stakeholder requirement. These interventions support the generation of innovative and practical solutions, while balancing risk, cost, time, quality, performance and environmental impact, to optimise deliverables and maximise the potential value/benefit.
- **Deal creation stage:** as part of the investment decision gate review, purchasers should satisfy themselves that all principal

risks identified during the procurement phase have been suitably addressed and that the potential supplier has adequate and realistic project, risk and value management plans to satisfy their requirements. Similarly, suppliers should incorporate risk analysis and value engineering into the bid preparation process. Also, all parties should satisfy themselves that the project/contract solution will deliver its anticipated value and return on investment (ROI).

- **Execution stage**: post-award risk and value management requires an understanding of and the ability to manage both contractual responsibilities/obligations and supplier/purchaser risk, for example:
    - **Processes and strategy**: including an acceptance that risk should be borne by the party best able to manage it, and the instigation of a formal risk identification, monitoring and mitigation process. Likewise, the application of value engineering and management approaches to ensure the project is still delivering its predicted value and return on investment (ROI).
    - **Contractual terms**: are understood and monitored by the contract/project manager.
    - **Ongoing supplier/purchaser risk and value management**: including the regular measurement of the supplier's/purchaser's financial status and project/business performance.

Best practice guidance

For additional sources of 'best practice' risk and value management guidance, see Chapter 7.

Summary

Risk (threat and opportunity) management enables individuals and organisations to identify, contextualise, analyse/assess/evaluate, quantify, understand, prioritise and communicate potential risks and opportunities associated with a purchase/sales prospect (asset, product or service). Accordingly, these risks may be retained (accepted) or transferred to a third party. Within the b2b context of exchange contracts, a level of risk-taking is anticipated and is clearly linked to value (profit) creation (an opportunity); for example, an organisation may accept an identified level of risk, at a premium. A generally accepted commercial principle is that risk (hazard) should be carried by the individual/organisation best able to control, manage or insure against the risk and its effects. On recognising or accepting a potential risk, a party will seek to mitigate and reduce its potential impact by formulating, validating and implementing a coordinated, monitored and controlled risk response.

Similarly, value management aids individuals and organisations identify, evaluate, understand, prioritise and communicate stakeholder requirements, generate innovative and practical solutions, while balancing cost, time, quality, performance and environmental impact, to optimise deliverables and maximise the potential value/benefit associated with a purchase/sales opportunity (asset, product or service) or organisational change.

Decision-support activities, risk and value management empower decision-makers to formulate informed, proactive management decisions, permitting a suitable balance between opportunity/value maximisation and the minimisation of potential threats and losses for each element of an exchange (contract or project).

Associated commercial tasks include identifying, responding to and managing the likely commercial, contractual and procurement risks associated with satisfying an organisational requirement or responding to an identified sales/supply opportunity. Generally, this involves drafting, negotiating, agreeing, managing and fulfilling any associated contractual commitment, with the aim of supporting the definition, creation and delivery of sustainable value (supply-side) or the identification, capture and exploitation of value (demand-side).

Undertaking timely risk and value management, as part of Front-End Loading (FEL) aka Left Shift – doing the 'best practical' project definition and planning early in the project/endeavour lifecycle, drives success.[3] Moreover, FEL is "… the single most predictive indicator of project success" (Merrow, 2011).

Personal reflection

Finally, consider the following questions:

- How might value management and risk management be combined into a single activity?
- What are the advantages and disadvantages of doing this?

Notes

1 For example, see Box 8.4: The London Underground PPP in in Lowe (2013).
2 For more details, see Box 8.6 Heathrow Terminal 5 (T5) case study and Case Study B in Lowe (2013).
3 See Box 1: Front End Loading in Waterworth and Gavin (2024) and Chapter 5 of this text.

Further reading

For additional information on the concepts covered in this chapter, see

Kähkönen K (2006) Management of uncertainty. In: D J Lowe (ed.) with R Leiringer, *Commercial Management of Projects: Defining the Discipline*. Blackwell Publishing, Oxford, pp. 211–233.

Maytorena E (2013) Perspectives on managing risk and uncertainty. In: D J Lowe *Commercial Management: Theory and Practice*. Wiley-Blackwell Publishing Ltd, Chichester, pp. 108–131.

Waterworth A and Gavin C (2024) Managing Projects, Routledge, Abingdon, Oxon. pp. 72–79.

Winch G W and Maytorena E (2011) Managing risk and uncertainty in projects: A cognitive approach. In: P W G Morris, J K Pinto and J Söderlund (eds.) *The Oxford Handbook of Project Management*. Oxford University Press, Oxford, pp. 345–364.

References

Ackermann F, Eden C and Cropper S (1992) *Getting Started with Cognitive Mapping*. Banxia Software, Kendal.

Association for Project Management (APM) (2019) *APM Body of Knowledge* 7th edition. Association for Project Management, Princes Risborough.

Association for Project Management (APM) (2024) *APM Glossary of Project Management Terms*. Association for Project Management, Princes

Risborough. https://www.apm.org.uk/resources/glossary/ (Accessed 10 July 2024).

AXELOS (2022a) M_o_R® *Management of Risk*: Creating and Protecting Value, 4th *Edition*. PeopleCert, Nicosia, Cyprus.

AXELOS (2022b) MoV® *Management of* Value, 2nd *Edition*. PeopleCert, Nicosia, Cyprus.

British Standards Organisation (BSI) (2020) *BS EN 12973:2020 Value management*. British Standards Organisation, London. https://knowledge.bsigroup.com/products/value-management (Accessed 10 July 2024).

British Standards Organisation (BSI) (2021) *BS 31100:2021 Risk management – Code of practice and guidance for the implementation of BS ISO 31000:2018*. British Standards Organisation, London. https://knowledge.bsigroup.com/products/risk-management-code-of-practice-and-guidance-for-the-implementation-of-bs-iso-31000-2018 (Accessed 10 July 2024).

Cabinet Office (2017) *Management of Risk in Government*. Cabinet Office, London. https://www.gov.uk/government/publications/management-of-risk-in-government-framework (Accessed 10 July 2024).

Chartered Management Institute (CMI) (2024) Risk Management: Checklist 266. Chartered Management Institute, Corby. https://www.managers.org.uk/~/media/files/resources/checklist-risk-management.pdf (Accessed 10 July 2024).

Cleden D (2009) *Managing Project Uncertainty*. Gower, Farnham.

Committee of Sponsoring Organizations (COSO) (2017) *Enterprise Risk Management - Integrating with Strategy and Performance*. Committee of Sponsoring Organizations. https://www.coso.org/enterprise-risk-management (Accessed 10 July 2024).

Corporate Finance Institute (CFI) (2024) *What Is Value*. Corporate Finance Institute, Vancouver, Canada. https://corporatefinanceinstitute.com/resources/valuation/value/ (Accessed 10 July 2024).

Government Finance Function and HM Treasury (2023) *Orange Book: Management of risk - Principles and Concepts*. Government Finance Function and HM Treasury, London. https://www.gov.uk/government/publications/orange-book (Accessed 10 July 2024).

Institute of Risk Management (IRM) (2002) *A Risk Management Standard*. The Institute of Risk Management, London. https://www.theirm.org/media/4709/arms_2002_irm.pdf (Accessed 10 July 2024).

Institute of Value Management (IVM) (2024) *What Is Value Management*. The Institute of Value Management, Leicester. https://ivm.org.uk/value-management/ (Accessed 10 July 2024).

International Organization for Standardization (ISO) (2021) *ISO 31000: 2018 – Risk Management – A Practical Guide* 1st Edition, International Organization for Standardization, Geneva, Switzerland.

Kim S D (2012) Characterizing unknown unknowns. Paper presented at PMI® Global Congress 2012—North America, Vancouver, British Columbia, Canada. Project Management Institute Inc, Newtown Square, PA.

Lowe D J (2013) *Commercial Management: Theory and Practice*. Wiley-Blackwell Publishing Ltd, Chichester.

Maytorena E (2013) Perspectives on managing risk and uncertainty. In: D J Lowe *Commercial Management: Theory and Practice*. Wiley-Blackwell Publishing Ltd, Chichester, pp. 108–131.

Merrow E W (2011) *Industrial Megaprojects: Concepts, Strategies and Practices for Success*. John Wiley & Sons, Hoboken, NJ.

Project Management Institute (PMI) (2021) *A Guide to the Project Management Body of Knowledge PMBOK® Guide 7th Edition and the Standard for Project Management*. Project Management Institute Inc, Newtown Square, PA.

RICS (2015) *Management of Risk*, RICS guidance note, UK, 1st Edition, Royal Institution of Chartered Surveyors (RICS), London. https://www.rics.org/profession-standards/rics-standards-and-guidance/sector-standards/construction-standards/black-book/management-of-risk (Accessed 10 July 2024).

RICS (2017) *Value Management and Value Engineering*, RICS professional standards and guidance note, UK, 1st Edition, Royal Institution of Chartered Surveyors (RICS), London. https://www.rics.org/profession-standards/rics-standards-and-guidance/sector-standards/construction-standards/black-book/value-management-and-value-engineering-1st-edition (Accessed 10 July 2024).

Williams T (2017) The nature of risk in complex projects. *Project Management Journal*, *48*(4), 55–66.

4

EXCHANGE GOVERNANCE

Contracts and legal, regulatory and governance issues

Introduction

In business, goods and services are predominantly procured using contracts to 'govern' the commercial interface (economic exchanges) between purchasers and suppliers. Similarly, these suppliers utilise contracts to acquire goods and services from their partners, subcontractors and suppliers.

To support these exchanges, senior leaders in organisations require an appreciation of a wide range of legal, regulatory and governance issues. For example, those associated with procurement/tendering (bid) processes (briefing, liaising with and managing internal and external legal advisers and consultants, etc.), contracting frameworks, contract formulation and award (drafting and negotiating contracts, licensing and confidentiality agreements), specific contract terms and conditions (rights and obligations, principle cost determinants, outputs and quality standards, time schedules, payment mechanisms and remedies for poor performance) and compliance with organisational legal requirements (interpreting legislation, regulatory frameworks and rights and obligations under contracts and agreements). Additionally, the increased globalisation of business relationships necessitates an awareness of the regulations that govern international trade and protect intellectual property (IP).

The aim of this chapter, therefore, is to develop an appreciation of some of the key legal, regulatory and governance issues that influence commercial practice. The intent is to provide an

DOI: 10.4324/9781003052159-4

overview of common contract provisions, plus an outline of the legalisation and regulations that impact business-to-business (b2b) exchanges. It covers contracts for the supply of goods and/or services in terms of generic contract provisions: the key components of contracts, and introduces procurement/acquisition regulations, competition and antitrust legislation, international trade law, IP, insolvency and employment rights on the transfer of an undertaking (TUPE).

Definitions

Contracts

A contract is an agreement, predominantly between two parties, whereby one party commits to do something for another in return for a consideration, usually a monetary payment. These parties comprise:

- **The purchaser:** the entity that acquires goods and/or services by payment or at some cost. Otherwise referred to as the buyer, client, customer, employer, owner, proposer, sponsor, etc.
- **The supplier:** the entity that provides the goods and/or services. Also termed the contractor, main supplier, main contractor, prime contractor, prime supplier, seller, vendor, etc.

Although the majority of b2b agreements are formed between two entities, bespoke contracts and some standard forms enable a multi-party approach. Additionally, while not a party to the contract, contracts may identify:

- **A project manager:** a named individual who leads the purchaser's contract management team. They may be an employee of the purchaser or an external consultancy. Alternatively, the terms architect, contract manager, engineer or supply manager may be used depending on the context of the contract.
- **Subcontractors:** suppliers to the main supplier (as defined above).

As there are no 'official' definitions (beyond those stated in individual contracts), care should be exercised where the descriptions above (or similar ones) are employed, as there is a range of possible meanings associated with each.

Contracts place obligations on both (all) parties to fulfil their part of the agreement (deliver on their commitments) and underpin the foundation for the relationship between the parties. For a contract to be deemed valid it typically requires the following elements:

- **Intention:** the agreement between the parties is intended to be legally binding (this can be implied in certain circumstances)
- **Capacity:** both parties must have the capacity to enter into the contract
- **Legitimacy:** the contract must be for a lawful purpose; to demonstrate this, in some legal systems, the intent of the contract must be clearly stated.

Essentially, the provisions of a contract:

- **State the responsibilities and obligations of each party:** relating to, for example, the contract's/project's objectives and priorities, plus its financing, innovation, development, design, quality, standards, procurement, scheduling, implementation, installation; project management, safety, inspection, testing, commissioning, operating and maintenance arrangements/requirements.
- **Distribute risk between the parties:** for example, risks associated with required investments in the project, design faults, missed performance requirements/levels, subcontractor default, productivity issues, delays, mistakes and uninsured incidents.
- **Establish effective payment terms:** associated with the project's development, design, construction, fabrication, implementation, management and other necessary services.

It is feasible, therefore, as a matter of law to construct and employ a concise contract, which states a scope of work, a price (perhaps with payment milestones) and some outline dates (illustrated by the Scottish and Newcastle Brewery's PathClearer Contract – see link included in the Further Reading section of this chapter). The rest of the arrangements would then be left to mutual agreement as the contract proceeds. Potentially, in a commercial environment, these negotiations may be guided by the 'insight' derived from the use of familiar standard form contracts.

Also, under English law, it could be argued that in many instances the parties only need to agree the scope of work and the law will cover the remaining issues. In business, this approach is commonplace, particularly between or with small firms. Moreover, there are good reasons why this approach may be preferable. For example, where:

- a good working relationship already exists between the parties,
- behaviours are adequately moderated by self-interest (where there is potential for the trading relationship to continue – the possibility of future work if all goes well) and
- the values involved may not warrant the effort/cost incurred in compiling (and/or agreeing) a more complete contract.

However, while it is possible that contracts may be formulated in a single document, commercial contracts generally comprise several documents (or distinct elements within documents). Common examples include:

- **The contract agreement:** includes the identities of the parties, the contract price and a schedule for its execution. It also itemises the documents that comprise the contract, such as that which sets out the scope of work.
- **General specification and scope of work, product or service:** details the scope of work to be undertaken (or product/service to be supplied) and the technical standards to be achieved.
- **General conditions of contract:** frequently, but not exclusively, a recognised standard form of contract. This document/element details the obligations/commitments made by the parties, allocates risk, itemises remedies for failure to fulfil obligations/commitments and includes appropriate commercial

arrangements (for example, concerning insurance, bonds, safety procedures, industrial relations, defects and disputes). It will also establish the administrative procedures to manage the execution of the contract: implement a project or deliver a service/product.
- **Special conditions of contract:** additions and amendments to the general conditions as required by the purchaser or the specific circumstances of the endeavour.

Due to the potential for discrepancies between these documents/elements, an order of priority is required.

Contract terms

The terms of a contract are essentially a record of all the commitments (rights and obligations) agreed by the parties, plus any terms implied by law. They can be classified as follows:

- **Express terms:** provisions that are stated (written) within a contract.
- **Implied terms:** provisions that form part of a contract but are not expressed. For example, in English Law these can include conformity with statutes, plus the supplier's responsibility for subcontractors, its duty to use reasonable skill and care in executing the work and its obligation to execute the work in a timely manner, having regard to the completion date.
- **Incorporation by reference:** where the contract, for example, refers to terms contained within other documents.

Contract management

Definitions of contract management include:

> ... the process that ensures both parties to a contract fully meet their respective obligations as effectively and efficiently as possible, in order to continually deliver both the business and operational objectives required from the contract.
>
> *(State Government of Victoria, 2024)*

> ... the process of creating, implementing, and reviewing contracts. Whether this is between a business and supplier, or partner, contract management is an essential part of your business. As your business grows, contract management can become complex. Therefore, the need for effective strategies and processes is important.
>
> *(CIPS, 2024)*

Starting with the identification of a purchaser's needs, the process concludes with the completion of the contract. Its principal characteristics are:

- Risk identification, apportionment and management – related to contract performance
- Relationship management – between the purchaser and the supplier
- Cost management – payment means and change management.

Contract management is covered in more detail in Chapters 7 and 8.

Letters of intent

A letter of intent is a device which is sometimes used as an interim arrangement to facilitate a supplier (successful bidder) commencing work prior to signing the eventual formal contract. They are generally utilised where there are elements of work that can be progressed with minor financial exposure on the part of the purchaser, or where certain products or components (for example, steel) have long lead times. To be valid, a letter of intent should contain all the properties of a contract (identified above) and should make clear which elements of the project/purchase have been agreed and which have not. If, however, it is merely an announcement of one party's present intentions, it may not be legally enforceable and could be revoked by the issuer without any redress.

To avoid the future potential loss of their 'bargaining position', associated with the use of letters of intent, a purchaser could utilise a 'Start-up' contract, which incorporates appropriate controls, limits and safeguards. For example, a specific agreement for the supply of pre-contract services.

Labels and descriptions

Legally, if properly formed, there is no distinction between the terms 'contract', 'order' and 'letter of intent', each refers to an enforceable agreement for the supply of goods and/or services. Therefore, care must be taken not to assume that a document with a particular title has a specific effect associated with its title. While the terms may have a particular meaning to the parties, courts are disposed to interpret the contents of a document rather than based their decisions on its title. Commercially, however, the term contract is predominantly used in relation to agreements executed over longer time periods and incurring greater expenditure than an order.

Subcontracts

In parallel to the (main) contract between the purchaser and the supplier (prime or main contractor), the supplier may employ third-party partners, subcontractors and suppliers of materials, plant, equipment and services, etc., via contracts. These agreements are often referred to as subcontracts. While the supplier is normally held responsible for any subcontracted work/service, the purchaser may retain the right to authorise subcontractors and/or to limit the extent of any subcontracted work. In some instances, the supplier may determine the terms of subcontracts, while in others the terms may (to varying degrees) be required to correspond (be 'back-to-back'), with those of the main contract. Purchasers may also nominate subcontractors, that is, require the supplier to enter into a subcontract with a subcontractor/supplier chosen by the purchaser or their agent, usually to carry out specialist work. In these instances, contract terms will need to address the specific risks created by nomination, for example, in relation to the default or non-availability of the nominated subcontractor, and to ensure that the supplier reimburses the nominated subcontractor.

Standard and model forms

As mentioned earlier, rather than construct bespoke contracts, many industry sectors use standard or model conditions of contract. The benefits of standard forms include:

- **Efficiency:** they save time, both in formulation and in negotiation.
- **Predictability:** they provide a recognised and predictable contractual basis.
- **Familiarity:** they are familiar to the project/contract management teams, resulting in smoother running projects, or at least in the avoidance of some misunderstandings that could disrupt progress.

Some organisations (including governments) devise their own standard conditions of contract. Invariably, these contracts are (to some degree) biased in favour of the party that generate them. Alternatively, those model conditions drawn up by an industry association (including representatives of all parts of the sector) are generally considered to be a reasonable basis upon which organisations may contract with each other – as risks are largely equitably distributed between the parties. Potentially, however, these forms can be complex, inflexible, unclear and unwieldy.

Legal interpretation of contracts

Contracts function in, and are subject to, a framework of applicable law. While globally legal systems may vary, many have shared 'roots', such as English 'common law', a code-based system or religious tenets (for example, Shariah Law). As a broad observation, therefore, the underlying principles of commercial contract law have significant commonality the world over, diverging mainly in their detail. International contracts must state which country's legal system or jurisdiction will apply, as the choice of law can have a significant impact. The designated law determines how (and whether) a contract is formed and provides guidance on how it should be interpreted. It also provides regulations within which the parties must function, for example, licensing of certain activities, safety, tax, etc. As a result, specialised legal advice should be obtained on the precise interpretation and implications of contract clauses under a particular legal system.

Where a contract is reproduced in more than one language, the contract needs to distinguish between a single ruling language and those language(s) used for communication purposes. This is imperative, as the exact words used in the contract will be scrutinised, say in the event of a dispute arising, to determine the terms of the agreement made (or deemed to have been made).

Contractual issues

Contract strategy and type

Frequently, contracts are categorised in terms of strategy (procurement approach or organisational choice) or by type (risk allocation and payment terms). These aspects should be addressed simultaneously.

Contract strategy

Contracts classified in terms of strategy include:

- **Design combined with production/execution:** include Design and Build and Turnkey contracts
- **Design separated from production/execution:** Two alternative organisational structures exist – sequential and parallel contracts. Parallel contracts (such as Management Contracting and Construction Management) are appropriate where an early project completion date is imperative, design requirements are initially uncertain, supplier design capability is beneficial or the identified work is of a specialist nature, suppliers have a limited capability, or the continuing operation of an existing installation/service is necessary.

- **Alternative organisational arrangements:** such as programme management, term contracting, and framework agreements. Term contracting is commonly utilised for the provision of a service, for example, repair and maintenance work, where the general nature of the work is known but the volume and exact nature of each work component is not. Individual orders issued under a term contract become a discrete contract governed by the umbrella terms of the main contract. Framework agreements, having similarities with term contracting, are primarily used where work packages (individual call-off orders) are more substantial and can be independently priced.
- **Cooperative arrangements:** include joint venture and partnering arrangements. Partnering arrangements are generally employed to facilitate collaborative and integrated working between multiple parties. Joint ventures are mainly established to enable a group of commercial organisations to form a single 'stand-alone' entity. In these circumstances, specific contract conditions are required to create a suitable organisational structure that will support the successful execution of the endeavour and provide safeguards in the event of the default or liquidation of one of the joint venture members, etc. Additionally, the diverse organisation culture, equalisation of power and potential for conflict between the joint venture partners will need to be addressed.

Contract type

Essentially, there are two categories based on the contract's payment terms:

- **Price based:** for example, Fixed Price, Measurement, Remeasurement and Target Price contracts. Fixed-price contracts remunerate the supplier a fixed-price or lump sum (a single tendered price), for executing the entire contract/project. However, the terms fixed, firm and lump sum have no 'official' meaning, while in practice a fixed-price contract is rarely truly 'fixed', as they often permit variations to the works, address the financial consequences of various risks/problems encountered or incorporate fluctuation clauses. Only the payment terms applied within the contract are determinative. Measurement forms of contract incorporate a provisional list of the items and quantities of the work to be executed (bill of quantities) as part of the bid/contract documentation. The purchaser pays a standard unit price based on agreed productivity rates and unit rates. Remeasurement forms require the actual work carried out (executed/implemented) by the supplier to be measured on completion and valued based upon either an approximate bill of quantities, a schedule of rates or a bill of materials. Target-incentive contracts, a variant of the reimbursable type of contract, enable the purchaser and supplier to set a target cost at contract award, additionally, they agree to share any cost savings relative to this target cost. Target price payment terms reimburse the supplier its actual costs incurred, including overheads and profit. If these costs exceed the pre-agreed target, the supplier will only receive part of its additional costs. However, if its final costs are lower than the target, the supplier will receive a percentage of the saving. Mechanisms are usually provided for the target cost to be amended if the scope of work changes or to cover risks retained by the purchaser. Target price contracts are considered less likely to result in disputes due to a more equitable distribution of risk and uncertainty between the purchaser and supplier.

While price-based contracts motivate suppliers (by working efficiently and controlling costs profit can be maximised), they are only incentivised to supply goods and/or services that meet the absolute minimum quality/service level specified. Concerning risk, under price-based contracts the supplier bears a comparatively high level of risk as they are required to execute all the necessary work to meet the specification within a determined timescale. Price-based contracts, however, create a relatively inflexible contract structure.

- **Cost based:** cost plus payment terms reimburse the supplier all its entitled expenditure plus an agreed overhead and profit margin. This can either be a percentage of the final cost (cost plus percentage fee), or a fixed amount (cost plus fixed fee). While engendering collaboration, cost-based contracts afford a much lower degree of control on the supplier, requiring more managerial oversight by the purchaser. Similarly, cost plus incentive fee payment terms permit the fee element to fluctuate either up or down within set limits and in accordance with a formula linked to permissible actual costs.

Compared with price-based contracts, the level of risk borne by the supplier decreases, while that retained by the purchaser will increase. Cost-based contracts, however, permit high levels of change.

Incentives and contract type

Incentive provisions, a combination of cost, schedule and performance inducements, can be incorporated in fixed-price and cost-reimbursable contracts. While there has been increased interest in and adoption of incentive contracts, they are not as extensively used as they perhaps could be. Moreover, there is a tendency for purchasers to resort to fixed-price contracts when budgets are limited due to economic conditions and often employ penalty systems to penalise late completion and poor performance, rather than incentivise supplier performance.

Choice of contract

Contract selection is a key strategic decision, as it determines how the supplier is paid and how risk is distributed between the parties. The link between risk allocation and payment terms is illustrated in Figure 4.1 as a contractual relationship continuum (from an arm's-length (market) to a collaborative (hybrid) approach), based on the allocation of risk to the parties derived from the perceived level of risk at contract formation.

As a broad assumption, the chosen contract should aim to provide the maximum likelihood of delivering an endeavour's/project's objectives. Further, the form of contract has been found to significantly impact project success. For example, where there is a high level of uncertainty, both contracting parties benefit from cost plus contracts, whereas where there is a higher degree of

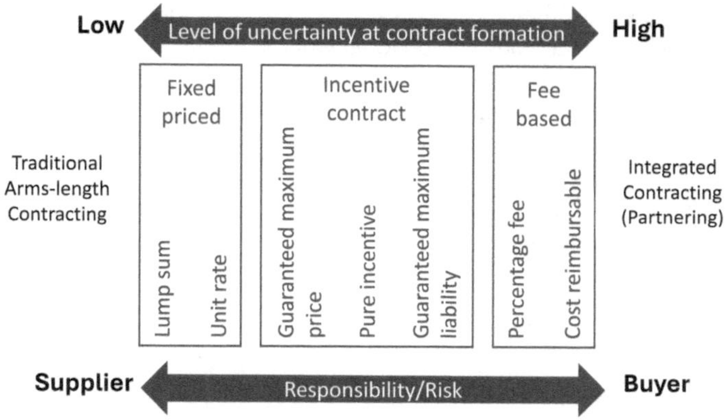

FIGURE 4.1 Risk allocation via contracts (Developed/adapted from Winch, 2010)

certainty, fixed-price contracts generate more benefits. Therefore, uncertainty in the process or final product determines the most appropriate type of contract.

Further, Turner and Simister (2001) suggest that, if the objective is to create a project organisation, based on cooperation rather than conflict, then achieving goal alignment is key. This is achieved, they advocate, by appropriately incentivising all the parties to the contract via the incorporation of suitable contract pricing terms. They conclude that the principal criterion for selecting contract pricing terms is goal alignment.

Globally, while fixed price remains a common approach, there has been a move towards guaranteed maximum price (GMP) contracts.

Frequently, a single contract type is adopted across the project lifecycle, although more complex projects may be divided into two stages:

1 **the preliminary design and feasibility study phases:** where uncertainty is frequently high, cost plus contracts are recommended.
2 **the full-scale design and development phases:** where a fixed-price contract may be preferable.

Further, on major projects it may be appropriate to allocate distinct contract types to individual work packages at the concept, assessment, demonstration, manufacture, in-service and disposal stages. The application section at the end of this chapter presents a decision-support tool that enables this, allowing decision-makers to reconcile the potentially conflicting issues of complexity, uncertainty, flexibility, context and governance to create a rational contracting strategy.

Contract provisions

Contracts:

- State precisely what product/services are to be provided and set appropriate performance/service levels.
- Define the roles of the purchaser and supplier (the parties). Additionally, they apportion roles, for example, relating to project management, design execution and integrity, production supervision and dispute determination.
- Establish transparent procedures for managing relationships and enabling contract management. While certain procedures will address routine contract management activities, others will only be initiated when needed.
- Record the rights and obligations of the parties to the contract and allocate risk between them (see Chapter 3).
- Address the key areas of time issues (commencement and completion dates, schedule/project progress and suspension of the works/service), payment provisions/terms (advance payments, payments on account – stage/milestone payments, bonuses/planned progress payments, price adjustments/variations, price fluctuations/adjustments for inflation, retention payments) and change mechanisms (value management and change management).
- Include provisions to manage the consequences of default by either party, for example, performance indicators, liquidated damages, rebates and termination.
- Incorporate bonds, guarantees and/or insurances, such as tender (bid), repayment, performance, retention, and parent

company guarantee, surety bonds and insurance requirements. Contracts typically stipulate insurance requirements (specifying the specific terms of the policies and limits of coverage) and identify which party is responsible for obtaining the policy.

- Provide a means of dealing with claims (usually a demand or request for an extra payment and/or additional time to execute the contract). Typically, a 'claim' is an assertion of a right conferred by the contract; however, in other circumstances it is the converse, a submission outside the terms of a contract. As an alternative to the more common term claim, some contracts use the phrase compensation events.

Personal reflection

For a recent contract you have been involved in, review any amendments made to this form. Reflect on the impact of these changes on contract execution/project delivery and the relationship between the contracting parties.

Adversarial and non-adversarial dispute resolution

Conflict and disputes can occur when executing contracts regardless of customer/supplier affinity (the relationship between the parties) or the type of contract/project. For example, they may arise because of one or both of the parties have conflicting objectives, fail to anticipate significant risks or variations, neglect to consult, or make invalid assumptions or errors. While conflict, an inescapable feature of organisational life, may have positive connotations, disputes negatively impact trading relationships.

A significant commercial activity is predicting likely problems or areas of conflict and interceding to avoid them turning into disputes. The impact of issues can be mitigated by establishing and observing transparent procedures, promoting collaboration and team-working and fostering a shared aim to resolve difficulties mutually.

Traditionally, litigation was the preferred approach to resolving contractual disputes; however, this is a slow, costly and uncertain process. Contracts, therefore, often include alternative means of dispute resolution, which seek to prevent disruption of the project/contract and determine any dispute in a just and timely manner, if the parties are unable to resolve an issue by mutual agreement. For example, this can include the utilisation of third-party determination either by a named agent (architect, engineer, etc.), mediation, conciliation, dispute review boards, adjudication or arbitration. Ultimately, if these approaches fail to produce a resolution the issue may be settled by litigation.

Personal reflection

For a recent contract/project you have been involved in where a dispute has occurred, reflect on how the dispute was resolved and consider whether the contract either supported or hampered the resolution process.

Flexibility, clarity, simplicity and collaboration

Commercial contracts are often highly complex documents, incorporating the legal, financial, and technical arrangements for the endeavour. As a result, the document itself can potentially be a source or risk/uncertainty. To minimise this, contracts should be evaluated for clarity, conciseness, completeness, internal and external consistency, practicality, fairness, and their potential impact on project implementation (in terms of quality, cost, schedule and safety).

Effective contracts, therefore, require flexibility, clarity and simplicity (including plain phraseology), be fair and should stimulate collaboration and include suitable/transparent management procedures. Unfortunately, many standard forms have previously been criticised for failing to incorporate these features. As a result, several contracts have been drafted to address these concerns, for example, the New Engineering Contract (NEC). A suite of contracts based on collaboration and mutual trust, the latest edition NEC4 launched in 2017 incorporates revisions to provide further *flexibility, clarity and ease of use*. It forms a manual of project management procedures rather than an agenda for litigation.

Regulations, legislation, etc.

Procurement/acquisition regulations

The procurement of assets and services by government bodies, utilities and agencies is generally regulated by statutes. For example, in the UK (excluding Scotland[1]) public procurement, is governed by The Procurement Regulations 2024 (Procurement Act 2023: effective from 24 February 2025). Likewise, the 'Federal Acquisition Regulation' (FAR) underpins a 'Federal Acquisition Regulations System', which codifies and issues standardised acquisition policies and procedures for use by all executive agencies in the US.

The UK Procurement Regulations outline the information required for transparency of procurements under the Procurement Act 2023. These include pipeline and planned procurement notices; tender notices (for open procedure, competitive flexible procedure, frameworks, dynamic markets and qualifying utilities dynamic market notices); associated tender documents; contract award/details notices; procurement termination notices; payments compliance notices; contract performance notices; contract change notices; and contract termination notices.

A comprehensive knowledge of the appropriate regulations is required by both public sector customers and suppliers seeking to trade with government entities. As contracting operations become increasingly global, knowledge of country-specific procurement and acquisition regulations is crucial.

Competition and antitrust legislation

Dynamic, open competition and fair exchanges within markets are widely considered to benefit consumers. To promote these principles, many countries have introduced competition or antitrust legislation that foster fair competition, curtail monopolies and inhibit restrictive commercial practices. For example, in the UK anti-competitive behaviour is prohibited under the Competition Act 1998. Primarily, the legislation proscribes anti-competitive agreements between businesses (or by trade associations), for example, price-fixing, cartels, apportioning contract opportunities within a market, restricting production, and unfairly discriminating between customers, plus the abuse of a dominant market position.

The Competition and Markets Authority (CMA) is responsible for enforcing competition legislation in the UK, although the regulators of specific sectors have been granted authority to implement and enforce the legislation within their remit. Breaching UK competition legislation can incur fines of up to ten per cent of an organisation's global turnover, while parties impacted by a breach can claim damages. Further, individuals found to have participated in a cartel can be imprisoned for up to five years and/or receive fines, while directors of organisation found to have engaged in such activities can be disqualified from holding directorships for up to 15 years.

An awareness of the implications of competition and antitrust legislation, both within home markets and globally, is therefore vital for those involved in commercial exchanges.

International trade law

The increased globalisation of trading relationships requires organisations to be mindful of the numerous regulations governing international trade. The following are the principal international conventions (and UK Legislation that implements them) and additional UK legislation, relating to the transportation of goods by:

- **Air:** the Warsaw and Montreal Conventions (implemented by the Carriage by Air Act 1961 and Carriage by Air and Road Act 1979).
- **Rail:** the Convention concerning International Carriage by Rail (implemented by the International Transport Conventions Act 1983 (amended 1985, 1992, 1994)).
- **Road:** the Convention on the Contract for the International Carriage of Goods by Road (CMR Convention) (implemented via the Carriage of Goods by Road (Parties to Convention) Order 1967). Additional UK legislation includes the Carriage by Air and Road Act 1979 and the Carriage of Dangerous Goods and

Use of Transportable Pressure Equipment Regulations 2009 (which incorporates the European Agreement concerning the International Carriage of Dangerous Goods by Road, generally referred to as ADR).

- **Sea:** the Hague-Visby rules (implemented by the Carriage of Goods by Sea Act 1971). Additional legislation includes the Carriage of Goods by Sea Act 1992.

International Commercial Terms (Incoterms®)

The Incoterms® rules devised by the International Chamber of Commerce (ICC) are a globally acknowledged set of definitions, standards and conventions used for interpreting commercial terms included in both international and domestic sale of goods contracts. The current version, Incoterms® 2020, became operable on 1st January 2020. Recognised by the United Nations Commission on International Trade Law (UNCITRAL) they are available in more than 29 languages. Their main function is to delineate the costs, risks and responsibilities involved in the transfer (delivery) of goods between suppliers and purchasers, thereby reducing the incidence of misinterpretation between the trading parties. An appreciation of these rules, therefore, is imperative for those involved in commercial exchanges commercial managers involved in international trade.

Letters of credit

A letter of credit, also termed documentary credit or letter of undertaking, is a guarantee underwritten, at a cost, by a bank. Often utilised for international trade exchanges, they provide collateral by transferring the risk of default to the underwriter. It provides assurance to sellers that they will receive payment (a fixed sum) from a purchaser within a stipulated timeframe. Payment is conditional, requiring strict conformity with the terms of the letter of credit and proof of compliance, for example, confirmation of transportation. While routinely benefiting buyers and sellers, in some instances they may prolong the transaction and/or result in administrative inconveniences.

Intellectual property

Responding to the opportunities and threats arising from globalisation and rapid technological change on economic exchanges, organisations are obliged to safeguard their competitive advantage. For example, by protecting the knowledge and expertise developed and held by the business. The applicable area of law that covers this is IP. IP includes any innovative (original) work (ideas and information) that has commercial value and can be traded, while IP rights refer to a collection of powers that promote and protect this work. Notably, IP incentivises knowledge creation: a source of competitive advantage and revenue for individuals, organisations and nations.

While there are various commercial mechanisms to protect an individual's or organisation's IP and stimulate innovation, the principal means are confidentiality agreements (confidentiality-disclosure agreements (CDAs) or non-disclosure agreements (NDAs)), secrecy (trade secrets), copyright, designs, patents and trademarks. The Copyright, Designs and Patents Act 1988 (as amended) is the principal legislation that deals with IP rights in the UK.

Usually, IP rights are exclusively acquired by the individual or group that originated the work. However, where it has been conceived by an employee under their contract of employment, the rights are normally held by their employer. Where work has been commissioned, for example as part of a supply contract, IP rights will often be retained by the creator (supplier), subject to any alternative arrangements. For example, commercial contracts may incorporate more complex arrangements, such as defining pre-existing (background) IP and foreground (emerging) IP as that developed in connection with the agreement. While suppliers generally retain rights to the former, customers seek either to obtain the rights to the latter or acquire a non-exclusive royalty free perpetual and irrevocable licence for them. Further, if the purchaser is dominant, they may impose terms that transfer all IP rights. Negotiation of IP terms is a key feature of the commercial activity during the deal creation phase.

When a contravention of an IP right has occurred or is believed to have occurred, actions for redress can only be submitted by the owner of the right (or an exclusive licensee). These rights are administered through a network of international organisations. In the UK, the Intellectual Property Office (an Executive Agency, sponsored by the Department for Science, Innovation and Technology), is accountable for all the key IP mechanisms.

Internationally, The Berne Convention for the Protection of Literary and Artistic Works (The Berne Convention), establishes a 'common framework and agreement between nations' regarding IP rights of authors, musicians, poets, painters, etc. It is administered by the World Intellectual Property Organization (WIPO). Additional agreements/organisations include the Universal Copyright Convention (UCC), the European Patent Organisation and the World Trade Organization (WTO) through the Trade-Related Aspects of Intellectual Property Rights Agreement (TRIPS).

Personal reflection

Examine the IP clauses of a recent contract your organisation has undertaken. Consider whether the treatment of the contracting parties' IP was dealt with equitably. If it was not, reflect on why this was the case.

Insolvency

Insolvency is commonly regarded as the inability of a company or individual to honour its/their debts and/or where its/their liabilities are greater than the value of assets held. Additionally, it refers to the various legal measures applicable when a company, partnership or individual is deemed insolvent. In the UK, insolvency is administered via, among others, the following legislation: the Insolvency Acts 1986 and 2000; Corporate Insolvency and Governance Act 2020; the Companies Acts 1985 and 2006; the Company Directors Disqualifications Act 1986; the Employment Rights Act 1996; and the Enterprise Act 2002 and 2016. Plus, a host of related secondary legislation. Additionally, the Cross-Border Insolvency Regulations 2006 introduced further amendments and establish the United Nations

Commission on International Trade Law (UNCITRAL) Model Law in the UK.

The legislation seeks to provide an objective process for managing the assets of an insolvent entity, settling creditors' claims and determining the eventual fate of the company, partnership or individual. The Insolvency Service, an Executive Agency sponsored by the Department for Business and Trade, oversees the framework and mechanisms used to manage financial failure in the UK and for dealing with any related misconduct.

Insolvency procedures

The following procedures are applicable in England, Wales and Northern Ireland:

- **Companies:** Administration, Administrative receivership, Company voluntary arrangement (CVA), Liquidation (Compulsory liquidation, Creditors' voluntary liquidation, Members' voluntary liquidation (MVL).
- **Individuals (personal insolvency), including an individual member of a partnership:** Bankruptcy, Voluntary arrangements (Individual voluntary arrangements (IVAs), Fast track voluntary arrangements) and Debt Relief Order (DROs).
- **Partnerships:** Administration, Bankruptcy (of individual members), Compulsory liquidation, Voluntary arrangements (company voluntary arrangements, individual voluntary arrangements (in respect of individual members)).

In lieu of liquidation, companies and individuals may seek to enter an informal arrangement with their creditors in an attempt to reach a mutually satisfactory settlement.

Invariably, commercial contracts include insolvency provisions that entitle buyers and sellers to terminate the contract if the other party becomes bankrupt or insolvent, enters liquidation, or has an administration or receiving order made against them. If germane the contract stipulates both the procedure to be followed and the amounts due on termination. However, as termination habitually has a major negative impact on the purchaser's ability to achieve their objectives (and depending on the stage of the project/contract), a purchaser may work with a receiver to permit the supplier to complete the contract.

TUPE regulations

The Transfer of Undertakings (Protection of Employment) (TUPE) Regulations 2006 (amend in 2014), generally referred to as the 'TUPE Regulations', have been effective since April 2006. They safeguard an employee's continuity of and terms and conditions of employment in the event of this being assigned to a new employer following a 'relevant transfer' (conditional on specific prerequisites). The regulations apply equally to private, public or third sector private sector organisations (undertakings), irrespective of their size. The Regulations are applicable to commercial exchanges that involve the transfer of an 'economic entity' (a discrete unit of a business or organisation) or an 'organised grouping of employees', following the outsourcing, insourcing or compulsory competitive tendering of a public service.

Application

Contracting strategy

The selection of an appropriate contract to facilitate a purchase/project is both a critical and significant strategic decision, as stated earlier, it determines the rights and responsibilities of the purchaser and supplier, how a supplier is paid (incentivised) and how risk is allocated between the parties. Additionally, contracting strategy:

- **Drives organisation success:** utilising suppliers, third parties, and partners, etc., to deliver organisational goals and strategic intent, for example, via outsourcing contracts and systems integration.
- **Fosters cohesion between the parties:** aligning the disparate interests of the parties so that their actions and behaviours contribute and support the contract's/project's intent.

Research by World Commerce & Contracting (2021), however, has identified ten common pitfalls in the contracting process, which can potentially impair relationships and lead to financial and schedule issues:

1. **Lack of clear scope and goals**: leading to disputes and claims.
2. **Late involvement of the commercial team**: producing inappropriate contracts and extended lead times.
3. **Failure to engage stakeholders**: resulting in misunderstandings, undermining trust and adversely impacting collaboration.
4. **Protracted negotiations**: causing competitive exposure and delaying revenue generation.
5. **Focus on risk allocation**: at the expense of creating economic benefits.
6. **Inflexible relationships and governance**: creating a blame culture in relation to performance management.
7. **Contract complexity**: leading to the contract being perceived as irrelevant by users.
8. **Poor handover to implementation**: resulting in misunderstandings and unmet commitments.
9. **Limited use of contract technology**: causing inefficient and poor-quality performance and analysis.
10. **Weak post-award governance**: ineffective procedures resulting in recurrent errors and defective work.

As presented above, a variety of contracting approaches exist – so, how do we select which approach to use? For many individuals and organisations, the decision is largely determined by familiarity (what they've previously always done), potentially leading to the selection of governance frameworks and contracts that are sub-optimal. Additionally, frequently a single contract type is adopted by purchasers across the project lifecycle or by suppliers across their supply base. However, on complex major projects it may be more appropriate for purchasers and suppliers to determine distinct contract types for individual work packages. In doing so, decision-makers need to reconcile the potentially conflicting issues of complexity, uncertainty, flexibility, context and governance to create a rational contract strategy. Moreover, key is the selection of commercial arrangements that are most likely to deliver successful outcomes (in terms of mission and scope).

The following section presents a decision-support tool that fosters objective decision-making, enabling the selection of an appropriate solutions from the continuum of contracting options available (see Figure 4.1) based on the specific circumstances impacting the project/commercial exchange.

Contracting strategy model

The following contacting strategy model (Figure 4.2), developed at Alliance Manchester Business School (AMBS) and utilised with several Executive Education clients, including BP and BAE Systems, can be used to determine appropriate contracting approaches at various stages throughout the procurement cycle (see Winch et al., 2023). It is frequently applied in the oil and gas sector.

The model considers the project, from inception to completion, identifying the various work packages involved in its execution/

Contracting Approach		Work packages							
		1	2	3	4	5	6	...	n
Project Management									
Procurement Cycle	Concept								
	Development								
	Execution								
	In-service								
	Disposal								

Commercial Key:

In In-house Inc Incentive (GMP/GML) Fee Fee-based Fixed Fixed price

FIGURE 4.2 Contracting strategy model

delivery. The aim being to evaluate each discrete work package at every stage of the procurement cycle and determine both the preferred supplier and the most appropriate contracting approach for the element of work to be undertaken. This may also involve appointing different suppliers to deliver the required service/product as the project progresses through its lifecycle.

The contracting strategy model can be used to derive an optimum contracting solution between the customer and the prime contractor/supplier. Similarly, it can be applied to establish appropriate contracts between the prime and the various suppliers, third parties and partners involved in delivering the project.

Overview of the model

Across the top of the model are the various work packages required to implement/execute the endeavour. Depending on whether it is being used to consider the interface between the customer and the prime or the prime and its various subcontractors it could comprise numerous work packages.

The left-hand side of the model is subdivided into stages of the project/procurement lifecycle, in this instance the following phases have been selected: concept, development, execution, in service and disposal. Alternatively, a procurement lifecycle that best reflects an industry sector can be adopted, for example, different stages would be more applicable for construction and infrastructure projects when compared to aerospace and defence. The UK Ministry of Defence, for example, uses the CADMID approach, which comprises the stages: Concept, Assessment, Demonstration, Manufacture, In Service and Disposal.

Why divide the project into packages? As a project progresses through the project/procurement lifecycle the degree of uncertainty and risk generally reduces. Similarly, not all work packages attract the same level of risk and uncertainty. For example, on construction projects a high degree of the risk is generally encountered in groundworks, as a contractor will not always know until they 'start digging' the precise ground conditions. Alternatively, with finishing trades, such as painting, there is a higher degree of certainty (the walls are built, their construction is known, as is their absorption factor, how much paint is required and how long it will take a painter to apply paint to the surface of the walls). Therefore, is it appropriate to use the same contract in both instances? Consequently, when proceeding through the procurement/project lifecycle, decision-makers should consider the most appropriate contract form given the prevailing circumstances.

Example: Figure 4.3

If we consider the first work package at the Concept and Development phases, it is assumed that there's a higher degree of uncertainty requiring a degree of flexibility. As a result, a fee-based contracting approach is adopted with Supplier A. During the Execution and In-service or Maintenance phases, a different supplier (Supplier B) is appointed using a fixed-price contract. At the final, Disposal, phase, a fixed-price contract is utilised with Supplier A undertaking the work.

Alternatively, for work packages three and four, once again fixed-price contracts are used for the Concept and Development

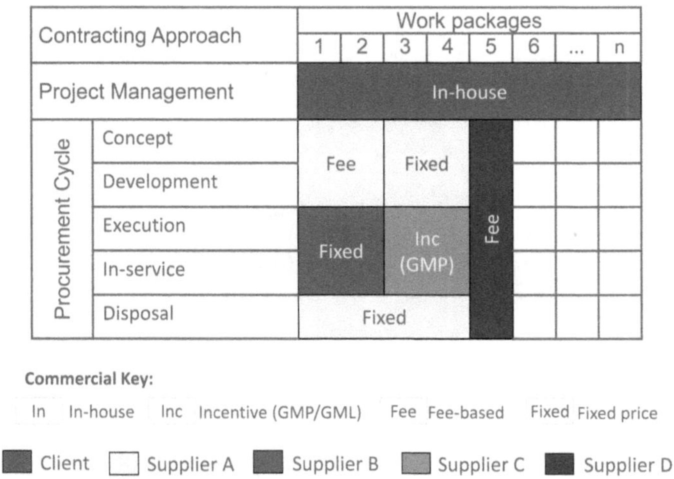

FIGURE 4.3 Example contracting strategy model

phases with Supplier A, then incentivised (GMP) contracts are placed with Supplier C for the Execution and In-service phases. Finally at the Disposal phase the purchaser reverts to Supplier A using a fixed-price contract. For work package five Supplier D is appointed throughout the project/procurement lifecycle utilising a fee-based approach.

The various work packages are, therefore, considered in isolation throughout the project/procurement lifecycle to determine the most appropriate procurement process and contracting strategy at each stage.

The following Contracting Strategy Model can be applied to support this decision-making process. It utilises four lenses (see Figure 4.4):

1 Nature of transaction
2 Nature of supply chain
3 Power dynamic, and
4 Environment

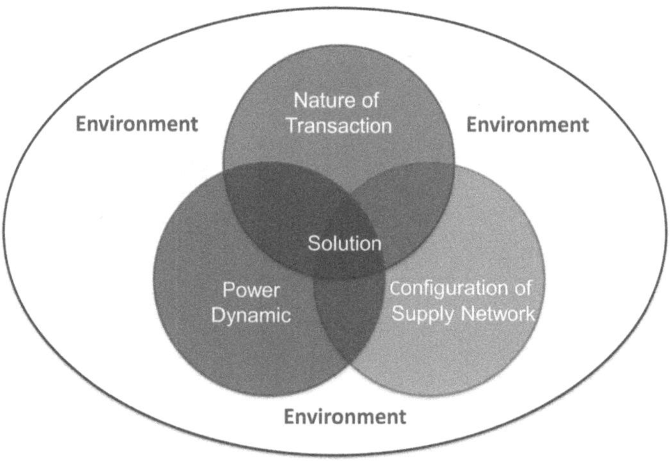

FIGURE 4.4 Contracting strategy model components

Appropriate contracting solutions are generated based on each of these four lenses/concepts:

1 **Nature of transaction:** The Contractual Governance Matrix (see Figure 2.6) based on the principles of Transaction Cost Economics can be used to derive an appropriate contracting solution for the nature of the transaction. For example, where the content of a work package (the final product and/or process) is highly uncertain or complex and the purchaser is highly dependent on the supplier, there is a strong likelihood that the supplier will behave opportunistically. In this instance the recommended contracting approach would promote cooperation and trust, such as a fee-based payment system.
2 **Nature of supply chain:** Kraljic's (1983) 'Portfolio Matrix' or Piercy and Lane's (2009) 'How buyers see suppliers' model (introduced in Chapter 1) may be used to inform the selection of an appropriate contracting solution based on the nature of the supply chain/network. For example, enabling the degree of competition in a market segment to be considered (Is there an adequate number of appropriately qualified suppliers, is it an oligopolistic or monopolistic market?). As an illustration, where there are numerous potential work package contractors and/or the market risk is negligible, combined with a potentially high impact of the product/service to be delivered on the project costs or the main contractor's competitiveness then an ideal contracting solution is one that leverages the best deal between the parties. Additional factors include the maturity and composition of the supply network (for example, is it highly fragmented or integrated?), the need to appoint local or global suppliers, and the financial, technological and collaborative capability of potential suppliers. Regarding, the technological and collaborative capability of potential suppliers, Kaufman et al.'s (2000) Strategic Supplier Typology that classifies prospective partners as either commodity supplier, technology specialist, contractor or problem-solver utilising the dimensions: Technology and Collaborative Capability could be used in lieu of Kraljic's 'Portfolio Matrix' or Piercy and Lane's 'How buyers see suppliers' model.

3 **Power dynamic:** The power dynamic between the two parties can be evaluated using Cox and Ireland's (2006) 'Power Matrix' (see Figure 2.5). For example, if the buyer has dominance pre-award a decision has to be taken as to whether or not they should extract the maximum value from the supplier. A factor to consider here is whether the buyer is also dominant post award – if not and dominance transfers to the supplier there is a potential for the supplier to behave opportunistically, enabling them to recoup value lost during the award stage negotiations. The contracting solution would need to mitigate against this possibility.
4 **Environment (atmosphere):** Data collated using the Pestle+R analysis (see Figure 1.2), concerning the political, economic, social, technological, legal, environmental and regulatory issues that may influence the project can be used to create a contracting solution to address/mitigate the effects of the exchange environment or atmosphere.

The four solutions, based on the Nature of transaction, Nature of supply chain, Power dynamic and Environment can then be consolidated to create an optimised contracting (governance) strategy (see Figure 4.5).

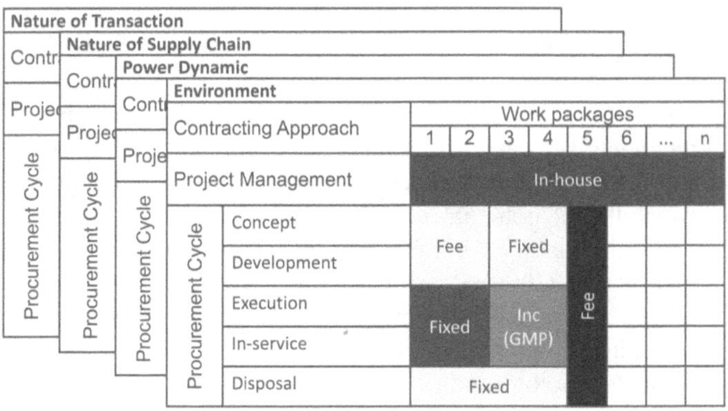

FIGURE 4.5 Contracting strategy model optimisation

Note

1 The Scottish Government has effectively retained the existing EU Procurement Directives.

Further reading/resources

For additional information on the concepts covered in this chapter, see

Generally

Jaeger A V and Hök G S (2010) *FIDIC - A Guide for Practitioners*. Springer-Verlag Berlin/Heidelberg [Provides an overview of English, Finnish, French and German Contract Law, and Islamic and Romanian Law].

Lowe D J (2013) *Commercial Management: Theory and Practice*. Wiley-Blackwell Publishing Ltd, Oxford [Chapter 6: Legal Issues in Contracting].

Contract type and choice

Hughes W (2006) Contract management (Chapter 15). In: D J Lowe with R Leiringer (eds.) *Commercial Management of Projects: Defining the Discipline*. Blackwell Publishing, Oxford, pp. 344–355.

Ten Pitfalls to Avoid in Contracting: in this video, Tim Cummins (President of World Commerce & Contracting) outlines these top ten pitfalls in contract management. https://www.futurelearn.com/courses/contract-management/0/steps/4086 (Accessed 20 July 2024).

Contractual relations

Clegg S, Bjørkeng K and Pitsis T (2011) Innovating the practice of normative control in project management contractual relations. In: P W G Morris, J K Pinto and J Söderlund (eds.) *The Oxford Handbook of Project Management*. Oxford University Press, Oxford, pp. 438–460.

Conflict management and dispute resolution

Fenn P (2006) Conflict management and dispute resolution (Chapter 11). In: D J Lowe with R Leiringer (eds.) *Commercial Management of Projects: Defining the Discipline*. Blackwell Publishing, Oxford. pp. 234–269.

Fenn P (2011) *Commercial Conflict Management and Dispute Resolution*. Taylor & Francis, Abingdon, Oxon.

Flexibility, clarity, simplicity and collaboration

The New Engineering Contract (NEC). https://www.neccontract.com/products/contracts (Accessed 20 July 2024).

Procurement/Acquisition Regulations

The Procurement Regulations 2024 https://www.legislation.gov.uk/uksi/2024/692/contents/made (Accessed 20 July 2024).

Competition and antitrust legislation

The Competition and Markets Authority (CMA) https://www.gov.uk/government/organisations/competition-and-markets-authority (Accessed 20 July 2024).

International trade law

International Commercial Terms (Incoterms®) https://iccwbo.org/business-solutions/incoterms-rules/ (Accessed 20 July 2024).

Intellectual property

Copyright, Designs and Patents Act 1988 (as amended) https://www.gov.uk/government/publications/copyright-acts-and-related-laws (Accessed 20 July 2024).

Insolvency

Insolvency Acts https://www.legislation.gov.uk/primary+secondary?title=Insolvency (Accessed 20 July 2024).

TUPE Regulations

The Transfer of Undertakings (Protection of Employment) (TUPE) Regulations 2006 (amend in 2014) https://www.legislation.gov.uk/uksi/2006/246/contents (Accessed 20 July 2024).

References

CIPS (2024) *Contract management.* Chartered Institute of Procurement & Supply, Stamford. https://www.cips.org/intelligence-hub/contract-management (Accessed 10 July 2024).

Cox A and Ireland P (2006) Strategic purchasing and supply chain management in the project environment – theory and practice. In: D J Lowe (ed.) with R Leiringer, *Commercial Management of Projects: Defining the Discipline*. Blackwell Publishing, Oxford, pp. 390–416.

Kaufman A, Wood C H and Theyel G (2000) Collaboration and technology linkages: a strategic supplier typology. *Strategic Management Journal,* 21(6), 649–663.

Kraljic P (1983) Purchasing must become supply management. *Harvard Business Review*, 61, 109–117.

Piercy N F and Lane N (2009) *Strategic Customer Management: Strategizing the Sales Organization*. OUP, Oxford.

State Government of Victoria (2024) *Contract Management: Goods and Services Guide*. State Government of Victoria, Australia. https://www.buyingfor.vic.gov.au/contract-management-goods-and-services-guide#what-is-contract-planning-and-management (Accessed 20 July 2024).

Turner J R and Simister S J (2001) Project contract management and a theory of organisation. *International Journal of Project Management,* 19(8), 457–464.

Winch G M, Sergeeva N and Lowe D J (2023) Owners managing the commercial interface on complex projects: A pluralistic theoretical perspective. *International Journal of Project Management,* 41(6), 102499.

World Commerce & Contracting (2021) *Overcoming the 10 Pitfalls of Contracting: How AI Can Transform the Value of Contracts*. World Commerce & Contracting. https://www.worldcc.com/Portals/IACCM/Resources/10655_0_Overcoming-the-10-pitfalls.pdf (Accessed 20 July 2024).

5

COMMERCIALLY DRIVEN DECISION-MAKING

A framework approach to support opportunity and investment decision-making

Introduction

Informed, reasoned and timely business decision-making is essential for organisational success. However, good decision-making is a competence where many business leaders would benefit from further development and support.

Drawing on and integrating concepts from earlier chapters and other books in this series, particularly 'Market-led Strategy' by Irene Roele, 'Measuring Business Value' by Julian Jones and Chapter 4: Project Initiating in 'Managing Projects' by Alec Waterworth and Carl Gavin, this chapter provides an overview of the 'Business Case Framework', which can be used to 'capture' pertinent information to support commercially driven business decision-making.

Commercially driven decision-making

While numerous decisions are left to individual leaders and managers, key decisions are usually determined by groups – requiring input from numerous stakeholders. These decisions include the following:

- establishing an organisation's strategy
- resolving managerial issues and challenges

DOI: 10.4324/9781003052159-5

- choosing between competing investment decisions
- determining whether to develop new products and services and
- selecting between competing business opportunities (invitations to tender, etc.).

Irrespective of the subject of the decision, effective decision-making involves the following stages:

- identifying the challenge/issue at hand (the focus of the decision)
- collating and synthesising information
- identifying potential options/available choices
- evaluating and prioritising these options – identifying the threats and opportunities of each
- selecting the most appropriate solution from the alternatives
- committing to a solution and taking action and
- reviewing the outcome of the decision/action taken.

In this chapter, we will focus on commercially driven decision-making in respect of organisational opportunities and investment decisions. It introduces a decision-support tool, the Business Case Framework, which has been successfully used with multiple clients across a range of industry sectors. The framework enables decision-makers to capture, collate and present information, allowing them to determine whether to respond or not to a sales opportunity/invitation to bid (opportunity screening and bid/no bid decision), to develop and launch a new product and/or service, or to initiate the procurement of an asset or service.

The need to draw upon the various underlying principles and concepts of commercial management, for example, relationship, legal, transaction and risk management to make informed commercial decisions at the various review points throughout the lifecycle of a business opportunity, is illustrated in Figure 5.1.

In Figure 5.1, the process has been simplified. In practice, there are multiple stage gates during a project's or value

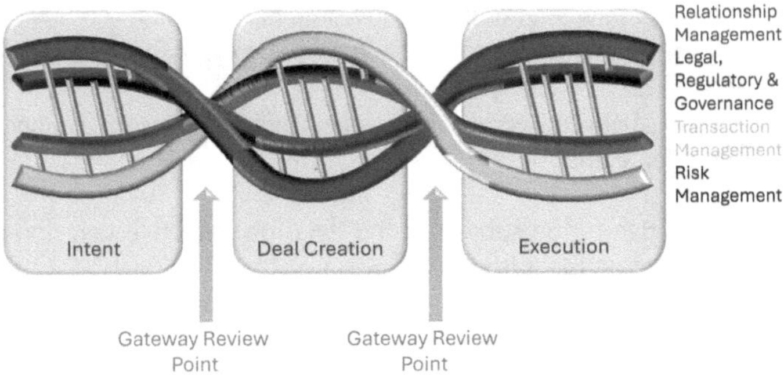

FIGURE 5.1 Interrelationship of commercial management activities

proposition's lifecycle, for example, where both customers and suppliers review and decide whether to proceed or not with a potential project or opportunity (see Figure 1.6). Later in Chapter 7 'The Gate Review Process', an independent, high-level, evaluation and review process is introduced, which can be applied to a programme or project at critical stages during its lifecycle.

Business case framework

Various models and frameworks can be used to capture and collate information to inform/support these stage gate decisions. An example is the following 'Business Case Framework', which enables organisations to evaluate how they identify, acquire and exploit value from its supply chain/value network, and define, create and deliver value for its customers.

There are two variants of the Business Case Framework:

1 **Proposition development:** utilised by supply organisations (for example, a supplier or main/prime contractor), captures the logic for responding (or not) to an externally conceived sales/bidding opportunity, where a customer seeks

to purchase an asset or service (instigate a project/contract). Initially, used during the pre-award stages of Opportunity Identification, Opportunity Development, Proposition Identification and Proposition Development to support the supplier's project screening: proceed/not proceed and bid/no bid decisions. Then, if a bid is submitted, at the deal creation and post-award stages to establish if the opportunity will/is still delivering the intended benefits/return on investment.

2 **Value/investment proposition:** utilised by supply organisations (for example, a manufacturer or consultancy), captures the reasoning for developing and launching (or not) a new internally conceived income-generating/value-adding product and/or service (Value Proposition). Again, initially used during the design/pre-launch stages of the product/service development: Opportunity Identification, Opportunity Development, Proposition Identification and Proposition Development to support opportunity screening: choosing between competing value propositions, then post-launch to establish if the value proposition is delivering the intended value/return on investment. This version can also be used by customers (buyers) to capture their rationale for initiating (or not) the procurement of an asset or service (Investment Proposition). Again, initially used during the pre-award stages of the procurement lifecycle: Requirement Identification, Requirement Specification, Solution Selection and Asset/Service Procurement to support the buyer's investment/purchase decision. Then, if the decision is to purchase the asset or service, at the award/deal creation and post-award stages to determine if the value asset purchase/service delivery will/is producing the intended value/return on investment.

As illustrated in Chapter 1, organisations that participate in b2b exchange relationships have both a supply (sell) side, which interfaces with its customers, the demand (buy) side of downstream businesses, and a demand (buy) side, which engages with its key partners and suppliers, the supply (sell) side of upstream businesses.

In the following explanation of the Business Case Framework, the term **organisation** is used to indicate the entity that is utilising the framework to capture either its:

1 logic for responding (or not) to an externally conceived sales/bidding opportunity (Proposition Development)
2 reasoning for developing and launching (or not) a new internally conceived income-generating/value-adding product and/or service (Value Proposition) or
3 rationale for initiating (or not) the procurement of an asset or service (Investment Proposition).

Additionally, **customer(s)** refers to downstream businesses and **external resources** (key partners and suppliers) denotes upstream businesses, while **opportunity** embraces the terms Proposition Development, Value Proposition and Investment Proposition.

The intelligence acquisition/collation process is iterative; information is recorded as/when it becomes available. The model, therefore, can be continually updated as the opportunity progresses. Moreover, as the framework is a live document: a strategy on a page, albeit a fairly large page, decision-makers are immediately aware of any information gaps. As a result, bid/development teams are encouraged to place large poster-sized copies of the Business Case Framework on their bid room/office walls as a visual aide-mémoire.

The Business Case Framework is divided into four parts. The first three, Overview and Context of the Opportunity, Analysis of the Opportunity and Risk and Opportunity Analysis, are identical in both variants of the framework. The fourth part has two alternatives: The Winning Solution (Variant 1: Proposition Development) or The Solution (Variant 2: Development/Investment Proposal). Figure 5.2 presents the Proposition Development variant of the Business Case Framework.

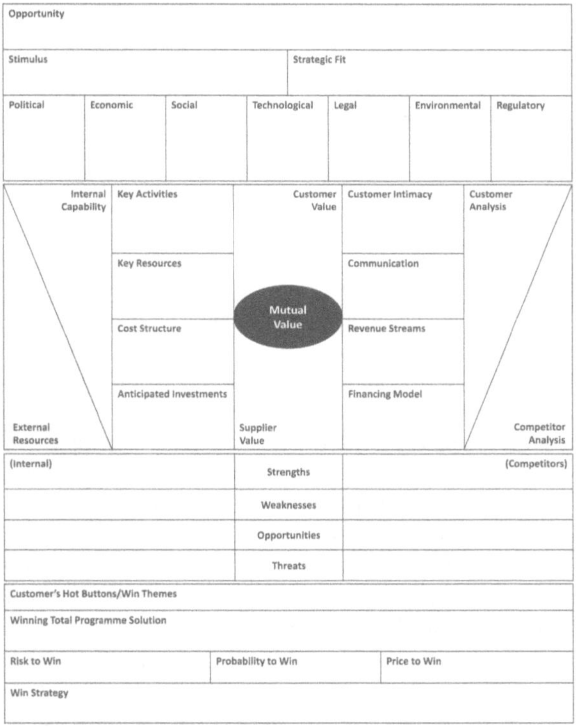

FIGURE 5.2 Business Case Framework (Proposition Development Variant) [NB: Part 2 Developed/adapted and extended from Osterwalder and Pigneur (2010) and Kalakou and Macário (2013)]

Part 1: Overview and context of the opportunity

The first part of the framework (Figure 5.3) comprises an overview of the opportunity and can be used to inform the initial screening activity – it contains four components:

1 **Opportunity:** requires the formulation of a clear succinct overview or statement of what the customer is trying to accomplish

Opportunity						
Stimulus				Strategic Fit		
Political	Economic	Social	Technological	Legal	Environmental	Regulatory

FIGURE 5.3 Part 1: Overview and context of the opportunity

via its purchase in the case of a sales/bidding opportunity (Proposition Development); or what the organisation is seeking to achieve via the introduction of a new income-generating/value-adding product and/or service (Value Proposition) or the procurement of an asset or service (Investment Proposition). The objective is to create a clear understanding of the aims and scope of the opportunity across the bid, development or procurement team. Essentially, it's an elevator pitch that can be shared with relevant stakeholders within the business and upstream suppliers.

2. **Stimulus:** entails the creation of a brief statement that encapsulates the motivation, rationale and justification of the originating organisation to initiate a new income-generating/value-adding product and/or service (Value Proposition) or procure an asset or service (Investment Proposition); or for the customer to purchasing an asset and/or service, or instigating a project in the case of a sales/bidding opportunity (Proposition Development). In both variants, it's an initial attempt to understand the customer's needs and desires.
3. **Strategic fit:** outlines how the opportunity is aligned to the organisation's strategy or enables it to deliver on its strategic intent. It informs the decision-making/screening process; for example, if the opportunity does not align with the organisation's strategic intent, why is it even considering it?
4. **PESTLE+R analysis:** the final section in this part of the framework collates the political, economic, social, technological, legal, environmental and regulatory issues that may influence the decision-makers' assessment of the opportunity. Additionally,

if media interest (of increasing importance due to social media) was deemed to be a significant issue, a separate media component could be included in the analysis. As mentioned in Chapter 1, exchange transactions take place within a context: the environment or 'atmosphere', this section enables the organisation to capture information concerning external and internal factors impacting the opportunity (see Environment in Chapter 1 for more details).

Decision-point: On completion of this section of the framework, the organisation can utilise the collated data to determine whether to proceed or not to proceed with a particular opportunity (for factors influencing this decision, see Chapter 8).

Part 2: Analysis of the opportunity

Part 2 (Figure 5.4) draws inspiration from Osterwalder and Pigneur's (2010) Business Model Canvas, which has been modified and extended to include additional features.[1]

I am always interested in how practitioners approach this part of the Business Case Framework. Coming from a commercial background, I am drawn to the middle section – the value

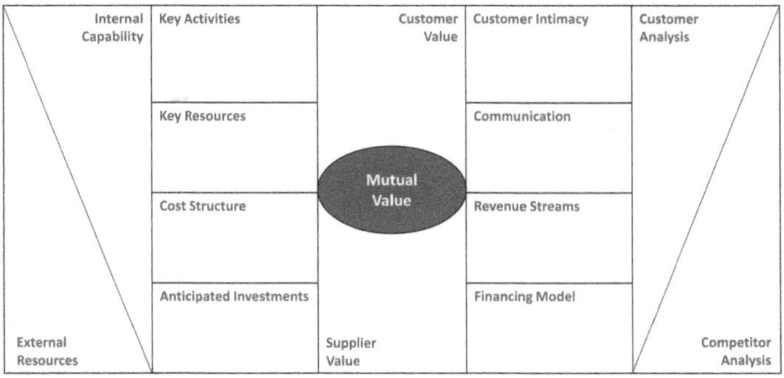

FIGURE 5.4 Part 2: Analysis of the Opportunity (developed/adapted and extended from Osterwalder and Pigneur [2010] and Kalakou and Macário [2013])

generated/derived from a potential opportunity for both the customer and supplier (organisation): the value proposition and expected returns. Whereas individuals with a sales/business winning focus tend to be drawn to the right-hand side, which captures information on the organisation's customers and competitors. While others proceed left to right because that's the way individuals generally work! The left-hand side captures information on the organisation's capability/efficiency to deliver value to its customer(s) via its value propositions: products and/or services.

Value

The central element of the model captures the potential value derived from the opportunity: value for the customer, supplier (organisation) value and the mutual value derived from the relationship/exchange.

- **Customer value:** comprises a statement of the value a customer will derive from the supply organisation, for example, via an innovative product, service or capability designed to meet a customer's desire or ease their pain. The features that attract customers: the supplier's value proposition.
- **Supplier value:** is a statement of the expected return for the organisation. For example, will the opportunity deliver the anticipated/forecasted return on investment, achieve acceptable or superior profits, obtain a greater market share or enhance their brand – enabling comparisons to be made with competing opportunities? Alternatively, will it regenerate the organisation's offerings, enabling it to counter 'wane depression', the decline stage of a product or service lifecycle by transitioning from one business model to another or motivate it to introduce a new value stream?
- **Mutual value:** recognition of the reciprocal value derived from the opportunity. As discussed in Chapter 1, central to commercial affinity and customer attractiveness is an acknowledgement of mutual value. If both parties perceive value in a relationship, then it will likely continue and be mutually rewarding. (See Commercial Affinity and Customer Attractiveness in Chapter 1 for more details.)

Models, such as Osterwalder et al.'s (2014) Value Proposition Canvas can be used to map the customer's pains and gains against the supplier's products or services (pain relievers and gain creators) to establish whether there is a mutually beneficial fit between the organisations. This exercise requires the identification and capture of the following customer factors:

- **Customer jobs**: the tasks a customer requires to be undertaken – their aspirations to be met or their issues to be resolved
- **Customer pains**: the negative aspects related to these activities (jobs, tasks)
- **Customer gains**: the benefits derived from the successful completion of these activities. For more information on this topic, see Christensen et al. (2016).

Plus, the identification and capture of the following supplier factors:

- **Product and services**: the features of the supplier's product or service that enable the customer to undertake their 'jobs' and create customer value
- **Pain relievers**: how the supplier's products or services relieve the customer's pains
- **Gain creators**: how the supplier's product or service create 'gains' – benefits for its customers.

Customers and competitors

Information on the supply organisation's customer (or customers) and competitors is captured on the right-hand side of the framework under the following headings:

- **Customer intimacy:** introduced in Chapter 1, an evaluation of the relationship with a particular customer, providing an assessment of the current level of customer intimacy, satisfaction, communication, collaboration, commitment and trust. (See Commercial Affinity, Customer Attractiveness and Customer Intimacy in Chapter 1 for more details). Tools, such as

Piercy and Lane's 'How buyers see suppliers' model or the Kraljic matrix presented in Chapter 1, can be used to establish how a supply organisation's customer views its relationship with the supplier: is the organisation considered a strategic partner or is the relationship based on price leverage, supply continuity or efficiency?

- **Communication:** the two-way communication channels between the organisation and its customer(s), through which a customer can raise issues/problems, demands and complaints or signal their satisfaction with the product and/or service. Plus, the methods used by the organisation to reach/engage customers and raise awareness of its products and services and communicate its value proposition. These channels can include personalised support mechanisms, automated interactions, co-creation activities and communities of interest.
- **Revenue streams:** notes how the organisation will generate an income through the opportunity. There are a variety of options, for example, through the successful completion of a contract, via payments based on delivery stage gates or based on selling products and services, capability, subscription or consultancy fees, leasing and licensing agreements, etc. A question: do Rolls-Royce sell aeroengines? The easy answer is yes, but they are often discounted. Rolls Royce tends to generate their primary return through selling in-service support – via their 'power by the hour' contracts.
- **Financing model:** identifies the method by which the implementation of the proposal will be financed. For example, if the opportunity will be directly financed by the customer or indirectly by them through the contract via payments on account. Alternatively, is the organisation expected to invest its own capital or raise finance to fund the opportunity?
- **Customer analysis:** as covered in Chapter 1, requires the organisation to clearly identify who their customer is, whether they are represented by an individual or group, if they are an experienced (repeat) client of the sector or an inexperienced, one-off purchaser, and who ultimately will be the key decision-maker. In addition, the supplier needs to consider the customer's profile, objectives (What are they seeking to

achieve through this opportunity? How the opportunity aligns with the customer's overall strategy?), current capabilities and assumptions, capacity to collaborate and co-create[2] and what future opportunities they offer (Is there potential for further contracts?).

Customers can be further segmented based on their geographical location, the products and services they purchase, the means (channels) through which they are engaged, their need for alternative forms of relationship management, whether the relationship is profitable, or whether they are disposed to pay for different features of an offer, etc. Our understanding of and how customers are segmented is based on the level of intimacy between the organisations that has been established (see Chapter 1). For example, is the organisation perceived to be a valuable supplier or trusted partner, and the purchaser a preferred customer?

- **Competitor analysis:** again, as addressed in Chapter 1, enables an organisation to objectively assess its competitive position within the market and evaluate potential outcomes if it were to competitively bid for a potential opportunity (Proposition Development), launch a competing value proposition (Value Proposition) or procure an asset or service (Investment Proposition). Competitor analysis requires the identification of the organisation's competitors, including their individual profiles, goals, current capabilities and assumptions, capacity to collaborate and co-create, and market strategy (plus, how these differ from its own). It also includes an assessment of how competitors react when competing against the organisation; plus, importantly an evaluation of their relationship with the customer, whether they have been able to influence the customer's purchasing requirements or procurement approach and how the organisation can respond/compete against them.

Internal capability and external resources

If the right-hand side of this part of the Business Case Framework is about the customer and potential competitors, the left-hand side is concerned with efficiency (productivity and operational effectiveness) and how the organisation delivers its products and services, and/or fulfils its contractual commitments. Information on the organisation's internal capability and external resources is captured under the following headings:

- **Key activities:** is an assessment of the major activities required to be undertaken/completed to deliver its products and services, and/or fulfil its contractual commitments.
- **Key resources:** collates the physical, intellectual, human and financial resources required to be expended to deliver its products and services, and/or fulfil its contractual commitments.
- **Cost structure:** an estimation of the costs incurred to deliver its products and services, and/or fulfil its contractual commitments.
- **Expected investments:** an evaluation of the anticipated/forecasted investment (internally sourced or from the financial market) and any associated costs required to deliver its products and services, and/or fulfil its contractual commitments.
- **Internal capacity:** an assessment of the capability found within the organisation to deliver its products and services, and/or fulfil its contractual commitments (see Chapter 1). Additionally, this component will identify those aspects the organisation will undertake internally 'make' and those it will look to third parties to perform – the 'buy' option. The classic 'make or buy' decision (see Chapter 2).
- **External resources:** identifies the key partners and suppliers the organisation will collaborate with to create, offer and deliver its products and services, and/or fulfil its contractual commitments (see Key Partners/Suppliers and Strategic Supply Chain Options in Chapter 1). These b2b economic exchanges may include strategic alliances (between non-competitors), strategic relationships (between competitors) and consortia/joint ventures to develop new business opportunities and buyer–supplier relationships. Again, models, such as Kraljic's (1983) 'Portfolio Matrix' and Piercy and Lane's (2009) 'How buyers see suppliers' model, can be used to identify appropriate exchange relationships with member of the upstream supply chain.

(Internal)	Strengths	(Competitors)
	Weaknesses	
	Opportunities	
	Threats	

FIGURE 5.5 Part 3: Risk and Opportunity Analysis

Part 3: Risk and opportunity analysis

Part 3 (Figure 5.5) incorporates SWOT analyses (introduced in Chapter 3): a consideration of the strengths, weaknesses, opportunities and threats involved, enabling the organisation to identify and analyse the risks and opportunities inherent in the particular venture. The framework requires the decision-makers to complete SWOT analyses from both their own internal perspective (labelled: Internal) and through the lens of the various competitors (labelled: External) to gain a better understanding of their position compared to their competitors.

An additional technique involves completing further Part 2 analyses (for the opportunity) from the perspective of each of the main competitors. Again, this enables the organisation to compare, for example, competing value propositions and the relative levels of customer intimacy. Alternatively, either Porter's Five or Six Forces (Porter, 2008) or Volatility, Uncertainty, Complexity and Ambiguity (VUCA) models could be utilised.

Part 4: The solution/the winning solution

As mentioned earlier, the final part of the Business Case Framework has two alternatives.

The solution (value/investment proposition)

The internally conceived income-generating/value-adding product and/or service (Value Proposition) or asset/service procurement

Customer's Hot Buttons
Total Solution
Opportunity Cost
Key Performance Indicators

FIGURE 5.6 Part 4: The Solution (Development/Investment Proposition)

(Investment Proposition) version (Figure 5.6) contains the following sections:

The first component of Part 4 enables the organisation to capture the customer's **hot buttons**. Shipley Associates define hot buttons as the "... highest priority topics that concern or motivate the customer for a specific procurement and influence a buying decision" (Newman, 2011). Customer hot buttons, therefore, are the comments, questions, symbols or images that instantly place an emotionally charged issue at the forefront of a prospective customer's mind. Consequently, they are linked to Emotional Intelligence (EQ) and Neuro-Linguistic Programming (NLP): the study of how individuals think and communicate, both internally and externally with others.

As mentioned earlier, hot buttons relate to the customer's issues (pains) to be resolved/off-loaded and their desires (gains) to be sated, which drive the buying decision. They are the lens through which a supplier evaluates their proposal or proposition. The objective is to identify the primary hot buttons that the opportunity will seek to address. Then generate responses to several potentially suitable hot buttons – selected based on their potential to stimulate an intense emotional response by the customer.

Importantly, these hot buttons, as raised in Chapter 1, are subject to change and can vary between individual decision-makers. It's crucial, therefore, to determine who the key decision-maker is and to establish what their particular hot buttons are. As motivators, hot buttons are specific to an individual/organisation, it is important, therefore, to use the customer's language (potentially utilising NLP) when identifying and responding to them.

To conclude, hot buttons are the collective issues and motivators that drive a customer's buying decision.

The second component, **Total Solution**, addresses how the organisation will deliver its product or service (value proposition) or procure an asset or service (Investment Proposition). It entails generating a statement of the evolving innovative, compliant, competitive, cost-effective, robust and profitable solution that includes a technical solution or service; implementation; project management; people; supply chain; commercial (partnering arrangements, contract structures, pricing/financials) and in-service support solutions (see Figure 5.7).

Various instruments can be used to assess the constituent parts of the Total Solution. For example, Kraljic's (1983) 'Portfolio Matrix', Piercy and Lane's (2009) 'How buyers see suppliers' model and the strategic supply chain options (outlined in Chapter 1) can be applied to establish the Supply Chain solution, while the Contracting Strategy Framework (introduced in Chapter 4) can inform

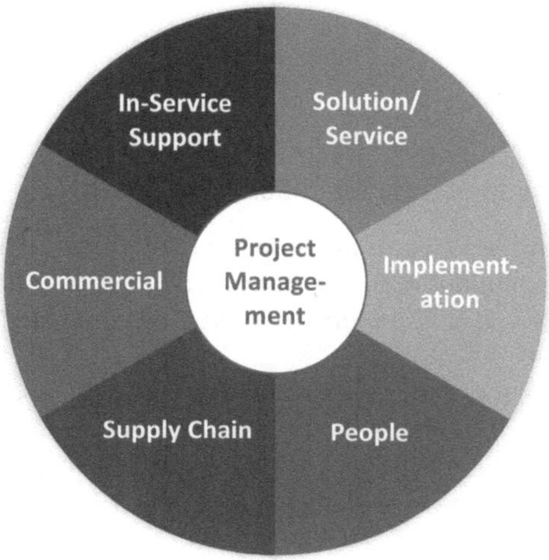

FIGURE 5.7 The Total Solution

the development of the Commercial Solution, determining appropriate contracting approaches across the procurement cycle.

The components of the Total Solution are considered in the round, generating an optimised response that best meets the needs of the customer(s), is deliverable and will generate an appropriate return on investment.

The third component, **Opportunity Cost**, enables the organisation to consider the impact of investing in the development of a new income-generating/value-adding product and/or service (Value Proposition); or the procurement of an asset or service (Investment Proposition). It is, therefore, a statement/evaluation of the potential benefit forfeited when one alternative is chosen over another, permitting the organisation to make informed decisions.

Finally, **Key Performance Indicators** allow the organisation to determine in advance what good looks like, identifying its vision (values), objectives and critical success factors, and establishing performance measurement metrics to assess its performance and ensure the development and supply of the product and/or service (Value Proposition) or evaluate and monitor the procurement of an asset or service (Investment Proposition). Ultimately, it can be used to establish whether the development/investment has been a success.

The winning solution (proposition development)

The **Proposition Development** version of Part 4 (Figure 5.8), where the solution forms the basis of the response to an externally conceived sales/bidding opportunity, contains the following sections:

As above, the first component of the Proposition Development version of Part 4 enables the bid team to capture the customer's **hot buttons.** These are then used to develop various **win themes** that can be incorporated into the bid/proposal submission. Underpinned by customer intelligence and intimacy, and addressing specific customer hot buttons, persuasive win themes contain three parts: an offer or feature, which can be either quantitative

Customer's Hot Buttons/Win Themes		
Winning Total Programme Solution		
Risk to Win	Probability to Win	Price to Win
Win Strategy		

FIGURE 5.8 Part 4: The Winning Solution (Proposition Development)

or qualitative in nature; a benefit, which directly responds to a customer's issue or desire; and evidence to back-up claims made, thereby establishing credibility and confidence in the offer/feature. As previously mentioned, to be effective, win themes need to adopt the customer's vernacular. Successful win themes convince the customer that the bidder understands and empathises with them to a greater degree than the competition.

The **Winning Total Solution** section is virtually identical to the Total Solution above, enabling an organisation to consider how it will deliver the project (asset/service) based on an optimised Total Solution (see Figure 5.7) that is well balanced, integrated, winning, executable and based on what the customer values.

The **Risk to Win** section collates the risk the organisation is prepared to accept in order to win a particular sales/bidding opportunity. The Risk Appetite/Johari Window model, introduced in Chapter 3, can be used to consider the risk to win.

Similarly, **Probability to Win** is the level of probability the organisation is prepared to accept in order to win the sales/bidding opportunity. There is an inverse relationship between the probability to win and price: a higher probability to win generating a lower bid price. This will require the organisation to value engineer their solution to meet this reduced price, accept a lower profit/margin or both.

Price to Win is essentially a top-down estimating approach, sometimes referred to as market pricing. Generally, organisations establish their bid price based on a bottom-up methodology. They initially establish their costs to deliver the project (asset/service) to which they add their required margin and overheads. This price must be market tested, as the bidder needs to consider what their customer is prepared to pay and what its competitors are likely to offer.

Alternatively, the **Price to Win** is an analysis of what the customer is prepared to pay: the Price to Compete and how competitors are likely to respond. From this, based on intelligence from the sales/marketing team, the organisation (bidder) generates a price that needs to be submitted to win the opportunity: the Price to Win. A total cost is established by subtracting the required margin, overheads and risk/management contingency from the Price to Win. This is based on judgement and business acumen. The figure left is the amount available to cover the bidder's solution. The bidder, therefore, needs to value engineer a solution within this cost that both meets the needs of the customer and delivers the required value propositions – **The Solution to Win**. The key principle here is that frugality, having a fixed cost, will drive innovation. Given the bidder has established its maximum costs, they can work with their supply chain and partners to develop novel solutions within the established cost constraint.

The major downside to this approach is where an organisation submits a bid that meets the customer's budget but without undertaking appropriate levels of analysis and value engineering. An example of this can be found on the Cardiff, Millennium stadium project – where John Laing, a preferred bidder, appears to have undertaken limited analysis and solutioning before submitting their tender – a price that met the customer's budget. This decision came back to 'bite them' during the delivery phase of the project, as they were unable to deliver the project within their tender price.

Allied to this point is the notion of Front-end Loading or FEL, a concept utilised in the oil and gas sector. Merrow (2011) has established from the analysis of over 21,000 projects that definition and planning deliver success; 'left-shifting' engineering and solutioning in a project's lifecycle have the most impact on project success.

The danger for suppliers when implementing FEL is that they are generally expected to undertake the work at their own risk; only receiving recompense if they are the successful bidder. Again, if we consider the Cardiff Millennium stadium, the customer, the Welsh Rugby Union (WRU), selected two preferred bidders John

Laing and Taylor Woodrow. Taylor Woodrow, unlike John Laing – who, as just mentioned, appear to have undertaken minimal engineering work to support their bid, implemented FEL and developed a fully engineered solution to support their tender. However, even though there was very little difference in the final bids submitted by the two suppliers – the customer selected the lowest bidder despite their lack of a supporting solution – appearing to have evaluated the options based on the lowest price principle. The potential lesson here is that before an organisation invests in FEL, they need to be assured that the work will be valued by the customer or that the engineered solution delivers the lowest price.

The final component of the model encapsulates the **Win Strategy**. This section collates the statements and specific actions that seek to put the organisation's (bidder's) proposal in a preferential position in the eyes of the customer when compared with its competitors. Further, it addresses specific responses to the customer's tender evaluation criteria.

Decision-point: On completion of the Business Case Framework, the organisation can utilise the collated data to determine whether to submit a bid (Proposition Development), launch a new internally conceived income-generating/value-adding product and/or service (Value Proposition) or procure an asset or service (Investment Proposition). For factors influencing these decisions, see Chapter 8.

Summary

The Business Case Framework enables an organisation to capture pertinent information relating to a potential opportunity (Proposition Development, Value Proposition or Investment Proposition). The capture process is iterative; the framework being continually updated as more data becomes available throughout the proposition's lifecycle. Also, if a physical copy is placed on the bid room/office wall it provides a visual prompt for all those aspects where information is missing, in addition to recording what is known. Essentially, it enables organisations to compile evidence to inform team review meetings and gateway reviews, where key decisions are made.

Frequently, there is a danger that decision-makers exhibit optimism bias during the early stage of an opportunity; this approach grounds the participants by identifying gaps in their information and knowledge.

Finally, the Business Case Framework is a further tool that can be used to support informed decision-making through the life of an opportunity. For example, the framework can be used to inform early stage opportunity/value proposition screening or the bid/no bid decision.

Personal reflection

Finally, for a project/contract that you are familiar with, consider how you might incorporate the Business Case Framework in your decision-making.

Notes

1 A detailed description of the Business Model Canvas can be found in Osterwalder and Pigneur (2010), while a brief introduction to the Business Model Canvas can be gained by viewing the following short (2 minute) YouTube clip: https://youtu.be/QoAOzMTLP5s or https://strategyzer.com/canvas/business-model-canvas

2 Work with one or more organisations to develop something – a product, component or service.

Further reading

For additional information on the concepts covered in this chapter, see

Osterwalder A and Pigneur Y (2010) *Business Model Generation: A Handbook for Visionaries, Game Changers, and Challengers*. John Wiley & Sons, Hoboken, NJ.

Strategyzer: The Business Model Canvas. https://www.strategyzer.com/library/the-business-model-canvas (Accessed 10 July 2024).

References

Christensen C M, Hall T, Dillon K and Duncan D S (2016) Know your customers' jobs to be done. *Harvard Business Review*, 94(9), 54–62.

Kalakou S and Macário R (2013) An innovative framework for the study and structure of airport business models. *Case Studies on Transport Policy*, 1 (1–2), 2–17.

Kraljic P (1983) Purchasing must become supply management. *Harvard Business Review*, 61, 109–117.

Merrow E (2011) *Industrial Megaprojects: Concepts, Strategies, and Practices for Success*. John Wiley & Sons, Hoboken, NJ.

Newman L (2011) *Shipley Capture Guide*. 4th Edition, Shipley Associates, Kaysville, UT.

Osterwalder A and Pigneur Y (2010) *Business Model Generation: A Handbook for Visionaries, Game Changers, and Challengers*. John Wiley & Sons, Hoboken, NJ.

Osterwalder A, Pigneur Y, Bernarda G, Smith A and Papadakos T (2014) *Value Proposition Design: How to Create Products and Services Customers Want*. John Wiley & Sons, Hoboken, NJ.

Piercy N F and Lane N (2009) *Strategic Customer Management: Strategizing the Sales Organization*. OUP, Oxford.

Porter M E (2008) The five competitive forces that shape strategy. *Harvard Business Review*, 86(1), 78.

6

INFLUENCING PARTNER BEHAVIOUR

Grounding successful commercial outcomes and trading relationships on the effective ethical application of persuasion, influence and negotiation

Introduction

The interrelated activities of persuading, influencing and negotiating are key elements of our daily lives, as we seek to interact with family, friends, colleagues, etc. As asserted by Voss and Raz (2017), everything is a negotiation. Moreover, they underpin effective management and leadership, and customer/supplier relationship management. For example, developing an effective win strategy or successfully executing a contract can be viewed as a process of internal and external persuasion, influence and negotiation.

As identified in Chapter 1, relationship management, especially influencing and negotiating with internal and external stakeholders (colleagues, customers, different business units within the organisation, partners, suppliers, etc.) is a key commercial activity. For example, commercial actors (both buy-side and supply-side) will seek to influence, both formally through contracts and agreements and informally via persuasion, the performance, actions and behaviours of other parties and stakeholders. Similarly, they will also engage in formal and informal negotiations during a project's, product's or service's lifecycle.

DOI: 10.4324/9781003052159-6

Rather than providing a best practice 'Negotiation 101', of which there are numerous good examples, this chapter will offer examples of influencing and negotiating across the exchange lifecycle from the commercial perspective, present the principles of influencing and persuasion, explore the impact of emotional and psychological aspects on negotiations and outline a nuanced approach to negotiation that aligns with the principles of TCE covered in Chapter 2.

If you are interested in studying the practice of negotiation in more detail, see the Further Reading section for additional resources.

Influencing partner behaviour

As discussed in Chapter 2, exchange parties seek to influence the behaviour of other participants via a combination of contractual and relational means (both formal and informal negotiations and persuasion) throughout a project/contract's lifecycle. This involves more than just negotiating the deal, contract or final account. Regarding relational means, see Ian Macneil's '10 common contract behavioural patterns and norms' outlined in Chapter 2 (Macneil, 2000).

There are multiple instances throughout an exchange that require the parties to negotiate or seek to influence/persuade. These include, for example, ensuring that the project team (buy-side and sell-side) have the appropriate resources to support a particular objective/opportunity, negotiate the 'deal' and execute the project/contract. Also, buy-side influencing activities will include obtaining agreement to a business case to support an investment/purchase (via a project/contract), securing approval for subsequent solutions, asset/service procurement and contracting strategy. While from a sell-side perspective, developing an effective win strategy or successfully executing a contract can be viewed as a process of internal and external persuading, influencing and negotiating. Further supply-side influencing activities include obtaining agreement to business cases to support an opportunity, securing approval at subsequent stage-gate reviews, such as bid screening, bid/no bid confirmation, bid approval, contract acceptance and subcontracting strategy.

Negotiating

In terms of negotiation, both buy-side and sell-side 'commercial' actors can undertake the following activities:

- Devising appropriate negotiation practices, forming negotiation teams, consulting internally and externally from initial enquiry to final settlement, objective setting and determining appropriate negotiation strategies then ensuring they are executed.
- Negotiating, within authorised limits, standard and/or bespoke contracts (commercial and legal terms and conditions, warranties, contractual risks and liabilities, etc.) for the supply or purchase of products and services and for aftermarket support/maintenance. These can include formal, short form, and annual contracts; agreements, for example, Teaming Agreements (TAs), Non-disclosure Agreements (NDAs), Intellectual Property Rights (IPRs) and commercial exploitation agreements. Plus, tenders, deals and prices, and various opportunities and business plans: the provision of commercial solutions.
- Negotiating and agreeing/resolving post-award contract variations (implications of scope changes: additions or omissions plus associated price adjustments and amendments to contract terms and conditions), disputes (conflict avoidance/management and dispute resolution), claims, liabilities, high value or complex subcontracts, and final accounts/contract close-out.
- Ensuring that the output of the negotiations reflect and are consistent with the organisation's strategic plan, objectives and requirements at the corporate/business unit/programme/project level, while simultaneously protecting business needs and interests, and delivering a commercially acceptable outcome. A result which generates the optimum return for the business, meets the customer's requirements, identifies and mitigates exposure to risk, supports and preserves equitable and balanced business relationships, delivers savings or efficiencies, and balances the drive for sales with business risk. (Lowe, 2013).

Influencing customers

During the initial stage of a potential opportunity (Opportunity Identification), the aim of the commercial function is to achieve visibility and customer awareness of the supply organisation's capabilities (products and services). While during the Opportunity Development and Proposal Identification stages its aim is to influence the customer's decision-making (Requirement Specification and Solution Selection) with the goal of securing the inclusion of the organisation's distinctive value propositions, technologies, solutions, products and capabilities (unique selling proposition) are integrated in the customer's proposal. Thereby, affording the organisation a competitive advantage over its competitors. Although if the customer has a stronger relationship/greater customer intimacy with a competitor, this places the supply organisation at a potentially significant disadvantage when competing for work. In this case, the disadvantage needs to be recognised and countered, via influencing and persuasion.

Simultaneously, a further objective is to secure a place on the customer's tender/preferred suppliers list or ultimately single bidder status. However, a generally held adage states that 'if the first time you hear about an opportunity is through an Invitation to Tender, you have probably lost the opportunity already'. Through the Deal Creation/Award stages the objective is to persuade the customer to appoint 'your' organisation (see section on Negotiation).

While implementing the project/contract (Execution Stage) a key facet of the commercial 'influencing' role, where an ongoing engagement is likely, is to seek to foster customer intimacy and attain trusted advisor status. This is principally achieved by ensuring that commitments made during the deal creation/negotiation phase are delivered.

Influencing suppliers

Likewise, contracts seek to influence behaviours by establishing transparent procedures to determine roles, relationships and responsibilities of and between the parties. As contracts are generally driven pre-award by the dominant party, as a form of governance structure, they tend to focus on protecting the interests of that party – frequently the purchaser. As discussed in Chapter 4, contracts state the rights and obligations of the purchaser and supplier, allocate risk and incorporate payment systems to incentivise supplier/partner performance. Approaches include, for example:

- **Payment on completion** is perceived to influence suppliers to fulfil their obligations on time or even earlier than stipulated in the contract, as contract completion is required before they can recoup monies/resources expended. Unintended consequences of this device can include poor execution due to suppliers rushing to complete the work in order to be paid, higher prices as suppliers may incur higher interest charges than the purchaser (particularly government clients) or lead to dispute if the supplier is delayed by the purchaser. Moreover, fixed-price contracts are generally held to lead to adversarial behaviour. Alternatives include payments on account, such as time-based stage payments or stage-gate payments, which seek to incentivise suppliers by requiring the completion of designated portions of the work to trigger payment.
- **Early completion bonuses** a further payment mechanism, which carries similar risks and unintended consequences as payment on completion. Plus, the tactic is ineffective if the supplier believes early complete is unattainable.
- **Liquidated and ascertained damages** are a predetermined estimation of the likely losses incurred by the purchaser due to non-completion by the supplier. The intention of such clauses is to incentivise suppliers to finish on time. Potentially, the approach has similar benefits and disadvantages as the previous two mechanisms. Plus, where contract time scales are considered to be unachievable, suppliers may increase their tender price to cover the imposition of such damages.
- **Key performance indicators:** where payments/rebates are linked to specific key performance indicators. For example, meeting service level agreements (SLAs) on outsourcing contracts. They are also associated with pain-share/gainshare

systems prevalent on target cost contracts, where savings against the target cost (gains) are distributed between the parties on a predetermined percentage basis. Likewise, if the supplier's costs exceeded the target, the increase (pain) is shared by the parties again by a predetermined proportion. KPIs can address a wide range of categories, however, the time and costs incurred in collecting and analysing performance measures increases proportionally with the number of categories selected. Additionally, KPI systems can be too complex or remote from the supplier's primary tasks, as a result diminishing their effectiveness. However, if chosen judiciously, they have been shown to be effective on long-term framework agreements.

Finally, in accordance with the principles of TCE (Chapter 2), the best approach to influencing supply behaviour positively is probably the ability to offer repeat/follow-on business, as it is in the supplier's self-interest to deliver on their commitments and abstain from opportunistic behaviour.

Conflict management and dispute resolution

While often used interchangeably, Fenn (2006) advocates that Commercial Managers should be able to recognise and distinguish between conflict management and dispute resolution, further suggesting that while conflict is inevitable, disputes are not. Conflict, therefore, can be viewed as a precursor to disputes. Fenn further asserts that it is in the interests of all parties to seek to avoid disputes by the effective management of conflict. Based on an aetiological approach to the investigation of commercial disputes, he proposes the following 'conflict management/dispute resolution' taxonomy (Fenn et al., 1997):

- **Conflict management:** conflicts are managed via non-binding avoidance/discursive approaches, such as dispute review boards, dispute review advisors, negotiation, quality matters (quality assurance, co-ordinated project information and total quality management), and procurements systems.

- **Dispute resolution:** alternatively, the resolution of disputes can be achieved by either non-binding or binding approached. Non-binding methods include conciliation, executive tribunal, and mediation, while binding approaches comprise adjudication, arbitration, expert determination, litigation and negotiation.

Again, requiring the application of advocacy (influencing and persuading) and negotiation skills:

Discourage litigation. Persuade your neighbour to compromise … the nominal winner is often a real loser.

Abraham Lincoln

Personal reflection

Select a project or contract that you are familiar with, then consider the following:

- What approaches did the buyer/supplier adopt when seeking to influence and persuade the other stakeholders. Was the approach consistent when engaging with internal and external parties? How successful were these approaches?
- Did the contract terms and conditions influence the behaviour of the parties as intended? Why was this?
- How were conflicts and disputes resolved?

Techniques of influencing and negotiation

There is a wealth of information available on how to negotiate successfully, including books and articles from academic, practitioner and 'personality' sources, and numerous training courses. You may well have attended one of the ubiquitous sessions on how to negotiate or influence. While many advocate a principled approach, such as Fisher and Ury (2012), others proffer a more positional perspective, for example, 'Trump: The Art of the Deal' by Trump and Schwartz (1987).

However, there are occasions where a more positional negotiation stance is warranted – as with earlier topics we've covered, there's a continuum of styles and techniques in this case from principled to positional negotiation. Our task is to select the most appropriate given the context of the exchange (Environment) and the specific circumstances we face. We will come back to this later in the chapter.

Superficially, some titles evoke military connotations, comparing negotiations to either a battle or a war, and that there will accordingly be a winner and a loser, as illustrated by the titles of 'Never Split the Difference: Negotiating as if Your Life Depended on It' by Voss and Raz (2017) and the best-selling 'Getting to Yes: Negotiating Agreement Without Giving In' by Fisher and Ury. Although win-win solutions are a major tenet of the latter text.

Influence and the science of persuasion

Science of persuasion

Similarly, there are numerous resources on how to influence people, for example, Dale Carnegie's classic book 'How to Win Friends and Influence People, while Robert Cialdini's (2001) HBR paper 'Harnessing the science of persuasion' introduces the following six fundamentals of persuasion:

1 **Commitment** (consistency) for example, if you can persuade a third party (a senior colleague, supplier or subordinate, etc.) to commit to an action, particularly when they are in a public arena, then it is far more likely that they will follow through and delivering on their promises. Experience supports this; generally, leaders do not want to be seen to lose face.
2 **Reciprocity** Generally, if someone does something good for you then you will normally respond alike. For example, research on tipping established that if a waiter gives a customer a sweet with their bill, the tip they receive is more generous than if they had not provided a sweet. Similarly, if the waiter places their hand on the customer's arm and then give them a couple of sweets with the bill the tip goes up even more. Apparently, if they move away and then come back with sweets this generates an even higher tip.

3 **Consensus** (social proof) is based on the principle that if something (a product or service) is good for other people then it's okay for me too! Archetypal 'keeping up with the Joneses'.
4 In terms of **authority**, we are all probably familiar with toothpaste adverts, where a white coated dentist extols the virtues of a particular toothpaste brand. We tend to be influenced by the opinion of experts, although due to politicians and others undermining the validity of expert knowledge, this may be declining.
5 **Liking** – while the Avon slogan from the 1960s 'Ding Dong, Avon's Calling' may be consigned to marketing history, its highly successful principle – utilising female agents to sell cosmetic products to their friends and neighbours, etc. – clearly illustrates this factor. People buy from people they like and relate to. Similarly, exemplified by supermarket chains using regional accents in their commercials.
6 **Scarcity**, either real or implied, research has shown that as a product, opportunity or service becomes less obtainable, it is perceived as being more valuable. This was clearly illustrated by the hording of scarce commodity items and the associated increase in their prices during the recent pandemic. Again, there are negative applications of this principle, for example, a common tactic of car sales executive is to offer or imply that a certain price is a one-off deal that will not be available in the future. Similarly, retailers use a variant of this ploy with their 'once it's gone – it's gone' sales slogans.

Likewise, the negotiation texts mentioned above invariably extol practical techniques for 'getting the deal you want'.

So why am I highlighting these principles, particularly their potential for misuse? Even though some authors, including Cialdini, suggest that we do not use these approaches unethically, they frequently are. Moreover, as we can all learn and apply these concepts and associated tactics, it can be obvious when the other partly utilises them. As a result, we may see through the manoeuvre. While this might prompt a predetermined response, the behaviour may well undermine trust, and the development of a collaborative relationship required to successfully implement lengthy and/or complex projects.

To illustrate the point, a former senior colleague had been trained and accredited to deliver Cialdini's 'Science of Persuasion' training material, however, when engaging with him, his use of the above principles and tactics was clearly apparent. Moreover, the individual came across as lacking authenticity. The impact was extremely negative, it undermined our working relationship and any trust we had in them. The issue, therefore, is that if you are blatant in the way that you utilise these principles, it is likely to have a negative impact on the interaction, be it a negotiation, an attempt to influence or the future long-term relationship/implementation stage of a contract.

The power perspective

Equally, how do you negotiate and apply these principles and tactics of influencing and persuasion when there's an unequal balance of power between the interacting/exchange parties? This problem raises further issues, for example: Is it always appropriate to extract maximum value from an exchange? What are the implications for the delivery of a contract or a project – if the dominant party fully exerts their power?

As discussed in Chapter 2, when either the buyer or supplier has relative power over the other, they face the choice of whether or not to fully leverage that power in pre- and post-award negotiations. If they take a positional approach, when negotiating a deal and extract as much value as possible due to holding a favourable power dynamic or imbalance of power, this might be advantageous and make perfect business sense if the purchase is a commodity or 'spot purchase'. However, where the negotiation is prior to entering a long-term relationship, a project or outsourcing contract that last for many years, that initial one-off win might bring with it future issues and conflict. For example, if a supplier is required to accept unfavourable terms in order to be awarded a contract, then they may well be inclined to behave opportunistically post-award. Moreover, if the power balance changes post-award, the supplier may have opportunities to extract their 'retribution'. That is, utilise tools and techniques at their disposal over the life of the project or engagement to recover some of the value lost during tender negotiations. The behaviour of the dominant party during the negotiation phase will often drive either positive or negative behaviours by the other party post-award. The strategy of exploiting maximum power during pre-award negotiations does not build good relationships and frequently results in conflict and disputes post-award, which, in turn, lead to significant contract management (enforcement) costs. Later in this chapter, we will examine how a party's negotiation approach can be focused on either striking the most advantageous deal or supporting the implementation/execution of projects and contracts.

Emotional and psychological aspects

Negotiation, particularly an appreciation of the emotional and psychological aspects of negotiation practice and the primary influencing techniques and strategies, is a fundamental 'commercial' capability. It is also associated with the ability to communicate and collaborate with key stakeholders both within and external to the organisation. Additional skills include determining and deploying negotiation strategies and tactics; being assertive but diplomatic, gaining the trust of others; and securing concessions/benefits without undermining relationships.

The dark side of personality

The following section considers the positive and negative impact of the dark side of personality (the dark triad of narcissism, psychopathy and Machiavellianism) on negotiations.

Utilising, the Hogan Development Survey (HDS) dimensions of Bold (which equates to narcissism), Mischievous (psychopathy) and Sceptical (Machiavellianism) as measures of the Dark Triad, Spain et al. (2014) identifies the behaviours associated with these personality traits and their potential impact on negotiations.

For those of you that have completed the HDS, now might be a good time to locate your results to see how you scored on these three dimensions. The survey seeks to describe an individual's traits as others perceive them not as how they see themselves. Feedback from the assessment can be used, therefore, to support your development as a negotiator and influencer, as it provides an indication how you may come across in a negotiation. However, bear in mind, just because an individual may have a high score on one or more of these dimensions does not necessarily mean that they are going to exhibit the following personality traits.

According to Spain et al., individuals that score highly on the **Narcissism (Bold)** dimension of the HDS exhibit the following behaviour. They are generally extraordinarily self-confident, reluctant to acknowledge mistakes, rarely listen to advice from colleagues and advisors and tend not to learn from their experiences. Additionally, they may have an inflated sense of their own importance or entitlement, come across as being arrogant, or adopt self-promoting behaviours and attitudes. Further, they may be extremely verbose: monopolising conversations.

I guess most of us have come across colleagues, suppliers or customers that exhibit some (if not all) of these traits and have experience their effect. To illustrate the point, in one meeting a former colleague talked nonstop for almost an hour. Normally when speaking at length individuals slow down or momentarily pause to draw breath, allowing others an opportunity to interject and participate in the conversation. Not in this instance. It does not take much imagination to realise the impact this had on the other participants in the meeting. Many were feeling irritated or annoyed, most if not all lost interest and disengaged, with one colleague openly scrolling through Facebook. While the colleague might have had an opportunity to present their proposals, unfortunately the message stopped landing shortly into his diatribe.

On a positive note, narcissists often create positive first impressions. However, this feeling can quickly wear off, as illustrated above, and ultimately lead to the individual being viewed as hostile.

So how can the bold or narcissism trait be applied to negotiation?

Initially, narcissists can come across as being positive and dynamic – but their self-interest can soon lead to their negotiation partners/opponents feeling frustrated, irritated, annoyed or even abused. Also, they frequently refuse to compromise, adopting positional approaches and failing to see the other party's perspective. They may fail to take counsel or adequately prepare for the negotiation. Additionally, they may lack empathy for the other negotiation party or parties and argue solely based on their own self-interests. In terms of negotiation tactics, they will probably exploit soft approaches, relying on their charisma and looks to influence others.

Individuals who scored highly on the **Psychopathy (Mischievous)** dimension often exhibit the following behaviours. Generally, they are great characters and often fun to be around. However, they tend to be risk-takers, who relish pushing boundaries. Spain et al. also suggests that they can be impetuous, may ignore inconvenient realities/truths, may fail to follow social norms and prepared to use unethical strategies. Moreover, during negotiations those that display psychopathy tendencies may be predisposed to employing hard tactics, particularly coercion and threats, to achieve their ends. As a result, they are probably not the most suitable individuals to lead negotiations or be responsible for influencing customers and partners.

The third dimension of the dark triad is **Machiavellianism (Sceptical).** Spain et al. observed that individuals that obtained high scores on this trait tended to be hypersensitive to criticism, cynical, suspicious and distrustful. They question the motives of others, often interpreting them in a negative way. This dimension is associated with intentional unprincipled decision-making and duplicity, particularly during interviews, Also, leaders with high scores on this trait are more likely to be viewed as abusive by their team members. However, individuals with Machiavellian tendencies can be highly effective negotiators. They relish the cut and thrust of the negotiation and are experts at establishing political connections and promoting a charismatic persona. They commonly resort to manipulating opponents, utilising both use hard and soft negotiation tactics. For example, they may ingratiate themselves and barter to get others to concede, compromise or buy in to their ideas and proposals.

Spain et al. (2014) consider the **Dark Triad** to be an antecedent of influencing tactics, with all three components associated with a willingness to use unethical negotiation tactics, particularly when these interactions are online and not face-to-face. Perhaps, inhibitions are diminished when people are online.

Finally, while an individual may score highly on the above dimensions (the dark triad), it does not necessarily mean that they will behave underhandedly or use the approaches cited. However, the findings above should be considered when forming negotiation teams. Plus, there are some positives to take from Spain et al.'s findings despite the negative connotations discussed.

The bright side of personality

Equally, bright side personality traits (linked to, for example, emotional intelligence and high IQs) are associated with constructive negotiation practice. In his HBR paper 'The Personality Traits of Good Negotiators', Chamorro-Premuzic (2017) claims that personality is a valuable predictor of an individual's ability to negotiate effectively. While some, as we have observed above exert a negative impact, other traits are clearly linked to good negotiation practice. The traits that improve an individual's negotiation performance, according to Chamorro-Premuzic, include:

Emotional intelligence (EQ): individuals that score highly in terms of emotional intelligence tend to produce positive environments in which negotiations can take place. Also, they generally ensure that when the other party's negotiators depart a negotiation, they are more content with the result. Even when they do not entirely secure what they set out to achieve. Further, they tend to be more self-cognisant, enabling them to comprehend how others perceive them (see Mueller and Curhan, 2006).

Also, a high **Intelligence Quotient (IQ)** is associated with greater levels of restraint and affability. Individuals who score highly on IQ adopt collaborative and two-way negotiation methods. Considering their opposite number to be an equal, they adopt win-win strategies. Aiming to ensure that all the parties get a fair share of the proverbial 'pie', rather than adopt a zero sums perspective they attempt to enlarge an opportunity, so all parties gain from the exchange/opportunity (see Sharma et al., 2013).

Self-monitoring is a key aspect of effective negotiation. Individuals, who are good at monitoring their behaviour, performance, non-verbal communication and how they are perceived, generally have a better understanding of how they appear to others. Ultimately, however, as human beings we are all free to determine how we act. We can decide to be collaborative, or we can adopt a more positional negotiation stance (see Sharma et al., 2013).

Culture

It's not enough to succeed others must fail.
Gore Vidal

The implication of this quote from Gore Vidal, is that for some it is insufficient to be successful, their opponents must be seen to fail. Not wanting to be controversial, to illustrate the point, we can see how a certain US politician over four years after winning the US Presidential election was still making play out of his opponent's failure. There is potentially both a personality dimension and cultural dynamic at play here. The inference being, that for some negotiators and within certain cultures, it is insufficient to win the other party must be seen to lose.

A few years ago, I was part of a team that undertook a study for the European Commission on voluntary collaborative arrangements across its member states (Rigby et al., 2009). It was interesting to observe that some states were culturally more attuned to collaboration, while others were more likely to adopt adversarial stances. Culturally, for example, the UK tends to be more confrontational in its processes and dealings (being inherent in its adversarial judicial and governmental systems, for example, first-past-the-post electoral procedures), while other European countries are perhaps more open to collaborative and relational approaches (possessing, for example, a more investigative judicial approach and adopting proportional representation to select its political representatives). Globally, we can observe similar regional and cultural differences.

Therefore, when considering our negotiating approach and potential outcomes, we should consider that certain negotiators may be inclined or inculcated to either win-win or alternatively win-lose scenarios and that some cultures are more aligned with the concept of win-lose than win-win, and vice versa.

Personal reflection

Select a project or contract that you are familiar with, then consider the following:

- How did the behaviour of the parties, both 'dark side' (Narcissism, Psychopathy and Machiavellianism) and 'bright side' (EQ and IQ) personality traits, impacted the project/contract and in particular the various negotiations that occurred?

Negotiation models and frameworks

Negotiation approaches

Fisher and Ury (2012) utilise the dimensions of cooperativeness/importance of the relationship (*x* axis) and assertiveness/importance of the outcome (*y* axis) for their 2x2 matrix to categorise four negotiation approaches. These comprise:

1 **Collaborating 'Win-Win'** (high cooperativeness/importance of the relationship and high assertiveness/importance of the outcome) a creative, problem-solving approach that recognises and seeks to meet the objectives and needs of both participants.
2 **Avoiding 'Lose-Lose'** (low cooperativeness/importance of the relationship and low assertiveness/importance of the outcome) utilised where the outcome for both parties is unimportant, and the potential gain/pain does not warrant the time and cost of a more exhaustive negotiation.
3 **Competing – Win at all Cost 'Win-Lose'** (low cooperativeness/importance of the relationship and high assertiveness/importance of the outcome) generally features coercion and intimidation and is associated with Gore Vidal's perspective. The approach is not conducive to the development of long-term

relationships and the creation of customer intimacy or trusted advisor status.

4 **Accommodating 'Lose to Win'** (high cooperativeness/importance of the relationship and low assertiveness/importance of the outcome) a compliant/cooperative approach adopted where maintenance or the establishment of a relationship is critical. However, it may also be embraced under duress to save a business relationship. In the long term, the latter will generally undermine trust and the degree of intimacy.

Additionally, they identify a fifth approach:

5 **Compromising 'Split the Difference'** (midpoint cooperativeness/importance of the relationship and midpoint assertiveness/importance of the outcome), which aims to minimise conflict rather than address/resolve underlying issues. While splitting the difference is taken to be an even division of the gap between the parties, this may not always be the case. Again, compromising may lead to both parties being dissatisfied to varying degrees with the agreement.

Finally, negotiators must be prepared to withdraw from a negotiation (**no-deal**) if the potential outcome of the deal does not align with the intent/requirements of their organisation. Unfortunately, this may be difficult to execute, as individuals can become fixated by the potential deal and lose objective, or alternatively senior leaders may having invested significant reputational credit be reluctant to withdraw, fearing loss of face.

Negotiating as if implementation mattered

In his HBR article, 'Getting Past Yes: Negotiating as if Implementation Mattered', Ertel (2004) presents a series of continuums reflecting the focus of a negotiator when negotiating a transaction. These continuums range from 'Deal-minded' to 'Implementation-minded' and include the following dimensions: surprise, information sharing, closing technique, realistic commitments, decision-making and stakeholders. He provides sample assumptions, approaches and behaviours to illustrate each continuum/dimension.

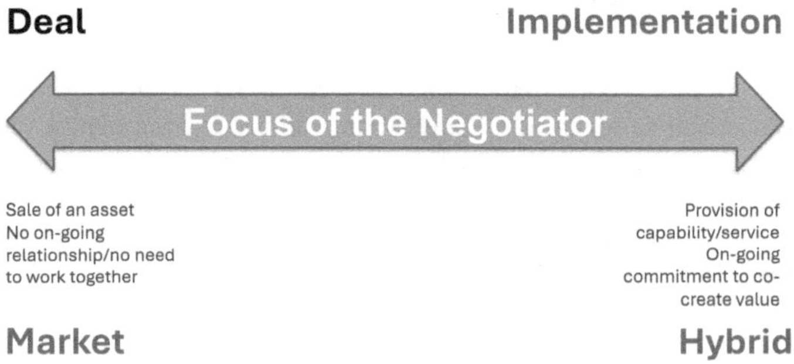

FIGURE 6.1 Focus of the negotiator (developed/derived from Ertel, 2004)

Figure 6.1 illustrates this deal-to-implementation continuum aligned with the TCE principles covered in Chapter 2. For instance, a positional 'deal focussed' stance may well be appropriate when buying/selling commodities or straightforward assets particularly where there is no ongoing relationship or requirement to collaborate. This is congruent with a TCE market-based approach and may be prevalent where the instigating party has power dominance (again, as discussed in Chapter 2 and earlier in this chapter). But even in these circumstances there may be instances that would preclude the adoption of deal-focused tactics. If an organisation gets a reputation for being an exceptionally hard or unprincipled dealmaker then that might influence the willingness of other entities to work with it in the future, or it might force these organisations to adopt similar aggressive negotiation (purchasing/sales) tactics in response.

Alternatively, an implementation focused principled negotiation perspective is aligned to a TCE hybrid approach. The practice supports partnering and collaboration, and, for example, the provision and purchase of capabilities and services or projects that involve/require an ongoing commitment to a relationship or a requirement to co-create value. In these circumstances, the adoption of a positional/deal focus will doubtless undermine the development of trust, which underpins effective relationships and the creation of customer intimacy or trusted advisor status.

The first dimension is **surprise.** A common tactic when focusing solely on the deal is for a negotiator to attempt to unnerve or disrupt their counterpart particularly during the latter or crucial stages of the process. This can take the form of making significant demands, raising crucial questions, requesting new information, revising their requirements. As an example of this, when selling my first house, the buyer contacted me just before we were due to exchange contracts to say that their surveyor considered my property required a new damp-proof course. They requested a price reduction to account for this. As far as I was aware the house did not require a damp-proof course; the request was purely a negotiation tactic. If I had challenged the surveyor's opinion or said no to a price reduction, I ran the risk of the other party walking away from the sale. They were a first-time buyer with no chain, while I had expended more money in legal fees, etc., was in the process of buying another house and about to move into it. Failure to agree the sale of my existing home would have resulted in my purchase falling through and abortive fees, etc. A classic example of TCE opportunism. In such a position, a choice is required on whether to say no to the proposed price reduction and risk losing the sale, or to be pragmatic and agree to one that meets their aspirations. Alternatively, at the implementation end of the 'surprise' spectrum, the emphasis of the negotiator is on actions and behaviours that seek to facilitate a mutually beneficial outcome by avoiding or minimising disruption of the negotiation activity, particularly during its final stages. According to Ertel, this can be achieved by establishing joint agendas, raising questions at the earliest opportunity, and creating joint teams to consider potential project/contract risks, etc.

The second dimension concerns **information sharing**. If the focus is on getting a deal, a negotiator may choose to withhold information or fail to correct misinformation or false assumptions. In terms of TCE, this approach exemplifies negative and unethical behaviours associated with bounded rationality and asymmetry of information. Instead, if the negotiator's aim is to support the ultimate implementation of the project, Ertel suggests that the parties should establish mutual information-gathering panels, commission consultants to undertake research and analysis, and question any latent assumptions. Thereby, exposing any issues or inappropriate impressions and expectations, enabling the parties to resolve them pre-award so avoiding the potential of undermining trust post-award.

In terms of **closing technique**, when the focus is on finalising the deal, common manoeuvres attempt to coerce the other party, by creating artificial deadlines or threatening to escalate matters to senior colleagues, to conclude the deal. Tactics include making a 'today only offer', for example using phrases, such as if you want to get it at this price, you will have to make the deal today it won't be around tomorrow (see Cialdini's Science of Persuasion). Whereas closing techniques that support project/contract implementation incorporate process that expose, define and resolve the issues/interests that need to be considered to enable the deal to be successfully finalised. These include creating joint communication strategies and collaboratively working to achieve a mutually beneficial conclusion.

The next dimension is **realistic commitments**. Again, a deal-centric approach will focus on capturing the decisions that have been reached and pressurising the other party to itemise their commitments. The emphasis is on protecting the organisations position via a robust contract (by defining precise terms and conditions and relying on penalty clauses to enforce delivery of commitments) rather than forge a collaborative relationship. Whereas an implementation focus requires the parties to raise difficult questions, engage in awkward conversations and make project implementation/contract execution a mutual interest pre-award. Potential actions can include establishing early warning signs and systems, forward planning, proposing agreeing actions to be taken in the event of specific occurrences and working to develop a reciprocal relationship to underpin the execution stage. Although possibly uncomfortable, it is constructive to engage in challenging conversations during the deal creation stage rather than having to initiate one for the first time once an issue has arisen during the execution of a project or contract. It is generally more problematic at a later stage and can potentially result in more impactful consequences for the parties.

The final dimension concerns **decision-making**. If the aim is to drive a deal, the negotiation team will endeavour to limit participation to the primary decision-makers. The aim being to exclude potential stakeholders that might derail the deal entirely or until their intervention is too late to influence the deal. At the implementation end of the spectrum, the parties will seek to establish and engage with all possible stakeholders, determining whose approval and/or cooperation is required, and identifying those who might obstruct the implementation of the project/contract and seek to involve them at an earlier stage.

Once again, there is no universal solution; rather, given the specific circumstances of the exchange/negotiation, the task is to understand the organisation's position and intent then objectively select an appropriate negotiation approach. Further, effective communication is fundamental to successful influencing and negotiation.

Summary

This chapter has discussed the importance of persuasion, influencing, and negotiation in developing successful commercial outcomes and effective trading relationships. It emphasised the ethical application of these skill sets in both personal and professional interactions. It also highlighted the impact of emotional and psychological traits on negotiations. The chapter covered strategies for influencing customers and suppliers, negotiating resources and agreements and managing conflicts and disputes. Various models and frameworks, such as Fisher and Ury's negotiation matrix and Ertel's deal-to-implementation continuum, were presented.

Further reading/resources

For additional information on influencing and negotiation, see

Cialdini's Science of persuasion: view https://www.youtube.com/watch?v=cFdCzN7RYbw (Accessed 10 July 2024).

Ertel D (2004) Getting past yes: negotiating as if implementation mattered. *Harvard Business Review*, 82(11), 60–68, 148.

Harvard Business Review (2019) *HBR's 10 Must Reads on Negotiation*. Harvard Business Review Press, Boston, MA.

References

Chamorro-Premuzic T (2017) The personality traits of good negotiators. *Harvard Business Review*. https://hbr.org/2017/08/the-personality-traits-of-good-negotiators (Accessed 10 July 2024).

Cialdini R B (2001) Harnessing the science of persuasion. *Harvard Business Review*, 79(9), 72–79.

Ertel D (2004) Getting past yes: negotiating as if implementation mattered. *Harvard Business Review*, 82(11), 60–68, 148.

Fenn P (2006) Conflict management and dispute resolution. In: D J Lowe (ed.) with R Leiringer, *Commercial Management of Projects: Defining the Discipline*. Blackwell Publishing, Oxford. pp. 234–269.

Fenn P, Lowe D and Speck C (1997) Conflict and dispute in construction. *Construction Management and Economics*, 15(6), 513–518. https://doi.org/10.1080/014461997372719

Fisher R and Ury W (2012) *Getting to Yes: Negotiating Agreement without Giving In*. Random House Business, New York.

Lowe D J (2013) *Commercial Management: Theory and Practice*. Wiley-Blackwell Publishing Ltd, Oxford.

Macneil I R (2000) Contracting worlds and essential contract theory. *Social and Legal Studies*, 9, 431–438.

Mueller J S and Curhan J R (2006) Emotional intelligence and counterpart mood induction in a negotiation. *International Journal of Conflict Management*, 17(2), 110–128.

Rigby J, Lowe D, Courtney R, Morrison K, Cox D, Chittenden F, Shaoul J, Winch G, Klepfisch G, Larsen J N, Lahdenperä P, Geraedts R, Wamelink H, Ingvaldssen T and Sandesten S (2009) *Study on voluntary arrangements for collaborative working in the field of construction services Final Report Parts 1–3*. Contract No SI2.ICNPROCE 015827500, Brussels: European Commission DG Enterprise and Industry.

Sharma S, Bottom W P and Elfenbein H A (2013) On the role of personality, cognitive ability, and emotional intelligence in predicting negotiation outcomes: A meta-analysis. *Organizational Psychology Review*, 3(4), 293–336.

Spain S M, Harms P and LeBreton J M (2014) The dark side of personality at work. *J. Organizational Behavior*, 35, S41–S60.

Trump D J and Schwartz T (1987) *Trump: The Art of the Deal*. Random House Publishing Group, New York.

Voss C and Raz T (2017) *Never Split the Difference: Negotiating as if Your Life Depended on It*. Random House Business, New York.

7

APPLYING RIGOROUS AND CONSISTENT COMMERCIAL PROCESSES AND PROCEDURES

Developing high-performing commercial management processes; implementing best-practice at the individual, team and organisational level

Introduction

The procurement and supply of complex goods (assets) and services (capabilities) through strategic acquisition projects impose significant demands on purchasers and suppliers alike. Failure of these commercial exchanges can often be attributed to poor demand-side oversight and decision-making.

In this chapter, we will explore the factors that lead to project/contract failure, plus those considered to support successful project/contract execution and delivery. 'Best practice' guidance in managing these exchanges (invariably delivered via projects and programmes) is identified, particularly that which is pertinent to commercial practice, as identified in Chapter 1. Derived from professional bodies, public sector and commercial organisations this includes an overview of the Infrastructure and Projects Authority (IPA) Assurance Review (Gate Review) process, the use of process protocols, such as Prince2®, Prince2 Agile®, Managing Successful

DOI: 10.4324/9781003052159-7

Programmes (MSP®), Management of Portfolios (MoP®) and the Portfolio, Programme and Project Management Maturity Model (P3M3®), plus guidance on best practice in commercial, contract, procurement, risk and value management, for example, the National Audit Office's (NAO) Commercial Audit Framework, and Axelos' Management of Risk (M_o_R®) and Management of Value (MoV®). Enabling you to assess what 'good' commercial practice looks like and similarly to potentially identify examples of sub-optimal practice within your organisation and team.

While not exhaustive, written primarily for an infrastructure and projects environment, and predominantly adopting a demand-side perspective, the underlying principles addressed are generic, applicable to both sides of an exchange transaction and valid across industry sectors and globally.

Project success/failure

Frequently, major asset and capability acquisition projects fail to deliver their anticipated benefits or meet their schedule and/or budget parameters. Negative media headlines proclaiming project fiascos or highlighting projects that have exceeded their cost and time budgets are ubiquitous, as illustrated in Figure 7.1. While the media may exaggerate negative news, bad news dominates the headlines and drives newspaper sales/boosts audience retention, they also influence public perception.

'MoD procurement disasters, delays and overspends'

The Guardian

'Hinkley Point C delayed by a year as cost goes up by £3bn'

BBC News

'HS2 in CHAOS as Tories won't deny £60bn rail scheme may not run to Euston'

Daily Mirror

FIGURE 7.1 Media headlines

While these examples concern construction and infrastructure projects, the issue is not solely restricted to these sectors. Numerous IT/IS, defence and engineering projects have suffered similar fates; for example, Concorde cost 12 times its predicted figure, while the aborted NHS IT System, terminated in 2011, cost the UK government £12.7 billion and only delivered benefits valued at £2.6 billion. Similarly, the UK's MoD has experienced a series of procurement disasters. Neither is the issue restricted to high profile, complex projects involving high levels of risk and uncertainty. A survey by KPMG (2015) found that 69% of construction projects exceed their budget by over 10%. Nor is it a recent phenomenon, as illustrated by the Houses of Parliament project.

Notable projects that have overrun their cost and time limits are included in Table 7.1.

TABLE 7.1 Examples of projects that exceeded their budget and schedule

Project	*Estimate*	*Final cost*	*Time overrun*
The Barbican	£8 million	£187 m (2,238%)	>3 years
Thames Barrier	£23 million	£534 m (2,222%)	N/A
Sydney Opera House	$7 million	$102 m (1,357%)	10 years
Holyrood Parliament Building	£10–40 million	£414.4 m (936%)	>3 years
Channel Tunnel	£2 billion	£8 billion (300%)	1 year
Berlin-Brandenburg International Airport	€2 billion	€7 billion (250%)	>9 years
Olkiluola Nuclear Plant (Unit 3)	€3 billion	€11 billion (267%)	>13 years
Boston 'Big Dig'	$2.8 billion	$8.08 billion (189%)	>8 years
Dubai Metro	AED 15.5 billion	AED 28 billion (81%)	>4 years
Houses of Parliament, London	£724,986	>£2 million (176%)	>24 years

But can all these examples be classified as project failures or disasters? Project failure is a vague concept. Moreover, perception of failure invariably changes over time and may differ between the various stakeholders. For example, while the Sydney Opera house may initially have been considered a failed project, it is now symbolic of Australia and regarded as an outstanding example of 20th-century architecture, gaining UNESCO World Heritage status in 2007. Alternatively, the Thames barrier has been protecting Greater London from high tides and storm surges for over 40 years. During that time, the barrier has been raised over 200 times, protecting approximately 48 square miles of London and over 1.25 million citizens. If we consider that without the barrier the damage resulting from a single storm surge is estimated to be approximately £50 billion at current prices, the Thames Barrier has been cost-effective. Another factor to consider when comparing the stated estimates and final costs is that we may not be equating 'like-with-like'. For example, the initial estimate for the Scottish Parliament (Holyrood Parliament) building was based on the refurbishment of an existing school, not the ultimate award-winning architectural design. Similarly, in addition to scope changes, cost can rise as a result of inflation especially when there is a long project gestation period. For example, the start of Heathrow Terminal 5 (T5) project was delayed by over 18 years due to a lengthy public inquiry.

Measures of success

Project success has traditionally been measured against the 'iron triangle' or 'triangle of objectives': time, cost and quality (specification/scope). While these dimensions are still crucially important, recent guidance has expanded the list to include, for example: funder satisfaction, stakeholder satisfaction, and overall project success (APM, 2015). Thus, accounting for the impact of the project and the value derived from it; plus, enabling the inclusion of fitness for purpose, equality and diversity, inclusivity, sustainable development, ethical sourcing and legacy benefits.

Project success factors

From the late 1960s, there has been significant interest in establishing the factors that underpin project success or lead to project failure. To illustrate the scale of research in this area, a recent search on Google Scholar produced 7.18 million hits for 'project success' and 5.46 million hits for 'project failure'. Two commonly cited sources are Baker et al. (1988) who identified ten factors affecting project success and Pinto and Slevin (1988) who established an alternative set of ten critical success factors. However:

> In spite of these well-known research results and despite column-miles of words that have been written about project management, despite decades of individual and collective experience of managing projects, despite the rapid growth in membership of project management professional bodies and despite a dramatic increase in the amount of project working in industry, project results continue to disappoint stakeholders.
>
> *Terry Cooke-Davies (2002)*

Following this pronouncement, Cooke-Davies (2004) produced a further list of four factors that are required to ensure that the 'right project is done right'. These focused on goal clarity, stakeholder commitment, effective processes and a contextualised project strategy. However, Winch (2003) considers the primary issue of project success/failure to be '... one of project management: specifically, a problem in how the interactions between the stakeholders in the process are governed'.

More recently, the Association for Project Management (APM, 2015) have proposed 12 project success factors, while the UK's Infrastructure and Projects Authority (IPA, 2020) identified eight components of success across the project lifecycle, which they subdivided into setting up for success, execution and entry into services. See Table 7.2.

TABLE 7.2 Project success factors

APM Project success factors	*IPA Components of success*
1. Effective governance	1. Focus on outcomes
2. Goals and objectives	2. Plan realistically
3. Commitment to project success	3. Prioritise people
4. Capable sponsors	4. Tell it like it is
5. Secure funding	5. Control scope
6. Project planning and review	6. Manage complexity and risk
7. Supportive organisations	7. Be an intelligent client
8. End users and operators	8. Learn from experience
9. Competent project teams	
10. Aligned supply chain	
11. Proven methods and tools	
12. Appropriate standards	

Common causes of project failure

Consistent with the views of Winch (2003), following a review of all its Value for Money reports, the NAO established that the key source of risk on UK government projects related to governance issues, while the rest were generally linked to the client organisation (NAO, 2004).

As with project success, there has been extensive research into the causes of project failure (for example, Pinto and Mantel, 1990; NAO/OGC, 2005), while some identify high-level issues, others provide extensive lists of potential sources of project failure (Kerzner, 2014). However, there is general agreement that project failure is associated with shortcomings in the following:

- **Project governance:** inappropriate contact selection/strategy. For example, where the contract is not aligned with project dependencies, the anticipated level of uncertainty, project scale or complexity, or where the customer lacks the expertise to manage/administer a complex contract. Other issues may include the failure to adequately incentivise project participants to keep within budget or complete on time, or to apply contract levers (penalties).

- **Communication and engagement:** inadequate and ineffective communication systems and relationship management. This can be evidenced by poor stakeholder engagement, failure to manage customer expectation, failure to communicate the project plan, lack of transparency, unclear points of contact, an inability to speak truth to power, unaligned or multiple communication channels/tools, cross-organisational/cross-team communication barriers – siloed teams, senior management and team members being kept in the dark concerning the implications of changes and updates, failure to identify and confirm key assumption, etc.
- **Vision, mission, values, goals, objectives and strategy:** misalignment between organisational and project intent (vision, mission, values, goals and objectives) and the approach (strategy and tactics) adopted to attain them. This can be associated with unclear or unrealistic stakeholder requirements and/or expectations, multiple interpretations of the project intent across team members, optimism bias, and undefined or unclear Key Performance Indicators (KPIs). This misalignment can also arise when a new executive team (buy-side or sell-side) with differing/conflicting expectations and/or objectives is installed.
- **Sponsorship/leadership:** issues arise when there is a lack of strong high-level ownership of the endeavour (project/contract), inadequate executive/high-level oversight or support, a remote and unapproachable project sponsor, ineffective leadership, unclear project accountability/responsibility, an inexperienced project sponsor, over involvement/micromanagement by a project executive, or too many significant and impactful stakeholders.
- **Competence:** incompetent or inexperienced management (project, commercial, contract, risk management, etc.). Demonstrated by the appointment of 'green' managers, the adoption of an inappropriate management style or approach, loss of authority and control, a reluctance or failure to make timely decisions and to delegate, and where potential problems are ignored.

- **Uncertainty:** the presence of high levels of risk and uncertainty. Arising from a poorly defined project scope/work definition (due to inadequate, incomplete or unclear customer requirements), conflicting stakeholder expectations and needs, the selection of novel, untried/untested or technologically impractical solutions, the inclusion of or need to avoid technological obsolescence, unidentified/unknown risks, an incomplete contract, etc.
- **Processes and practices:** inadequate or poorly implemented management tools, techniques and approaches, for example:

  - *Market research*: including the failure to establish a market need for the product/asset to be purchased or sold; lack of market awareness (supply-chain capability and capacity), lack of senior level (buy-side) supply chain contact.
  - *Business case*: including the failure to prepare/or an inadequate business case, or to evaluate on-going/changes to business requirements and the appropriateness of the business case over the project lifecycle.
  - *Planning and resource management*: including poor resource scheduling/forecasting (financial/budgets, time, staff, plant and equipment, materials/components, facilities and space, etc.) resulting from the lack of a systemised planning process and/or resource management plan, inadequate work breakdown structure: a failure to create a delivery-oriented plan or break the project's development and execution stages into manageable phases, a lack of a systematic on-going planning activity, inadequate design review/red teaming, failure to hold 'kick-off' meetings, insufficient attention given to establishing the project infrastructure, overallocated, misaligned or inexperienced resources, insufficient or inadequate resources to complete activities, overly optimistic or inadequate budgets, cost estimates and deadlines, failure to enforce deadlines or hold teams/managers accountable, poor cost control and performance measurement.
  - *Risk Management*: including poor analysis, allocation, mitigation and management of risk, failure to adopt accepted

risk management tools and techniques, risk and opportunity analysis omitted from the design and planning process, project warning signs (across the project lifecycle) ignored, and the failure to inform senior leaders of a potential risk incident once identified.

- *Change Management*: including failure to instigate a robust change-management process and culture, failure to adequately evaluate proposed changes in terms of their potential impact on cost, time, risk and quality prior to its authorisation, unrestrained/untracked changes and revisions (inadequate change control process), failure to manage customer expectations, establishing unrealistic deadlines and budgets, and operatives/managers committing to undertake unapproved work. Resulting in scope creep (continuous and/or uncontrolled changes to project deliverables: where a project exceeds its initial parameters), over extended teams, financial (budget/cost) overruns, missed milestones – time/schedule delays, poor quality and failure to meet client expectations.

- **Funding:** insufficient funding. For example, due to the customer failing to secure or allocate appropriate funds to finance the project or the supplier having inadequate funds to finance project execution between stage payments or completion of the works in the case of lump sum contracts, failure to allocate an appropriate contingency sum to cover potential cost overruns, etc.
- **Award criteria:** the adoption of unsuitable award criteria. For example, embracing a lowest price mentality, i.e., where the proposal (project award) evaluation for the purchase of a complex asset (as opposed to a readily available or specifiable commodity) or when commissioning a service (acquiring a capacity or the delivery of business benefit) is driven by initial price (lowest price) rather than whole-life value for money.
- **Integration and collaboration:** poor team assimilation and cohesion. Exhibited by ineffective project team integration between client, client representatives, tier one contractor(s) and the wider supply chain, and the failure to promote and/

or reward collaboration, resulting in ineffective teamwork, poor collaboration, and conflict within and between teams/organisations.
- **Culture and ethics:** misaligned organisational culture and work ethics, miscommunication due to language barriers and geographic time zone issues.
- **Project visibility:** a lack of visibility/transparency across the project team, resulting from non-transparent project activity status, unclear/multiple communication channels, and poor document/information management. Leading to poor communication with stakeholders/decision-makers, substandard feedback and performance measurement and monitoring.

We can observe a converse relationship between the above and the factor that drive project success.

This begs the question: If we know the drivers of project success/failure, why do contracts/projects continue to fail? In other words: why do exchange participants keep repeating the same mistakes? Further, what impels them to behave in sub-optimal ways?

Therefore, if we are to improve our track record in project delivery, it is necessary to fully understand the reasons for project failure and know whether success factors and best-practice guidance are effectively implemented within our organisation (and if not, why not?).

Personal reflection

Select a project or contract that you are familiar with, then complete the following tasks:

- Using the measures of project success identified above, evaluate the success or otherwise of the project/exchange.
- Similarly, using the project success factors and common causes of project failure as a template, identify features of the project that enhanced or undermined project performance.
- What lessons have you gained from this exercise?

Best-practice guidance

One definition of 'Best Practice' is as follows:

> ... a procedure that has been shown by research and experience to produce optimal results and that is established or proposed as a standard suitable for widespread adoption.
>
> *(Merriam-Webster.com)*

Others refer to optimal methods of working, standards, series of guidelines or compilations of exemplars, etc., generated externally by government, professional or trade bodies or internally by a public or commercial organisation. Adherence to these principles is often voluntary, alternatively it may be a requisite of professional membership or prescribed by a government body/agency or internal functional authority.

The benefits derived from the application of 'best-practice' approaches and methodologies include:

- The establishment of a recognised/agreed framework of operation/practice
- Enhanced efficiency and productivity through work, activity or process rationalisation
- Improved performance and quality of work/output
- Time and resource optimisation and cost reduction
- Improved/optimised decision-making.

Potentially, enabling individuals and organisation to benefit from the experience and practice of others, leading to the development of competitive advantage, cost leadership, increased market share or new business and underpinning key business/commercial decisions. Following such guidance or gaining certification from the sources of best practice may raise the status of individuals or enable organisations to demonstrate their capability to customers and stakeholders.

However, the notion of 'best practice' has its critics. For example, some question the appropriateness of the term 'best' (suggesting that it is merely customary practice), the applicability of the guidance beyond its specific context and the veracity of the advice provided.

Good guidance, therefore, should be based on research, supported by clear evidence, experience and capable of being scaled, tailored and contextualised.

Various 'best practice' approaches, frameworks, methodologies, principles, processes, procedures and guidance have been developed that can be utilised to support commercial practice. Bearing in mind the caveats above, the remainder of this chapter provides examples of these.

Gate review process

Developed and introduced in January 2001 by the Office of Government Commerce (OGC) and originally termed the Gateway Project Review Process, the review methodology was primarily aimed at improving the delivery of UK public services. It sought to ensure that central government procurement projects and acquisition programmes delivered their anticipated benefits more effectively and with greater cost and outcome certainty. The underlying principles and methodology of the approach are equally applicable to both local government and private sector organisations. Moreover, the Gate Review approach has since been adopted and adapted by numerous governments and commercial entities.

The IPA, which reports to the Cabinet Office and HM Treasury, is now responsibility for the approach. Rebranded as the Gate Review Process, the latest version was published in July 2021 (IPA, 2021).

The review process is designed to be appropriate for a broad range of complex and high-risk projects and programmes, including infrastructure, transformation, defence and digital/IT. It involves an independent, high-level, evaluation of a programme or project at critical stages during its lifecycle – in particular, its progress to date and chances of delivering the intended benefits on time, to cost and at the agreed quality. The aim of the process is to provide assurance to the programme/project senior responsible owners (SRO) that the undertaking can proceed to the next phase. The SRO (the project owner) is the senior individual who is personally responsible for the successful conclusion of the programme/project. Further, it assists the SRO to deliver their business goals.

During the lifecycle of a project/programme, there are five reviews and associated review workbooks, three before contract award:

- Gate 1 Review: Business Justification
- Gate 2 Review: Delivery Strategy
- Gate 3 Review: Investment Decision

and two which focus on service implementation and the verification of operational benefits:

- Gate 4 Review: Readiness for Service Version
- Gate 5 Review: Operations Review and Benefits Realisation

Each Gate Review document contains a series of core and sector specific questions that need to be addressed together with sample evidence required to demonstrate compliance, etc.

Recurring over the life of the programme, the Gate 0 Review: Strategic Assessment is a programme-only review which takes a broader corporate or policy perspective.

Additional guidance documentation includes:

- **Review Team:** briefing note – provides members with pertinent information on their role in the review process and outlines their responsibilities and the actions required to fully participate in a successful review.
- **Programme Team and Senior Responsible Owners:** briefing note – similarly, provides the SRO and Project/Programme Manager with pertinent information on their role in the review process and outlines their responsibilities and the actions required to fully participate in a successful review.
- **Assurance Review:** administration – contains details of the general administration requirement before and during the Assurance Review.
- **Assurance of action plan guidance and templates** – provides guidance on how to complete an assurance of action plan (AAP) review. A re-assessment of a project or programme that considers actions taken when a Stage Gate Assessment has

been assessed as Red, following a Government Major Project Portfolio (GMPP) assurance review.

- **Project assurance review guidance and template** – provides guidance on how to undertake a project assessment review.
- **Assurance Workbook:** Portfolios and Portfolio Management – provides guidance on the IPA's approach to assuring portfolios.

Project, programme and portfolio management

> Project management is the *application of processes, methods, knowledge, skills and experience to achieve specific objectives for change.*
>
> Programme management is the *coordinated management of projects and business-as-usual (steady-state) activities to achieve beneficial change.*
>
> Portfolio management is the *selection, prioritisation and control of an organisation's projects and programmes in line with its strategic objectives and capacity to deliver.*
>
> *(Murray-Webster and Dalcher, 2019; APM, 2024)*

The following interrelated management best practices, referred to as the Global Best Practice Portfolio, are provided by Axelos. Originally developed by the UK OGC but incorporating feedback from the public and private sectors, it aims to improve the delivery and control of projects. In July 2021, PeopleCert acquired Axelos, a joint venture company created in 2013 by the Cabinet Office and Capita plc (CPI.L) to develop, enhance and promote several best-practice methodologies for professionals working globally in project, programme and portfolio management, IT service management and cyber resilience roles. These include the following:

- **PRINCE2®** (Projects in Controlled Environments): a flexible and scalable process-based project management methodology/approach to the management of projects that can be tailored to meet the needs and complexity of specific projects. Three distinct guides are available: Managing Successful Projects with PRINCE2®

(AXELOS, 2021d) Directing Successful Projects with PRINCE2® (AXELOS, 2021a), and PRINCE2 Agile® (AXELOS, 2021g).

- **MSP®** (Managing Successful Programmes): provides a governance approach and a lifecycle protocol for the management of programmes linked to the strategic intent of the organisation (AXELOS, 2021e).
- **MoP®** (Management of Portfolios): a guide for senior leaders on the principles and techniques of portfolio management (AXELOS, 2022b).
- **P30®** (Portfolio, Programme and Project Offices): consistent with PRINCE2®, MSP® and M_o_R®, P30® provides a suite of principles, processes and techniques that underpin effective portfolio, programme and project management (AXELOS, 2021f).
- **ITIL®** (IT Infrastructure Library) – an approach to IT service management for which four guides are available: *ITIL® Foundation* (AXELOS, 2022a), *ITIL® Digital and IT Strategy* (AXELOS, 2021c), *ITIL® Create, Deliver and Support (*AXELOS, 2021b)*, and ITIL® Direct, Plan and Improve* AXELOS (2021h), providing guidance on the creation, delivery and on-going improvement of technology-enabled products and services across their lifecycle.

For an introduction to the above see Axelos' short videos for which links are provided in the Further Reading/Information section of this chapter.

Further sources of best-practice guidance can be obtained from the various project management institutes and associations, for example, the Project Management Institute (PMI) PMBOK® 7th edition and the Association for Project Management (APM) APM Body of Knowledge 7th edition. Additionally, the International Organization for Standardization (ISO) publishes extensive guidance on project, programme and portfolio management:

- **ISO21500 Project, programme and portfolio management** – Context and concepts
- **ISO21502 Project, programme and portfolio management** – Guidance on project management
- **ISO21503 Project, programme and portfolio management** – Guidance on programme management

- **ISO21504 Project, programme and portfolio management** – Guidance on portfolio management
- **ISO21505 Project, programme and portfolio management** – Guidance on governance
- **ISO/TR21506 Project, programme and portfolio management** – Vocabulary
- **ISO21508 Earned value management in project and programme management**
- **ISO21511 Work breakdown structures for project and programme management**

Personal reflection

By adopting a systemised approach to project and programme management, as advocated in the guidance above, there is a danger that managers will be overburdened with bureaucracy, resulting in the various principles, processes and reviews becoming merely paper exercises. Either:

a Appraise the benefits and disadvantages of introducing the above approaches on a project within your own organisation. Or
b If your organisation utilises the PRINCE2®, MSP or MoP® methodologies evaluate their efficiency and effectiveness.

Procurement

> Procurement involves the buying of goods and services that enables an organisation to operate their supply chains, in a profitable and ethical manner.
>
> *(CIPS, 2024b)*

Best-practice procurement guidance is prevalent. Sources include central and local government departments and agencies, financial institutions such as the World Bank and the International Monetary Fund, and professional organisations representing the procurement and supply chain management function, for instance, The Chartered Institute of Procurement & Supply (CIPS). Within the UK, collectively, the Cabinet Office, Efficiency and Reform Group, and Crown

Commercial Service provide best-practice procurement guidance and documentation for the UK's public sector organisations.

The main requirement of the UK government's procurement policy, in line with common best practice, is that procurement should be based on value for money, which is defined as 'the best mix of quality and effectiveness for the least outlay over the period of use of the goods or services bought'. The guidance determines that value for money is achieved via competition unless there is persuasive justification to use other means.

This includes, for example, the following:

- **New models of construction procurement**: which provides guidance on:
  - *Cost Led Procurement:* seeks innovative solutions from the supply chain within a challenging cost limit, output specification and competitive framework environment. Plus, continuous improvement is encouraged by working collaboratively with the supply chain.
  - *Two Stage Open Book:* stage one – potential integrated teams are invited to competitively tender for a project based on their capability to deliver an outline brief and cost target. The successful team in conjunction with the client develops a proposal, following which the contract is awarded – stage two.
  - *Integrated Project Insurance:* enables the creation of holistic and integrated project teams; the aim being to eradicate a 'blame/claim' culture. The approach also limits the risk for individual team members, fostering joint project ownership and reducing the likelihood of cost and time overruns (Cabinet Office, 2014).
- **The Construction Playbook** provides guidance on sourcing and contracting public works projects and programmes (Cabinet Office, 2022a).
- **The Consultancy Playbook** provides guidance on how to commission and engage with consultants more effectively, achieving better outcomes, better value for money and supporting internal capability through the creation of knowledge and skills (Cabinet Office, 2022b).

- **The Digital, Data and Technology Playbook** provides guidance on sourcing and contracting for digital, data and technology projects and programmes (Cabinet Office, 2023a).
- **The Sourcing Playbook** provides guidance on service delivery, including outsourcing, insourcing, mixed economy sourcing and contracting (Cabinet Office, 2023b).

The principal takeaway from 'Key insights on public sector procurement best practice' (NAO, 2023) was:

> To maximise the benefits of effective competition, decision makers will need to have consideration for multiple aspects of procurement throughout a contract's lifecycle, especially prior to signing a contract when the requirements and approach to engagement are still being determined.

Additionally, the ISO publishes the following:

- **ISO 20400:2017 Sustainable procurement** – Guidelines
- **ISO 22058:2022 Construction procurement** – Guidance on strategy and tactics
- **ISO/DIS 10845-4 Construction procurement** – Parts 1–8

As stated in Chapter 4, the procurement of assets and services by government bodies, utilities and agencies in the UK (excluding Scotland) is generally regulated by The Procurement Regulations 2024 (Procurement Act 2023: effective from 24 February 2025). The Act presents the Government's post-Brexit public procurement principles, which comprise value for money, the public good, transparency, integrity, efficiency, fair treatment of suppliers and non-discrimination. The document includes an 'open procedure' a competitive approach for use in procuring commodity items, etc., and a 'flexible competitive procedure' that enables buyers to negotiate and innovate to obtain best value from suppliers. Additionally, a 'direct award' may be permissible under specific conditions, for example, when an urgent response is required. The legislation also establishes a Central Digital Platform (CDP) to support potential suppliers identifying tender opportunities.

Elsewhere, CIPS provides open access resources, for example, on procurement strategy and its Procurement and Supply Cycle, plus member only access to a series of guides, including Strategic procurement, Procurement strategy development guide, High-performance procurement guide, The role of strategic procurement and supply management in risk management guide (see https://www.cips.org/intelligence-hub/procurement Accessed 10 July 2024).

As noted in Chapter 2, while collaborative working, incorporating integrated project teams (design and delivery) and collaborative procurement processes, is suitable for long-term engagements and large complex projects, and particularly where there is a potential for repeat business and a requirement for cocreation, etc., it may not be appropriate for all contracts/projects, for example, in respect of commodity purchases.

A collaborative relational approach may come at a premium, costs are incurred by all parties in maintaining the relationship. Therefore, the parties need to consider if it is worthwhile putting the necessary effort and resources into building strong relationships, particularly if the exchange is based on a one-off market-based contract or one with little or no potential of an on-going/long-term trading relationship. Nevertheless, there is a tendency to assume that collaboration is de rigueur, particularly regarding procurement.

Personal reflection

While suitable in some circumstances, the collaborative/integrated approach promoted by best-practice guidance may not be appropriate for all projects. Consider under what circumstances the collaborative/integrated approach would be appropriate for projects within your organisation.

Contract management

Contract management has been defined as:

> ... the process of creating, implementing, and reviewing contracts. Whether this is between a business and supplier, or partner, contract management is an essential part of your business.

> As your business grows, contract management can become complex. Therefore, the need for effective strategies and processes is important.
>
> *(CIPS, 2024a)*

While effective contract management has been shown to be delivered when the commercial capability has been involved both pre- and post-award and incorporates the proactive monitoring of all the activities required to ensure that goods/services are delivered in accordance with the agreed contract (Crown Commercial Service, 2022). However, many descriptions of contract management and, therefore, practice still tend to focus on the post-award nature of the function/activity, as illustrated below:

> Contract management refers to all the activities undertaken by an entity, after the contract has been signed or commenced, to manage the performance of the contract (including any corrective action) and to achieve the agreed outcomes.
>
> *(Australian Government Department of Finance, 2019)*

Additionally, the following are evident in a proficient contract management capability: clear contract administration procedures, which are underpinned by senior executive support and are enabled by contract lifecycle management (CLM) software, plus the use of standardised contract language and risk assessment. CLM has been defined as: '... the process of systematically and efficiently managing contract creation, execution and analysis for maximising operational and financial performance and minimising risk' (Aberdeen Group, 2004).

Contract Management Cycle and frameworks

CIPS's contract management guidance is based around its Contract Management Cycle, see Table 7.3, which comprises 12 steps allocated to four stages. Acknowledging that contract management can be separated into pre-award and post-award stage, CIPS'

TABLE 7.3 Components of CIPS' Contract Management Cycle (CIPS, 2022)

Strategy, structure and resources:	**Development:**
1. Plan and Scope	8. Contract Development
2. Stakeholders	9. Supplier Development
3. Administration	10. Supplier Relationship Management (SRM)
4. Relationship Management	
Implementation:	**Lifecycle Management:**
5. Performance Management	11. Exit and Termination
6. Payment and Incentives	12. Asset Management
7. Risk and Resilience	

best-practice guidance provides advice for both buy-side and sell-side parties to the contract.

At each step practitioners, according to CIPS, should consider the following themes: developing and managing contracts, risk assessment and mitigation, sustainability, corporate social responsibility (CSR), ethics, procurement cycle, category management, procurement systems and technology, strategy and policy. For more information on CIPS' contract management best-practice guidance and a link to short video summarising the Contract Management Cycle, see the Further Reading/Information section of this chapter.

Similarly, the NAO's Good practice contract management framework and associated guidance identifies essential contract management activities. Having much in common with the CIPS Contract Management Cycle, NAO have identified eleven areas of practice that are collated into four blocks. These comprise:

Structure and resources

1 *Planning and governance*: preparing for contract management and providing oversight.
2 *People*: ensuring the right people are in place to carry out the contract management activities (subdivided into 'The contract manager' (or contract management team) and 'Wider staff issues').

3 *Administration*: managing the physical contract and the timetable for making key decisions.

Delivery

4 *Managing relationships*: developing strong internal and external relationships that facilitate delivery (subdivided into 'Roles and responsibilities' and 'Continuity and communications').
5 *Managing performance*: ensuring the service is provided in line with the contract (subdivided into 'Service delivery' and 'Feedback and communications').
6 *Payment and incentives*: ensuring payments are made to the supplier in line with the contract and that appropriate incentive mechanisms are in place and are well managed (subdivided into 'Payment and budgets' and 'Payment and incentive mechanisms').
7 *Risk*: understanding and managing contractual and supplier risk (subdivided into 'Processes and plans', 'Contractual terms' and 'Ongoing supplier risk management').

Development

8 *Contract development*: effective handling of changes to the contract (subdivided into 'Change processes' and 'Processes for different types of change').
9 *Supplier development*: improving supplier performance and capability (subdivided into 'Processes' and 'Improvement activities')

Strategy

10 *Supplier relationship management*: having a programme for managing and developing relationships with suppliers.
11 *Market management*: managing the wider market issues that may impact the contract but lie beyond the appointed supplier. (NAO, 2016a)

Also, the guidance acknowledges that, in addition to requiring good contract management, contact/project success or failure is contingent on having a sound commercial strategy, capable client personnel, and a robustness procurement approach. Moreover, the NAO framework is consistent with its 'Commercial and contract management: insights and emerging best practice' (NAO, 2016b). This is covered later in this chapter.

Contract management principles

Complementing the NAO's contract management framework and guidance, the Crown Commercial Service (2021) promotes a set of principles that underly the UK government's approach to contract management. These comprise the following headline directives:

1. Make sure the contracts are understood by all those who will be involved in their management [Comprehension]
2. Be clear about accountability, roles and responsibilities [Project Governance]
3. Set up and use strong governance arrangements to manage risk and allow strategic oversight [Project Governance]
4. Take a differentiated approach based on risk [Risk]
5. Manage contracts for business/public service outcomes [Deliverables/Benefits]
6. Accept that change will happen and plan for it [Change Management]
7. Measure and report on performance [Performance Measurement]
8. Work for continuous improvement, value for money and capture innovation [Leveraging Value]
9. Success is best achieved through working as a fully integrated team [Collaboration]
10. Make sure that links are made with organisation and/or government wide SRM programmes [Supplier Relationship Management]
11. Encourage mature commercial behaviours, understand what drives suppliers' behaviour and know how to assess profit vs. excess profit [Commercial Awareness]

These principles are expanded to provide additional advice. Note, I have added the labels in square brackets to link these principles to the concepts covered in this text.

Commercial management

Published in 2016, the RICS guidance note 'Commercial management of construction' outlines the function of commercial management in the construction sector, specifically that of supply-side commercial managers (those employed by contracting/supply organisations). The note provides a framework of best-practice advice on the following areas:

- understanding estimates
- value engineering
- supply chain management
- valuing work
- understanding cost
- cost/value analysis
- cash and cost flow analysis, and
- commercial decision-making.

Additionally, it includes:

- a practical guide to contract administration for a cost/value reconciliation (CVR) and a forecast model, and
- an exemplar risks and opportunities register (RICS, 2016).

This document was followed in January 2017 with the publication of a further guidance note 'The role of the commercial manager in infrastructure'. Similarly, it seeks to present current commercial management best-practice and establish professional competency levels for those commercial managers engaged on infrastructure projects. The document outlines how supply-side commercial managers should apply their expertise and influence throughout a project's lifecycle. Further key elements include the significance of being aware of and converting the business case into systematic procedures, plus adapting their cost, risk and supply chain management approaches to meet the challenges of the scale, complexity and uniqueness of a given project.

The note includes sections, such as:

- *What is commercial management?* considered to be associated with "... effective decision making and thereafter successful delivery of any infrastructure project. The role of the professional commercial manager is to provide the stewardship at the heart of the investment, and ultimately the benefit realisation processes" (RICS, 2017a).
- *The role of the commercial manager in infrastructure*:
- *Key commercial management roles*: comprising:

  1 Project initiation
  2 Cost planning and benchmarking
  3 Procurement
  4 Post contract delivery

Links to both documents are provided in the Further Reading/ Information section of this chapter.

Commercial audit framework

The NAO published *'Commercial and contract management: insights and emerging best practice'* in 2016, which draws on their audits of government contracts (NAO, 2016b). The document delineates seven key judgements associated with commercial relationships. Based on these seven components/headings, the document presents a 'Commercial Audit Framework', which consists of a series of questions. While not an exhaustive performance checklist, these questions can be used by organisations to evaluate its compliance with emerging commercial and contract management best practice. These questions have been adapted in the following list to align with the Commercial Management Framework and to apply to both buy-side and supply-side commercial operations.

1 *Commercial strategy*: *Is there an overarching commercial strategy, with a clear rationale and linkage to organisational strategy, and which targets VFM* (buyer) or expected return/ROI (supplier)?

2 *Commercial capability*: Does the entity [buyer: organisation/ business unit/department or supplier: contractor] have the commercial *capability needed to manage the contract and is it developing capability for the future?*
3 *Market management & sourcing/procurement*: Has procurement/sales *supported the commercial strategy and followed recognised good practice to optimise VFM* or expected return/ROI?
4 *Contract approach*: *Has the contract set up risk and reward dynamics that will encourage the parties to delivery* on their commitments, *minimise perverse incentives*/opportunistic behaviour *and promote good relationships?*
5 *Contract management*: *Is the contract being managed well, with costs and benefits* or expected return/margin/ROI *being realised as* anticipated?
6 *Contract lifecycle*: *Is the contract delivering value for money* or expected return/margin/ROI *and will it continue to* do so *through its lifecycle?*
7 *Termination and transition*: *Is the* buyer (commissioner) *ready* to accept the asset *or move into a new contract*/Is the supplier ready to take on follow-on business, re-bid or handover the asset? (Adapted from NAO, 2016b)

For each of the above questions, the document provides additional supplementary questions and illustrative case studies.

Early warning signs

Williams et al. (2012) demonstrate how project assessments can identify early warning signs (EWS) in complex projects, which, if ignored, may result in underperformance, cost overruns, disputes, or project failure. They note that project participants often fail to recognise and act on these signs. Their recommendations aim to help project leaders detect EWS and act promptly to support project success. Although Williams et al. focus on project owners, their approach is also adaptable for supply-side participants. They categorise EWS under 'project setup', 'early stages', and 'project execution', which correspond with the Intent, Deal Creation, and Execution stages adopted in this text. EWS are further classified as process assessments and intuition. Similarly, the NAO have developed warning indicators (signs) for each of their seven commercial and contract management components. Again, while the guidance is from a government project owner's perspective, it is equally applicable and adaptable for supply-side participants.

Value and risk management

As noted in Chapters 1 and 3, the management of risk and value are key aspects of commercial management practice. Again, there are numerous sources of 'best practice' guidance in these interconnected areas. For example, Axelos, provide the following guidance and certification programmes:

- **M_o_R®** (Management of Risk: Creating and Protecting Value): provides a value-focused framework and practical guidance to risk management at the strategic, programme, project or operational level (AXELOS, 2022c).
- **MoV®** (Management of Value): a guide to value management practice on portfolios, programmes and projects, providing guidance on value maximisation and resource optimisation (AXELOS, 2022d).

Similarly, various professional bodies provide guidance and standards in these areas. For example, The RICS provides the following professional guidance and recommended best practice:

- **Management of risk**: which contains the following sections:
    - *General principles (knowing)*: key principles of risk management – response/mitigation strategies (risk avoidance, reduction, transfer, sharing and retention), procurement routes and risk, risk quantification techniques, effect of risk on programme and cost
    - *Practical application (doing)*: risk identification techniques, qualitative risk assessment and management, risk ownership v procurement route, contributing data for quantification
    - *Practical considerations (doing/advising)*: advising on appropriate procurement route.

It also provides a list of key risk terms/definitions and sample risk registers (RICS, 2015).

- **Value management and value engineering:** which covers the following sections:
    - *Introduction*: earned value management.
    - *General principles (knowing)*: definitions and introduction to the concepts, the benefits of VM and VE to clients and delivery teams, a comparison of the features of VM and VE studies, relationship to other project management activities.
    - *Practical application (doing)*: How and when to carry out VM and VE, determining the value criteria for a project, identifying what does and what does not add value, prioritising and weighting alternative technical solutions, what resources are needed to carry out VM and VE? Reporting the outcomes of the study.
    - *Practical considerations (doing/advising)*: potential problems when carrying out VM and VE studies, appropriate facilitation skills and VM workshop techniques, designing large-scale VM programmes (RICS, 2017b).

Additionally, the ISO publishes the following standards and guides:

- **ISO 31000 Risk management** (ISO 31000:2018 Risk management – Guidelines, IEC 31010:2019 Risk management – Risk assessment techniques, ISO Guide 73:2009 Risk management – Vocabulary)
- **ISO 21508:2018 Earned value management in project and programme management**

Summary

As alluded to earlier in the chapter, a frequent criticism of best-practice guidance and frameworks is that by adopting a systemised approach to project, programme, commercial management, etc., we run the danger of it becoming a bureaucracy exercise – turning the process into merely a box ticking activity, So, rather than being considered a benefit, it's perceived as a drain on resources. As a result, practitioners do not spend an appropriate length of time preparing for and undertaking the required activities and stages, for example, resorting to cutting and pasting solutions from previous projects in order to get a particular process 'out of the way'.

However, a scaled, tailored and contextualised application of these methodologies can enable commercial practitioners to deliver value across a contract's/project's lifecycle. In the following final chapter, I will illustrate how these principles can be applied.

Personal reflection

Consider the benefits, drawbacks and applicability of the foregoing best-practice guidance to your organisation, sector or geographical location. If appropriate, reflect on the value of introducing aspects of this guidance on projects within your business.

Further reading/resources

For additional information on applying rigorous and consistent commercial processes and procedures, see

PRINCE2® https://www.youtube.com/watch?v=j02r5H6wCzo (Accessed 10 July 2024).

PRINCE2® Agile https://www.youtube.com/watch?v=SyewYk1TP5U (Accessed 10 July 2024).

MSP® https://www.youtube.com/watch?v=8iS8ygW0nak (Accessed 10 July 2024).

MoP® https://www.youtube.com/watch?v=XqE6TuDADjU (Accessed 10 July 2024).

CIPS Contract Management Cycle https://www.youtube.com/watch?v=mlpfHcN2opg (Accessed 10 July 2024).

CIPS The 4 Stages of Procurement Maturity https://www.youtube.com/watch?v=P38alqwPQc4&t=43s (Accessed 10 July 2024).

References

Aberdeen Group (2004) *Best Practices in Contract Management: Strategies for Optimizing Business Relationships*. Aberdeen Group Inc., Boston, MA.

Association for Project Management (APM) (2015) *Conditions for Project Success: APM Research Report Association for Project Management,*

Princes Risborough https://www.apm.org.uk/v2/media/jqwlj5oj/conditions-for-project-successwebfinal0.pdf (Accessed 10 July 2024).

Association for Project Management (APM) (2024) *APM glossary of project management terms*. Association for Project Management, Princes Risborough https://www.apm.org.uk/resources/glossary/ (Accessed 10 July 2024)

Australian Government Department of Finance (2019) *Australian Government Contract Management Guide*. Commonwealth of Australia. https://www.finance.gov.au/sites/default/files/2019-12/Contract%20Management%20Guide%20January%202020.pdf (Accessed 10 July 2024).

AXELOS (2021a) *Directing Successful Projects with PRINCE2®*, 6th Edition. PeopleCert, Nicosia, Cyprus.

AXELOS (2021b) *ITIL® Create, Deliver and Support*, 4th Edition. PeopleCert, Nicosia, Cyprus.

AXELOS (2021c) *ITIL® Digital and IT Strategy*, 4th Edition. PeopleCert, Nicosia, Cyprus.

AXELOS (2021d) *Managing Successful Projects with PRINCE2®*, 6th Edition. PeopleCert, Nicosia, Cyprus.

AXELOS (2021e) *MSP® Managing Successful Programmes*, 5th Edition. PeopleCert, Nicosia, Cyprus.

AXELOS (2021f) *P3O® Portfolio, Programme and Project Offices*. PeopleCert, Nicosia, Cyprus.

AXELOS (2021g) *PRINCE2 Agile®*. PeopleCert, Nicosia, Cyprus.

AXELOS (2021h) *ITIL® Direct, Plan and Improve*, 4th Edition. PeopleCert, Nicosia, Cyprus.

AXELOS (2022a) *ITIL® Foundation: ITIL 4 Edition*, 4th Edition. PeopleCert, Nicosia, Cyprus.

AXELOS (2022b) *MoP® Management of Portfolios*. PeopleCert, Nicosia, Cyprus.

AXELOS (2022c) *M_o_R® Management of Risk: Creating and Protecting Value*, 4th Edition. PeopleCert, Nicosia, Cyprus.

AXELOS (2022d) *MoV® Management of Value*, 2nd Edition. PeopleCert, Nicosia, Cyprus.

Baker B N, Murphy D C and Fisher D (1988) Factors affecting project success. In: D I Cleland and W R King (eds.) *Project Management Handbook*, 2nd Edition. Wiley, New York, pp. 909–919.

Cabinet Office (2014) *New Models of Construction Procurement*. Cabinet Office, London. https://www.gov.uk/government/collections/new-models-of-construction-procurement (Accessed 10 July 2024).

Cabinet Office (2022a) *The Construction Playbook*. Cabinet Office, London.

Cabinet Office (2022b) *The Consultancy Playbook*. Cabinet Office, London.

Cabinet Office (2023a) *The Digital, Data and Technology Playbook*. Cabinet Office, London.

Cabinet Office (2023b) *The Sourcing Playbook*. Cabinet Office, London.

CIPS (2022) *Contract Management Cycle*. Chartered Institute of Procurement & Supply, Stamford. https://www.cips.org/intelligence-hub/contract-management/cycle (Accessed 10 July 2024).

CIPS (2024a) *Contract Management*. Chartered Institute of Procurement & Supply, Stamford. https://www.cips.org/intelligence-hub/contract-management (Accessed 10 July 2024).

CIPS (2024b) *Procurement*. Chartered Institute of Procurement & Supply, Stamford. https://www.cips.org/intelligence-hub/procurement/what-is-procurement (Accessed 10 July 2024).

Cooke-Davies T (2002) The "real" success factors on projects. *International Journal of Project Management*, 20(3), 185–190.

Cooke-Davies T (2004) Project success. In: P W G Morris and J K Pinto (eds.) *The Wiley Guide to Managing Projects*. John Wiley and Sons, Hoboken, NJ.

Crown Commercial Service (2021) Guidance: Contract management principles. https://www.gov.uk/government/publications/commercial-capability-contract-management-standards/contract-management-principles (Accessed 10 July 2024 – content is available under the Open Government Licence v3.0).

Crown Commercial Service (2022) *Effective Contract Management – Procurement Essentials*. https://www.crowncommercial.gov.uk/news/effective-contract-management-procurement-ccs (Accessed 10 July 2024 – content is available under the Open Government Licence v3.0).

Infrastructure and Projects Authority (2020) *Principles for Project Success*. Infrastructure and Projects Authority, London.

Infrastructure and Projects Authority (2021) *Assurance Review Toolkit*. Infrastructure and Projects Authority, London. https://www.gov.uk/government/collections/infrastructure-and-projects-authority-assurance-review-toolkit (Accessed 10 July 2024).

Kerzner H (2014) *Project Recovery: Case Studies and Techniques for Overcoming Project Failure*. John Wiley & Sons, Hoboken, NJ.

KPMG (2015) *Climbing the Curve: 2015 Global Construction Project Owner's Survey*. KPMG International Cooperative. https://assets.kpmg.com/content/dam/kpmg/pdf/2015/04/2015-global-construction-survey.pdf (Accessed 10 July 2024).

Murray-Webster R and Dalcher D (eds.) (2019) *APM Body of Knowledge*, 7th Edition, Association for Project Management, Princes Risborough, Buckinghamshire.

National Audit Office (NAO) (2004) *Getting Value for Money from Construction Projects through Design*. The Stationery Office, London. https://www.nao.org.uk/wp-content/uploads/2013/02/VFMfromConstruction.pdf (Accessed 10 July 2024).

National Audit Office (NAO) (2016a) *Guidance: Good Practice Contract Management Framework*. NAO External Relations, London.

https://www.nao.org.uk/wp-content/uploads/2016/12/Good_practice_contract_management_framework.pdf (Accessed 10 July 2024).

National Audit Office (NAO) (2016b) *Commercial and Contract Management: Insights and Emerging Best Practice*. NAO External Relations, London. https://www.nao.org.uk/wp-content/uploads/2016/11/Commercial-and-contract-management-insights-and-emerging-best-practice.pdf (Accessed 10 July 2024).

National Audit Office (NAO) (2023) *Lessons Learned – Competition in Public Procurement HC1664*. NAO Communications Team, London. https://www.nao.org.uk/insights/competition-in-public-procurement-lessons-learned/#downloads (Accessed 10 July 2024).

OGC (2005) *OGC Best Practice - Common Causes of Project Failure*. OGC, London.

Pinto J K and Mantel S J (1990) The causes of project failure. *IEEE Transactions on Engineering Management*, 37(4), 269–276.

Pinto J K and Slevin D P (1988) Critical success factors across the project life cycle. *Project Management Journal*, 19(3), 67–75.

RICS (2015) *Management of Risk*, RICS guidance note, UK, 1st Edition, Royal Institution of Chartered Surveyors (RICS), London. https://www.rics.org/profession-standards/rics-standards-and-guidance/sector-standards/construction-standards/black-book/management-of-risk (Accessed 10 July 2024).

RICS (2016) *Commercial Management of Construction*, RICS guidance note, UK, 1st Edition, Royal Institution of Chartered Surveyors (RICS), London. https://www.rics.org/profession-standards/rics-standards-and-guidance/sector-standards/construction-standards/black-book/commercial-management-of-construction (Accessed 10 July 2024).

RICS (2017a) *The Role of the Commercial Manager in Infrastructure*, RICS guidance note, UK, 1st Edition, Royal Institution of Chartered Surveyors (RICS), London.

RICS (2017b) *Value Management and Value Engineering*, RICS professional standards and guidance note, UK, 1st Edition, Royal Institution of Chartered Surveyors (RICS), London. https://www.rics.org/profession-standards/rics-standards-and-guidance/sector-standards/construction-standards/black-book/value-management-and-value-engineering-1st-edition (Accessed 10 July 2024).

Williams T, Klakegg O J, Walker, D H T, Andersen B & Magnussen O M (2012) Identifying and acting on early warning signs in complex projects. *Project Management Journal*, 43(2), 37–53.

Winch G M (2003) Models of manufacturing and the construction process: The genesis of reengineering construction. *Building Research and Information*, 31, 107–118.

8

REALISING VALUE AT THE COMMERCIAL INTERFACE

Identifying/defining, acquiring (capturing)/creating and exploiting/ delivering value throughout an exchange's lifecycle

Introduction

This chapter identifies and considers commercial practices throughout the contract/project lifecycle from both supply and demand perspectives. It connects demand-side procurement practices with supply-side bidding and implementation cycles. Given that most organisations engage in both buy and sell-side activities, it's crucial for senior leaders to be aware of the processes, techniques and frameworks that support these activities and of the numerous action points and decisions that are required to be made.

Also, it examines how purchasers can clearly define their needs for new assets and services, and effectively manage the process of identifying, defining and acquiring/managing these assets and services to gain value. From the sell-side, it covers how suppliers can discern potential opportunities, shape and present their proposals, manage the contract negotiation/deal creation phase, and ensure the profitable delivery of their commitments and generate customer value. It refers to and utilises tools and frameworks introduced in earlier chapters.

For brevity, the chapter adopts a project-based (complex products and services) perspective although the generic principles presented, when tailored, apply equally to the procurement/supply of

DOI: 10.4324/9781003052159-8

less involved products and services. It is divided into three parts: Intent, Deal Creation and Execution aligned with the Commercial Management Framework (see Figure 1.6 in Chapter 1).

Intent

The intent phase of the Commercial Management Framework connects a proposed acquisition (buy-side project conception) or potential opportunity to supply (sell-side pre-request for proposals) with an organisation's strategic intent (formulation and implementation).

Buy-side activities

> How do we identify/define value during the requirement identification/specification and solution selection stages?

From a demand (buy-side) perspective, Intent encompasses requirement identification, requirement specification and solution selection. This section explores how purchasers can effectively articulate their requirements for a new asset and/or service, and then select a suitable procurement system to facilitate its acquisition/delivery.

The aim of the procurement process is to fulfil the needs of the purchaser and/or user, considering factors such as quality (fitness for purpose and specific service level requirements), adherence to schedules (meeting time constraints), cost considerations (cost certainty, value for money, and affordability), and anticipated benefits. Additional elements include environmental impact, ethical trading, and the collaborative, co-creation, and innovative capability of the parties. The procurement process is typically initiated by the purchaser; they are responsible for choosing the procurement methodology and setting the tone for the transaction. Consequently, it can be said that buyers 'acquire' the suppliers they deserve.

Requirement identification involves recognising, analysing, and confirming a requirement (need, opportunity, or issue). After identifying a potential requirement, a high-level business validation review ensures its alignment with the organisation's strategy. The Infrastructure and Projects Authority's (IPA) Gate Review Process – Gate 0 Review: Strategic Assessment (IPA, 2021a) can be utilised or adapted as part of this decision process. Depending on the buyer's capability and/or experience, advice may be sought from consultants and contractors. If the review outcome is positive, the purchaser moves to the next procurement phase.

Requirement specification entails understanding and documenting (specifying) the internal customer's needs in detail. After identifying and validating a requirement, the next step is to create a clear and comprehensive Project Brief, which is crucial for the project's success. The resulting specification documentation generally includes design details, specific materials or components, service levels, and standards to be attained. In addition, mapping the entire procurement process at an early stage leads to improved planning and management of the endeavour, identifying non-value-adding aspects, potential disruptions, and alternative delivery methods. During this phase the project's viability is evaluated and a business case generated.

Once suitable project objectives have been determined, a stage gate review is recommended to review their alignment with the organisation's intent and to assess the business justification for proceeding. The review seeks to assure decision-makers (the Project Board) that the proposed approach has been well-researched and is feasible, and to verify that the project's risks and benefits are identified and manageable/achievable and will be tracked using a defined methodology. Plus, that ample resources and funding are available. The IPA Gate 1 Review: Business Justification (IPA, 2021b) offers a template for developing a pro-forma to support this review. Additionally, sample questions on policy, business context, stakeholders, risk management, and delivery strategy are provided along with examples of the expected evidence needed to corroborate compliance.

During the requirement specification stage, commercial practitioners assess, select and formulate appropriate procurement, contracting and tendering strategies/methodologies plus strive to accurately capture organisational requirements in tender documentation and contracts. They also engage in assessing the feasibility of projects/purchases, reviewing and revising business cases, applying risk management, financial decision-making, and value management techniques. Additionally, they may evaluate (pre-qualify) potential solution providers, forecast procurement costs, prepare cost plans and undertake value management for potential solutions.

Solution selection comprises identifying and selecting the best approach to meet the organisation's specified need, considering what the market can supply (the preferred solution), and determining the method to acquire the chosen products or services (the sourcing strategy). First, organisations must address the make or buy decision, that is decide whether to produce assets/deliver services internally or procure them from external sources (suppliers). While historically sources have differentiated between purchasing assets and capital goods versus services and capabilities (Rathmell, 1966; Baily et al. 2008), globally, the lines between production and service-oriented organisations are increasingly becoming blurred. Transaction cost economics (TCE), introduced in Chapter 2, can be utilised to inform the decision.

When selecting a procured solution, choosing an appropriate procurement strategy is crucial. In project environments, procurement options (procurement systems) for acquiring assets and services can be categorised as follows:

- **Separated Procurement Systems:** these involve procuring design aspects separately from delivery (production/implementation). Examples include design-bid-build, with sequential and accelerated options.
- **Integrated Procurement Systems:** which combine design and delivery, options include:
  - *Design and Build*: where a single supplier is responsible for both design and production.
  - *Package Deal*: where the supplier designs and produces the asset under one contract, often utilising standardised solutions.
  - *Turnkey Contract*: where a single organisation designs and produces the asset – ready for immediate use.

- *Build-Own-Operate-Transfer (BOOT)*: where the supplier operates the facility for a set period before transferring it to the purchaser. Alternatives include Build Own Operate (BOO) and Design Fund Build Operate (DFBO).
- *Design and Manage*: while one organisation designs and delivers the project, specialist contractors handling specific tasks. Two variants exist: contractor-led and consultant-led approaches, which entail varying degrees of risk transfer.

Additionally, prime contracting involves a single supplier (Prime Contractor) acting as the sole point of responsibility between the client and the supply chain. Collaborative arrangements include project partnering, strategic partnering, alliances, framework agreements, and construction consortia.

The choice of procurement system is inherently associated with the purchaser's objectives, with each system offering distinct advantages and disadvantages in delivering quality, cost and schedule certainty, fitness for purpose, innovative solutions, post-award flexibility, single point responsibility, team working, and purchaser participation. A key factor in selecting a procurement system is the purchaser's attitude to risk, particularly their willingness to retain or transfer risk to the supply chain. Risk transfer ranges from design and build (higher) to construction management (lower).

The following questions may be used by senior leaders to inform and probe this decision/approach:

- How crucial is early completion for project success?
- Once started, is the project scope likely to be modified?
- Does the project incorporate advanced or complex technical solutions?
- What level of quality (design and workmanship) is required?
- Is price/cost certainty important?
- Are we mandated to select suppliers/subcontractor by price-based competition?
- Have we the capability/capacity to manage multiple suppliers, or do we require a single point of responsibility?
- Is direct accountability from our professional advisors critical?

- Are we content to pay for transferring the risk of cost and time overruns?
- Is post-award co-creation and supply chain collaborate a requirement?
- Are we likely to issue similar contracts in the future? (adapted from Bennett and Grice, 1990).

During this stage, the solution is refined and appraised, potential providers assessed, and a tendering methodology selected. Purchasers can choose from a range of options: open competition to direct negotiation, guided by factors such as commercial imperatives, market conditions, bespoke solution needs, and the ability to specify requirements in advance. Additionally, the business case is reviewed and revised. A stage gate review is recommended to appraise the delivery strategy.

Sell-side activities

How do we identify/define value during the opportunity/proposal identification and development stages?

From a supplier (sell-side) perspective, Intent includes opportunity identification, opportunity development and proposition identification. This initial stage of the bid cycle starts with identifying a lead and ends with either winning or losing the opportunity. The goal is to aid suppliers in understanding how to create greater value for purchasers and effectively screen potential opportunities.

Opportunity identification comprises discerning potential customer needs that the organisation can satisfy. A high-level business validation review assesses the lead's (opportunity's) viability and alignment with the supply organisation's strategy, forming the basis of a screening exercise (the bid/no bid or proceed/decline decision). The IPA's Gate 0 Review: Strategic Assessment (IPA, 2021a) can be adapted to support a supply-side business validation review.

Commercial organisations must be selective, choosing the most advantageous projects to pursue/bid. However, while few suppliers decline invitations to tender, believing a negative response would result in being excluded from future opportunities, they must decide whether to submit a genuine (*bona fide*) bid. In theory multiple factors are considered to influence the decision to bid (see Lowe, 2013), although in practice organisations can make objective/informed decisions by answering the following four questions (see Figure 8.1):

1 Is it real (funded)? (Is this a genuine opportunity that the purchaser can finance – rather than merely 'kite flying' or market testing an incumbent supplier?)
2 Is it worth it? (Will the organisation derive an appropriate benefit/value from undertaking the opportunity?)
3 Is it winnable? (Is the organisation competitive in the market?)
4 Can we deliver it? (Has the organisation the requisite capability and experience to bid for and successfully fulfil the contract?)

At this stage of the exchange lifecycle, the decision outcomes are generally either to proceed or not to proceed with the opportunity.

After a positive decision, the potential supplier promotes their capabilities and seeks to influence the buyer's decision-makers. During this phase, commercial practitioners seek to identify and

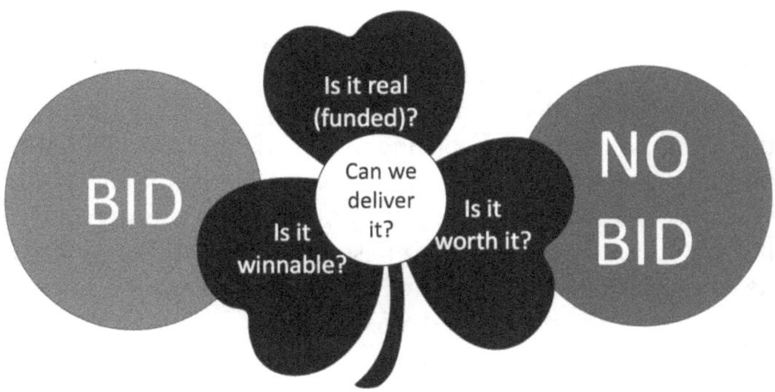

FIGURE 8.1 Bid screening

comprehend the purchaser's requirements, drivers and expectations: essential for proposition (bid) development and drafting contracts. They also contribute to evaluating the feasibility of the opportunity using risk management and financial decision-making techniques.

Opportunity development entails building relationships with potential customers and developing/marketing solutions for them. Suppliers aim to influence the buyer's choice, ideally to become the sole supplier or preferred bidder. Plus, they seek to shape the buyer's invitation to tender (ITT) or request for proposal (RFP) to their advantage. During this stage, client managers gather information on the potential customer's requirements and expectations, particularly their 'hot buttons', to create a 'win' strategy.

A robust bid strategy combines business and competitive strategies into a persuasive 'win' plan. Key features include:

- **Purchaser factors:** preferences/preconceptions, buying power and award criteria.
- **Supplier factors:** price, supply chain and alternative work sources.
- **Competitor factors:** economic environment, new entrants, rivals and emulators.

Note, unanticipated ITTs or RFPs often indicate prior competitor influence on the customer's requirements/solution.

This phase should conclude with a stage gate review to evaluate the business justification for proceeding with the opportunity. The IPA Gate 1 Review: Business Justification (IPA, 2021b) can be modified to support a supply-side review.

Proposition identification encompasses verifying and refining a solution to meet a customer's requirements. This stage includes identifying/determining bid team members, formulating a bid management (win) plan, and initiating appropriate bid processes. It concludes with a stage gate review to reassess the business justification, re-evaluate the bid/no bid decision, and appraise the bid strategy. IPA's Gate 2 Review: Delivery Strategy (IPA, 2021c) can be revised to support a supply-side bid strategy review, incorporating relevant decision support tools, such as those introduced earlier in the text.

Commercial activities

Common commercial activities during the Opportunity Development phase include building business investment cases, selecting procurement strategies, assessing costs and risks, constructing business cases for deals, and obtaining legal and regulatory approvals. Commercial practitioners may undertake briefing presentations, demonstrations, site visits, and develop contacts/advocates. Additionally, during the Opportunity Development and Proposition Identification stages, key sell-side activities include continuing the sales campaign to influence customer procurement solutions, developing a bid strategy, and conducting a formal opportunity screening (bid/no bid) appraisal.

At this stage, sell-side commercial practitioners attempt to expand their understanding of the purchaser's requirements, hot buttons and expectations, manage pre-qualification, draft contract terms, and support bid strategy development. They also contribute to project screening, applying strategic thinking, risk management, and financial decision-making techniques.

The following questions and allied early warning signs (EWS) can be utilised by senior leaders at the Intent (Business justification) stage to evaluate their organisation's commercial capability and its commercial performance on a contract/project basis, and support decision-making. They are framed and apply to both the buy-side and sell-side of organisations. Moreover, the term 'entity' refers equally to both the buyer (organisation/business unit/department) and the supplier (contractor).

Q: Is the identified requirement and preferred solution (buy-side) or potential opportunity (sell-side) aligned with the strategic intent, policies and standards, and, where appropriate, programme goals of the organisation?

EWS: The proposed solution/purchase (buy-side) or opportunity (sell-side) is inconsistent with the business needs or objectives.

Q: Are the entity's business objectives and how the purchase/ project or opportunity will deliver them clear, agreed and fully understood?

EWS: The project/opportunity is poorly defined, lacking clarity in its objectives, design/scope and perceived benefits, which can potentially lead to uncertainty and post-award claims and disputes.

Q: Have all potential stakeholders been identified and consulted? Plus, have their needs been clearly articulated, understood and addressed?

EWS: Failure to effectively engage with stakeholders can lead to misunderstandings and undermine trust between the parties, and/ or result in the sponsor(s) forming false expectations or being unclear as to their role.

Q: Has the feasibility study (buy-side)/initial opportunity screening (sell-side) examined sufficient potential solutions that meet the business/customer needs?

EWS: Inadequate business planning, invalid assumptions and ambiguous or ill-defined reasons for the purchase/undertaking the project.

Q: Have the risks associated with each potential solution (buy-side) and opportunity (sell-side) been identified and evaluated?

EWS: Key risks overlooked or disregarded, inadequate consideration of the potential impact of innovative/untried solutions

Q: Have critical success factors been identified and can these be measured and evaluated?

EWS: Standard, inappropriate, unwieldy or unmeasurable metrics selected.

Q: Has the organisation the necessary capability/capacity to procure (buy-side) or respond to and deliver the opportunity (sell-side)?

EWS: Uncertainty over the magnitude of the project/opportunity and what resources will be required.

Q: Specifically, does the entity (buyer/supplier) have the commercial competence (skills and systems) required to manage the contract and is the competency effectively integrated within the organisation?

EWS: Unbalanced or late deployment of the commercial team, leading to delays or the utilisation of inappropriate forms of contract.

Q: Is there a clearly articulated commercial strategy for the endeavour that drives VFM (buy-side) or expected return on investment (ROI) (sell-side) and is it consistent with the organisation's intent? Has sufficient time been allocated to developing the commercial strategy?

EWS: Inconsistent and unclear views of what the contract is producing (buy-side) and how it will be delivered (sell-side), and what the optimal commercial relationship (contract type/strategy) should be and how it ought to be managed?

Q: Has the entity undertaken sufficient market research/sourcing analysis, plus does procurement/sales support the commercial strategy? Has it followed recognised good practice to optimise VFM/anticipated ROI?

EWS: Pressure to circumvent approved processes and best practice.

Q: Has an overall project structure/governance framework been established for the delivery/execution phase?

EWS: An absence of an implementable contract/project oversight/governance framework.

Further potential questions and EWS's can be obtained from the following sources: NAO (2016), IPA (2021a-c), World Commerce & Contracting (2021), and Williams et al. (2012).

Personal reflection

For a project/contract that you are familiar with, evaluate the Intent stage activities undertaken and decisions made.

- What tools and techniques were used and how effective were they?

Deal creation stage

> How do we acquire (capture)/create value during the deal creation stage and handover/start up stage of a contract/project?

The deal creation stage is directed towards forming an agreement (primarily a contract) between the exchange parties for mutual benefit. Often called brokering or 'striking' the deal, this phase includes the following elements.

Buy-side activities

Asset/service procurement entails acquiring assets, products, or services by implementing the chosen sourcing strategy and tendering process, including conforming where required to UK procurement legislation (for example, public sector purchases), and negotiating the exchange agreement. This includes preparing tender documentation (including commercial terms and condition, and technical specifications) and issuing ITTs to suppliers. After deciding on a 'buy' solution and selecting a procurement method, the purchaser must decide on procedures for selecting and appointing a supplier.

There are three principal procurement procedures:

1 *Open Tendering*: with no restrictions on who can submit a tender, except possibly a requirement to post a refundable deposit. Although, tenderers may be excluded post-submission.

This approach is considered to generate maximum competition. Public advertisements invite tenders, often placed in trade journals, national press, and official publications.

2 *Restricted Tendering*: alternatively referred to as selective or closed tendering, includes a pre-selection (pre-qualification) stage where suppliers are shortlisted based on their capacity, competence, and experience to undertake the project. This list can be established from existing preferred suppliers or generated through advertisements. The purchaser then invites tenders only from qualified suppliers.
3 *Direct Negotiation*: where the purchaser negotiates terms directly with one or more supplier. This method is used when there are few competent suppliers, the market is saturated, or the client has a well-established relationship with a supplier. However, the approach may not be permissible under an organisation's operating system.

Except for open tendering, purchasers are required to pre-qualify suppliers using objective criteria such as project personnel strength, reputation, industry expertise, price, delivery reliability, financial stability, flexibility, customer relationships, and capability to innovation.

Additionally, there are three main tendering approaches:

1 *Single stage tendering* involves submitting proposals/bids via a one-step competition.
2 *Two-stage tendering* is recommended for projects where early contractor involvement is advantageous, such as in developing the solution or design. This process involves the purchaser or their lead consultant negotiating with a few potential suppliers (typically three or four) on all aspects of the project. After these discussions, price competition is introduced through a schedule of prices or an approximate bill of quantities, with additional criteria to select a suitable contractor. Most clients opting for a design and build approach would benefit from this procedure.
3 *Multi-stage tendering* as above but with multi-staged negotiations or dialogue, possibly following an initial competition stage.

After receiving proposals, the purchaser evaluates them and selects a winning bid, a preferred bidder, or decides to cancel the project. Conventionally, contracts were awarded to the lowest bidder among pre-selected suppliers who met the customer's procurement goals and submitted a complaint bid based on an equivalent detailed design or specification. This 'lowest-price wins' approach faced criticism for focusing solely on price. In response, best practice procurement guidelines generally recommend that bids should be evaluated based on value for money, not just price. Value for money has been defined *as the optimum combination of whole-life cost and quality (or fitness for purpose) to meet user requirements* (NAO, 2024), aligning with the MEAT (Most Economically Advantageous Tender) principles.

An evaluation panel typically assesses proposals (bids) and recommends which supplier should be awarded the contract. Bid evaluation (award) criteria can be categorised as follows:

- *Commercial*: compliance with the RFP, delivery requirements, tender validity period, acceptance of contract terms and conditions, payment arrangements, and product range/design market duration.
- *Technical*: performance and productivity standards, quality (fitness for purpose), inspection requirements, operational and maintenance costs, professional competence, technical support, standardisation, after-sales service, availability of spares/consumables, manuals and training provision, and warranties.
- *Financial*: lifecycle costing comparisons, financial benefits, pricing (fixed or variable), cost of components, spares, consumables and servicing, financial qualifications, risk analysis, and financial appraisal.

To facilitate effective and transparent bid evaluation, award criteria should be agreed before issuing an ITT/RFP or quotation request. When not employing the lowest bid principle, detailed evaluation criteria should be included in the tender documentation.

Sell-side activities

Proposition development focuses on bid management. It involves generating and submitting a proposal in response to a buyer's RFP, RFQ or RFT (request for proposals/quotations/tenders) for the supply of assets, products or services, with a particular emphasis on determining a bid price. During this stage suppliers will additionally re-evaluate their decision to bid, scrutinise tender documents, assess resource needs and risks, perform necessary design work, estimate costs, prepare proposal documents, and, if required, prepare a supporting presentation. This stage seeks to ensure a comprehensive and competitive bid submission.

The stage necessitates the supply organisation assessing its capability and capacity to manage/execute the project or supply the product or service. Crucially, early determination of the proportion of the project to be subcontracted to third parties and partners (a 'make or buy' decision) will be undertaken. Additionally, considering whether forming a joint venture (JV), teaming agreement (TA) with partners, or a consortium with multiple companies may be appropriate/beneficial.

Deciding whether to bid for a project is strategic, involving the consideration of the organisation's strategic intent, competency, and long-term goals. The decision is crucial for suppliers due to resource allocation and the significant cost of preparing a bona fide tender, investment that is only recovered if they are selected. While various decision outcomes have been proposed, such as declining the ITT, provisionally accepting and prioritising the opportunity, submitting a 'cover price' (an inflated 'non bona fide' tender) or unconditionally accepting an RFP, in practice (due to time constraints) the choices are generally accept or reject, although rejection may not exclude the submission of a bid. Again, the bid/no bid decision can be informed by answering the following questions Is it real (funded)? Is it worth it? Is it winnable? Can we deliver it? posed earlier in the chapter.

The supplier's bid price should leverage the organisation's strengths and address its weaknesses, the competition and the purchaser's award criteria. Pricing systems include:

- *Cost-related approaches*: standard-cost pricing (variable and fixed costs, plus profit, adjusted for the level of competition), cost-plus-profit (markup on total cost), break-even analysis (price that will deliver a specific level of profit), and marginal pricing (marginal cost per unit).

- *Market-related approaches*: perceived value pricing (based on purchaser's value perception), psychological pricing (price used to influencing purchaser perceptions), promotional pricing (discounting to drive high turnover), and skimming (exploiting a niche, high pricing strategy).
- *Competitor-related approaches*: competitive pricing (challenging the sector's price leader), discount pricing (stating high prices, which are then discounted), and penetration pricing (undercutting competitors to increase turnover).

Suppliers may also employ the following bidding tactics:

- *Tactical withdrawal*: adopted only after considering the impact of the action on current and future relations with the purchaser.
- *Requesting an extension*: adopted only when there are compelling reasons to do so, this option is deemed better than missing a deadline or submitting a flawed bid.
- *Submitting a non-compliant offer*: the approach may be received positively if cost savings for both parties can be demonstrated, such as through value engineering. An innovative solution can produce a competitive advantage.

Additionally, suppliers may adopt specific pricing tactics, including:

- *Overpricing*: suppliers who are not interested in bidding but fear exclusion from future opportunities may submit inflated prices. A variant of this practice, cover pricing (collusion), involves obtaining an artificially high price from a competitor. The approach results in fewer bona fide bidders, higher average prices, and reduced bid variance. Once a common practice, it is now prohibited under the UK's 1988 Competition Act.
- *Unbalanced allocation of profit*: when detailed bid breakdowns are required, suppliers can distribute the profit element in various ways within the tender.

- *Tactical pricing*: stage payment regimes enable bid manipulation, such as front-end loading, item spotting, back-end loading and maximising the net present worth of cashflow.

Risk analysis, an integral part of bid preparation, can be utilised to evaluate uncertainties associated with a contract/project and to formulate bids that balance the risk of not winning a particular contract with the potential profit and losses the organisation may incur if the contract is secured.

Before submitting a bid or proposal, a stage gate review (adjudication meeting) is recommended to re-examine the business justification for submitting a tender and once more reconsider the bid/no bid decision. If a decision to proceed is taken, a commercial offer (price) or proposal (price and design/specification) is determined and approved. The aim is to formulate/submit a bid that positions the firm as the preferred bidder at the right price, considering the purchaser's scope, quality expectations, schedule and contract terms. The IPA Gate 3 Review: Investment Decision guidance (IPA, 2021d) can be adapted to support this review, incorporating factors influencing the bid/no bid decision, bid price determination, and relevant decision support tools.

Between proposal submission and the announcement of a preferred supplier, suppliers aim to keep communication open with the prospective customer, if allowed, to gauge how their proposal is received and suggest alternative solutions if appropriate.

Buy-side/sell-side activities

Award: This stage involves the evaluation of the submitted proposals (offers, bids or tenders), negotiation of an agreement and the subsequent award of a contract to the successful (winning) bidder (supplier).

After initiating the procurement process and receiving suppliers' proposals, the purchaser evaluates them to select a winning proposal or preferred bidder. Alternatively, they may decide to abort the project/purchase. If a preferred bidder is chosen, purchasers typically negotiate with the selected supplier to agree on the most advantageous or mutually beneficial contract terms before awarding a contract. This may involve discussion over the amendment of a standard contract form identified in the ITT/RFP or a prolonged contest to impose a company's precedent document, often biased towards the originator.

Globally, according to World Commerce & Contracting (2023), the ten most negotiated contract terms (in descending order) across all sectors are Limitation of Liability, Price/Charge/Price Changes, Indemnities, Liquidated Damages, Termination, Scope and Goals/Specification, Payment/Payment Options, Warranties, Cybersecurity/Data Privacy, Intellectual Property. The term 'battle of the forms' refers to resolving disputes over contract terms when both parties acknowledge a contract exists but disagree on its specific terms. For complex projects, pre-award negotiations can take months or even years to close.

If pre-award negotiations result in a mutual agreement (a 'meeting of minds') on contract terms and conditions and a subsequent investment review is positive, the contract is awarded to the successful bidder.

Before entering an exchange contract, a stage gate review is recommended to support the investment decision. The IPA Gate 3 Review: Investment Decision guidance (IPA, 2021d) offers sample questions for assessing the proposed solution, business case, stakeholders, risk management, current phase review and readiness for the next phase.

Contract award marks the transition to the implementation stage, where parties are required to deliver on their commitments made during the deal creation phase. Following the award of the contract, both the purchaser and bidders (successful and unsuccessful suppliers) should conduct a post-award review to capture lessons learnt. Prince2 offers a template (Lessons Report) and a process (Managing Stage Boundaries) for this analysis.

Commercial activities

Common commercial activities during the Deal Creation stage include:

- Constructing business cases
- Implementing procurement strategies

- Assessing costs and risks
- Drafting, negotiating, and agreeing complex contracts
- Preparing bids and leading or participating in bid teams
- Managing bid and commercial authorisation procedures
- Selecting, formulating or publishing standard contract terms
- Arranging subcontract terms to mirror main contract provisions
- Obtaining legal and regulatory sign-off for business opportunities

Activities undertaken by sell-side commercial practitioners during this stage include:

- Preparing a proposal development plan
- Convening a kick-off meeting for all participants
- Collating information on the purchaser, agents, potential subcontractors, and competition
- Updating preliminary 'win plan' themes and strategies
- Maturing the proposition's implementation, financial, contractual, and performance components
- Conducting formal and informal reviews, such as value management exercises ('red teaming'), and revising the draft proposal based on feedback
- Discussing the proposed solution with the purchaser and stakeholders, if permitted
- Drafting the proposal document
- Holding a post-publication review meeting to capture lessons learnt.

During the deal creation stage, buy-side commercial practitioners prepare tender documentation, including drafting complex contracts or selecting standard terms, writing technical specifications, and compiling bills of quantities. They select and implement the procurement strategy, issue ITTs, RFP, etc., and distribute tender documents to suppliers. Plus, evaluate tender submissions, report on each bid's merits and shortcomings, and advise on supplier selection. They also negotiate with preferred suppliers on contract terms and obtain legal and regulatory sign-off before contract award. These activities involve applying risk management tools and financial decision-making techniques, as well as best practices in procurement, risk, and contract management. A detailed understanding of legal and contractual issues is also essential.

Similarly, during this phase, sell-side commercial practitioners lead or participate in bid management teams. Their activities include reviewing and analysing tender documentation (ITT, RFP, etc.), capturing customer requirements, and assessing resource needs, risks, and opportunities. They prepare teaming and joint venture agreements (if needed), draft complex contracts, and define the customer proposition. Plus, write technical specifications, estimate costs, conduct value management exercises, and develop the commercial response. They also establish pricing and payment policies, obtain necessary bonds, guarantees, insurance, and export control licences, and oversee proposal documentation publication. Further tasks include managing the bid authorisation process, arranging subcontract terms, and securing legal and regulatory sign-off for bid submissions. Additionally, they ensure effective CRM techniques are implemented, prepare bid presentations, evaluate bid processes and performance, playing a key role in adjudication meetings.

The following questions and allied EWS can be utilised by senior leaders at the Deal Creation (Investment decision) stage to evaluate their organisation's commercial capability and its commercial performance on a contract/project basis and support decision-making. Again, they are framed and apply to both buyers and suppliers.

Q: Have the suppliers or partners submitted fully compliant bids? Additionally, have any alternative solutions been proposed? Will the proposed solution deliver the anticipate business benefits?

EWS: Failure of suppliers to submit compliant tenders may indicate an oversaturated market, or an unattainable solution.

Q: Are there sufficient resources to enable the entity to fulfil its contractual commitments?

EWS: Competency/capability gaps in the project team (particularly commercial/contract management expertise) and/or overreliance on external capability (consultants/contractors).

Q: Have all major risks been identified, evaluated and mitigated/managed? Plus, are retained/accepted risks appropriate and manageable?

EWS: Ignoring or failing to identify, evaluate and mitigate/manage risk at an early stage. Unidentified risks emerge later in the process, failure to allocate risk to the party most able to manage it.

Q: Does the proposed contract incorporate appropriate incentives to encourage the parties to delivery on their commitments, deter opportunistic behaviour and promote good working relationships?

EWS: An overreliance on contractual terms that compel compliance or overly penalise non-performance, rather than encourage appropriate performance and reward exceptional performance.

Q: Are the supplier's contract/project risk management proposals rational and credible?

EWS: Failure of supplier to complete requisite risk registers. Key risks overlooked.

Q: Have all mandated procurement (buy-side)/sales and tendering (sell-side) and technical checks been undertaken, and approvals/signoffs obtained?

EWS: Pressure to circumvent approved processes and best practice.

Q: Have all outstanding contractual issues been negotiated/resolved?

EWS: Again, pressure to circumvent approved processes and best practice or presence of optimism bias.

Q: Has the organisation previously worked with the proposed customer/supplier? How would you rate the degree of customer/supplier intimacy? Do the pre-award interactions with the customer/

supplier suggest that a successful working relationship will be established? Are appropriate relationship management mechanisms in place to support the parties?

EWS: Inadequate communication channels and/or interactions between the parties are frayed.

Once more, further potential questions and EWS's can be obtained from the following sources: NAO (2016), IPA (2021d), World Commerce & Contracting (2021) and Williams et al. (2012).

Personal reflection

For a project/contract that you are familiar with, evaluate the Deal Creation stage activities undertaken and decisions made.

- What tools and techniques were used and how effective were they?

Execution stage

How do we exploit/deliver value during the execution stage and at the close/retendering of a contract?

The execution stage, also known as project implementation, requires the parties to fulfil the commitments made during the deal creation stage concerning the required asset, products and/or services. The term 'execution' signifies that the contract provisions have been fully performed by both parties. Depending on the detail of the purchase and sourcing strategy, this phase includes various components.

For product or asset product purchases, the following elements are involved:

- **Asset supply** (sell-side activity) involves designing, manufacturing, constructing, providing, and delivering the procured asset or product(s) in compliance with the contract, including managing supply chains. Maintaining good relationships with the customer during this phase is crucial, as contract performance can impact future opportunities, potentially leading to follow-on contracts. After contract completion, a post-contract review is recommended to capture lessons learnt.

- **Asset receipt** (buy-side activity) comprises receiving/managing and accepting the procured asset or product(s) in fulfilment of the contract terms. On completion of a supply contract, the purchasing organisation should conduct a readiness for service review to assess the asset's/product's fitness for purpose. The IPA Gate 4 Review: Readiness for Service Version guidance (IPA, 2021e) provides sample questions on the business case, stakeholders, risk management, and readiness for the next phase (service).
- **Asset usage** (buy-side activity) involves applying or utilising the procured asset or product(s). During this stage, the customer will maintain and service the asset or product, often through term contracts with suppliers. Stage gate reviews throughout the asset's/product's lifetime and before disposal are encouraged to evaluate operational capability, assess benefits delivered, and capture lessons learnt.
- **Asset maintenance** (sell-side activity) incorporates the care and maintenance of the asset or product(s). Throughout their lifespan and on termination of maintenance contracts, suppliers should conduct reviews to capture lessons learnt.
- **Asset disposal** (buy-side activity) involves divesting property and assets at the end of their lifespan.

Alternatively, service acquisition entails the following phases:

- **Service implementation** (sell-side activity) comprises executing and delivering services in line with the contract terms. Throughout the service contract and following its completion, suppliers should conduct reviews to capture lessons learnt.
- **Service management** (buy-side activity) involves receiving, utilising, monitoring, and managing services consistent with the contract. Throughout the service duration and before its termination, stage gate reviews are recommended to evaluate operational capability, assess benefit delivery, and capture lessons learnt.

Commercial activities

Common commercial activities during these phases focus on managing and administering complex contracts and agreements (post-award contract management). They include:

- Advising and providing business support to project management teams on contractual issues to ensure project delivery conforms to the contract terms.
- Managing/administering commercial/contractual issues and instigating correspondence, including:
  - Processing contractual correspondence, variations, and claims.
  - Producing and maintaining financial reports and forecasts.
  - Processing and ensuring timely receipt of interim payments.
  - Liaising with accounts to ensure timely payments to suppliers
  - Valuing, preparing, submitting, assessing, negotiating, and approving additional payments (fees) and extensions of time for contractual changes.
  - Arranging insurance provisions.
  - Resolving disputes and managing conflict.
  - Finalising accounts.

Additionally, commercial activities undertaken by suppliers include:

- Procuring subcontractors and materials:
  - Establishing trading relationships with subcontractors/tier two suppliers.
- Managing/administering subcontracts and tier two suppliers.
  - Processing subcontract interim payment claims and final accounts.
  - Ensure timely payments to subcontractors/tier two suppliers).

The management of subcontract and supply contracts closely mirrors the management of the main contract between the purchaser and the main contractor/supplier.

Chapter 7 outlined best practices in contract management, emphasising the roles and responsibilities of both parties (purchaser and suppliers). It highlighted five key components:

Establishing the contract management team, ensuring the right people are in place at the right time. Often, a discrete post-award execution/implementation contract management team replaces those involved pre-award. Effective transfer of commercial oversight requires well-documented pre-award decisions and agreements to minimise misunderstandings later in the project.

Contract administration during the post-award execution stage comprises two key aspects:

1 *Managing the contract*: This includes establishing a contract repository, maintaining a timetable for key decisions and action points, and administering contract changes and closure/termination. It may well involve utilising IT/IS for enterprise contract management.
2 *Payment and incentivisation*: Ensuring interim payments are made in line with the contract and managing agreed incentive mechanisms.

Performance Measurement: Managing supplier and subcontractor performance is crucial for both demand-side and supply-side contract management teams to ensure service/project delivery in accord with the contract. There are two main components:

1 *Service delivery*: Involves establishing a performance management framework and SLAs, plus collating and providing timely performance information.
2 *Communication and feedback*: Providing performance feedback and conducting formal performance reviews.

Benchmarking assesses the effectiveness and efficiency of an organisation's strategies, procedures, portfolios, programmes, projects, products and services, comparing results obtained with industry peers or standards. Its objective being to discover best practices, and their associated factors, which can then be used as standards to promote performance (efficiency and quality) improvement and generate lessons learnt for application on subsequent projects. On one-off projects, performance improvement can be encouraged by incorporating target cost incentive payment terms. The activity is closely linked to continuous improvement. However, in outsourcing and managed services, benchmarking is often misinterpreted as merely cost-cutting.

Relationship management focuses on building strong relationships with strategic participants and stakeholders to support successful project/service delivery. Integral features are:

1 *Roles and responsibilities*: Ensuring all project participants understand their roles and are engaged.
2 *Communication and Continuity of Engagement*: Establishing clear communication channels and expectations, ensuring effective stakeholder interaction, and instituting dispute resolution and conflict management mechanisms.

Risk Management: Post-award risk management involves understanding and managing contractual and supplier/purchaser risks. This includes:

- *Processes and strategy*: Assigning risks to the party best able to manage them and implementing formal risk identification, monitoring, and mitigation processes.
- *Contractual Obligations/Responsibilities*: Ensuring contracts are understood and monitored.
- *Continuing risk management*: Assessing the supplier's/purchaser's commercial status and performance.

Post-contract/execution

Conducted by the procuring organisation, the 'operations and benefits realisation review', an iterative exercise, especially on projects with a service contract element. Multiple reviews may occur during the project's operational life. The review's extent is adaptable based on the nature of the project. For long-term contracts and strategic partnerships, four reviews might be held over the contract period. For IT-enabled projects, two or three reviews could occur during a five-year contract. An initial review is conducted 6–12 months after receiving an asset or launching a new service to collate evidence of derived operating benefits. The review emphases the Business Case and the effectiveness of service delivery and contract management procedures.

An IPA Gate 5 Review: Operations Review and Benefits Realisation follows a post-implementation review by the purchasing organisation, using internal review conclusions and organisational learning from the project. Additionally, while not mandated, a full 'future plan' review may be undertaken. Further Gate 5 Reviews ascertain if the projected value for money and anticipated benefits are being produced. IPA guidance (IPA, 2021f) provides sample questions on the business case, stakeholders, risk management, and readiness for the next phase.

For a supply or service contract, a post execution stage gate review is recommended for suppliers to capture lessons learnt. Prince2 offers a template (Lessons Report) and a process (Closing a Project) for this purpose.

Asset disposal/service termination

Asset Disposal refers to divesting or disposing of property and assets at the end of their economic life, while Service Termination indicates the conclusion of a service contract. Additionally, termination can also denote the premature end of a contract or releasing parties upon fulfilment of their obligations, by mutual agreement, or due to breach or frustration of the contract. On conclusion of a service contract, the purchaser should reassess the business case to determine if there is a continuing need for the service. This review should form part of the Operations and Benefits Realisation reviews. If a requirement remains, the purchaser must decide whether to renew, renegotiate, or terminate the agreement, and either appoint a new provider or insource the activity

During asset disposal, the buy-side commercial function advises on sales or disposal, such as facility demolition, and where required, liaising with in-house or external legal teams. In respect of Service Termination, they support the decision process by providing supplier performance data and advising on the contractual aspects of service termination, reappointing the incumbent supplier, transitioning the service to an alternative provider or insourcing the activity. If an alternative provider is chosen, the commercial function participates in the procurement process and oversees the service transfer. If the service reverts to an in-house capability, they manage the contractual process to facilitate this transition.

The following questions and allied EWS can be utilised by senior leaders during the Execution Stage, including the asset disposal/service termination phases, to evaluate its commercial performance and support decision-making. Again, they are framed and apply to both buyers and suppliers.

Q: Does the contract/project still support the entity's (buyer and supplier) strategic intent? Is the Business Case that underpins the contract/project still valid?

EWS: The chosen solution/purchase (buy-side) or opportunity (sell-side) is no longer consistent with the business needs or objectives. Alternatively, doubts are expressed over its viability.

Q: Is the contract/project well managed? Is it performing to budget and schedule? Is the service/capability being delivered as contracted? Is the contract delivering value for money or its expected margin/ROI? Are processes in place to monitor their achievement (performance measurement)?

EWS: Unfulfilled commitments – missed targets/service levels. Lack of transparency. High levels of claims. Loss of value/profit due to poor post contract governance and oversight.

Q: Are project/contract sponsors fully engaged?

EWS: Disengaged sponsor. Stakeholders unaware of who their sponsor is.

Q: Are changes to the contract being effectively managed?

EWS: Inadequate control of variations and changes: poor record keeping and failure to cost control.

Q: Are sufficient resources and capable personnel allocated to the contract/project?

EWS: Failure to delegate responsibility to project managers, inadequate staff numbers or missing competencies.

Q: Are relationships being appropriately managed?

EWS: Failure to implement relationship management mechanisms. Poor communication and/or interactions between the parties are awkward.

Q: Has a commissioning inspection been undertaken? Have all identified defects been resolved? Does the asset or service/capability meet predetermined acceptance criteria?

EWS: Incomplete assessments or inadequate inspection regimes. Defects unresolved. Failure to meet asset or service/capability acceptance standards.

Q: Has a lessons learnt review been undertaken? Have appropriate recommendations for improvement been made?

EWS: Time constraints. Withdrawal of personnel or staff encouraged to move on to the next opportunity/project before completing the review.

Q: Has an operations/benefits realisation review been undertaken? Is the purchaser ready to manage/operate the delivered asset? Are appropriate maintenance contracts or inhouse capability in place?

EWS: Failure to adequately prepare for the handover of an asset. Maintenance contracts or inhouse staff not in place.

Q: Is the purchaser satisfied with the performance of the incumbent service provider? Is the supplier still delivering value? Do they wish to reappoint the supplier, retender or bring the service in house? Is the service provider still receiving the anticipated benefits/value from the contract? Do they wish to continue the relationship or are there more lucrative opportunities available?

EWS: Poor service delivery. Lack of potential alternative suppliers. Poor returns from the investment of resources. A buoyant market. Insufficient time allocated to consider service contract termination or transition.

Once more, further potential questions and EWS's can be obtained from the following sources: NAO (2016), IPA (2021e,f), World Commerce & Contracting (2021), and Williams et al. (2012).

Personal reflection

Finally, again for a project/contract that you are familiar with, evaluate the Execution stage activities undertaken and decisions made.

- What tools and techniques were used and how effective were they?

Summary

Chapter 8 emphasised the importance of effective commercial practices and decision-making throughout the contract/project lifecycle. Structured around the Intent, Deal Creation and Execution phases, it provided a guide and essential insights for both buyers and suppliers, plus practical approaches/tools for managing commercial activities across each stage. It stressed the importance of strategic alignment, effective procurement, and robust contract management in achieving successful and sustainable commercial outcomes.

The chapter also provided a series of questions and allied EWS that can be utilised by senior leaders at each stage of contract/project to evaluate their organisation's commercial capability and its commercial performance on a contract/project basis and inform commercially driven decision-making. Enabling them to further develop their commercial capabilities, leading to better project outcomes and value realisation.

Further reading/resources

For additional information on applying rigorous and consistent commercial processes and procedures, see

Cummins T, David M and Kawamoto, K (2011) *Contract and Commercial Management: The Operational Guide*. Van Haren Publishing, Zaltbommel.

Lowe D J (2013) Commercial strategies and tactics. In: D J Lowe *Commercial Management: Theory and Practice*. Wiley-Blackwell Publishing Ltd, Chichester, pp. 288–378.

Lowe D J and Skitmore M (2006) Bidding. In: D J Lowe (ed.) with R Leiringer, *Commercial Management of Projects: Defining the Discipline*. Blackwell Publishing, Oxford, pp 356–389.

National Audit Office (NAO) (2016) *Commercial and Contract Management: Insights and Emerging Best Practice*. NAO External Relations, London.

References

Baily P, Farmer D, Jessop D and Jones D (2008) *Purchasing Principles and Management,* Tenth Edition, Financial Times/Pitman Publishing, Harlow.

Bennett J and Grice T (1990) Procurement systems for building. In: P S Brandon (ed.) *Quantity Surveying Techniques – New Directions*. Blackwell Scientific Publications, Oxford.

Infrastructure and Projects Authority (IPA) (2021a) Gate Review Process – Gate 0 Review: Strategic Assessment. Infrastructure and Projects Authority. https://assets.publishing.service.gov.uk/media/60f01860e90e0764cb10bd8a/1174-APS-0-CCS0521656666-001_IPA_Gateway_Web.pdf (Accessed 20 July 2024).

Infrastructure and Projects Authority (IPA) (2021b) Gate Review Process – Gate 1 Review: Business Justification. Infrastructure and Projects Authority. https://assets.publishing.service.gov.uk/media/60f0188dd3bf7f568e1f6463/1174-APS-1-CCS0521656666-001_IPA_Gateway_Web1.pdf (Accessed 20 July 2024).

Infrastructure and Projects Authority (IPA) (2021c) Gate Review Process – Gate 2 Review: Delivery Strategy. Infrastructure and Projects Authority. https://assets.publishing.service.gov.uk/media/60f018b3e90e0764ce826745/1174-APS-2-CCS0521656666-001_IPA_Gateway_Web1.pdf (Accessed 20 July 2024).

Infrastructure and Projects Authority (IPA) (2021d) Gate Review Process – Gate 3 Review: Investment Decision. Infrastructure and Projects Authority. https://assets.publishing.service.gov.uk/media/60f019678fa8f50c7745827f/1174-APS-3-CCS0521656666-001_IPA_Gateway_Web1.pdf (Accessed 20 July 2024).

Infrastructure and Projects Authority (IPA) (2021e) Gate Review Process – Gate 4 Review: Readiness for Service Version. Infrastructure and Projects Authority. https://assets.publishing.service.gov.uk/media/60f019b0e90e0764ccfbd7b1/1174-APS-4-CCS0521656666-001_Gateway_Web1.pdf (Accessed 20 July 2024).

Infrastructure and Projects Authority (IPA) (2021f) Gate Review Process – Gate 5 Review: Operations Review and Benefits Realisation. Infrastructure and Projects Authority. https://assets.publishing.service.gov.uk/media/60f019e58fa8f50c75b6aded/1174-APS-5-CCS0521656666-001_Gateway_Web.pdf (Accessed 20 July 2024).

Lowe D J (2013) *Commercial Management: Theory and Practice*. Wiley-Blackwell Publishing Ltd, Oxford.

National Audit Office (NAO) (2016) *Commercial and Contract Management: Insights and Emerging Best Practice*. NAO External Relations, London.

National Audit Office (NAO) (2024) *Successful Commissioning Toolkit: Glossary of Terms*. NAO External Relations, London. https://www.nao.org.uk/successful-commissioning/glossary-of-terms/#V (Accessed 20 July 2024).

Rathmell J M (1966) What is meant by services? *Journal of Marketing*, 30, 33–34.

Williams T, Klakegg O J, Walker D H T, Andersen, B and Magnussen O M (2012) Identifying and acting on early warning signs in complex projects. *Project Management Journal*, 43(2), 37–53.

World Commerce & Contracting (2021) *Overcoming the 10 Pitfalls of Contracting: How AI Can Transform the Value of Contracts*. World Commerce & Contracting. https://www.worldcc.com/Portals/IACCM/Resources/10655_0_Overcoming-the-10-pitfalls.pdf (Accessed 20 July 2024).

World Commerce & Contracting (2023) *Most Important Terms 2022/23: Negotiating for marriage or divorce?*, World Commerce & Contracting. https://www.worldcc.com/Portals/IACCM/Resources/11487_1_Most%20Important%20Terms%202022.pdf (Accessed 20 July 2024).

INDEX

Note: Page numbers in **bold** and *italics* represent tables and figures respectively.

Kolibri 360 GmbH
Ferdinand-Jühlke-Straße 7
99095 Erfurt, Deutschland
produktsicherheit@kolibri360.de